# Real Business Plans & Marketing Tools

...including samples to use in starting, growing, marketing, and selling your business

Anne McKinney, Editor

PREP PUBLISHING

FAYETTEVILLE, NC

**PREP Publishing**

1110 ½ Hay Street
Fayetteville, NC 28305
(910) 483-6611

Library of Congress Cataloging-in-Publication Data

McKinney, Anne, 1948-
Real business plans & marketing tools : including samples to use in starting, growing, marketing, and selling your business / Anne McKinney.
        p.  cm. -- (Business success series)
     ISBN 1-885288-36-0
     1. Business planning. 2. Proposal writing in business.  3. Business enterprises--Planning. 4. Marketing--Planning. I. Title: Real business plans and marketing tools. II. Title. III. Business success series (PREP Publishing)

     HD30.28.M3847 2003
     658.4'012--dc21                                                           2003042943
                                                                                      CIP

Printed in the United States of America

## By PREP Publishing

*Business and Career Series:*

RESUMES AND COVER LETTERS THAT HAVE WORKED

RESUMES AND COVER LETTERS THAT HAVE WORKED FOR MILITARY PROFESSIONALS

GOVERNMENT JOB APPLICATIONS AND FEDERAL RESUMES

COVER LETTERS THAT BLOW DOORS OPEN

LETTERS FOR SPECIAL SITUATIONS

RESUMES AND COVER LETTERS FOR MANAGERS

REAL-RESUMES FOR COMPUTER JOBS

REAL-RESUMES FOR MEDICAL JOBS

REAL-RESUMES FOR FINANCIAL JOBS

REAL-RESUMES FOR TEACHERS

REAL-RESUMES FOR STUDENTS

REAL-RESUMES FOR CAREER CHANGERS

REAL-RESUMES FOR SALES

REAL ESSAYS FOR COLLEGE & GRADUATE SCHOOL

REAL-RESUMES FOR AVIATION & TRAVEL JOBS

REAL-RESUMES FOR POLICE, LAW ENFORCEMENT & SECURITY JOBS

REAL-RESUMES FOR SOCIAL WORK & COUNSELING JOBS

REAL-RESUMES FOR CONSTRUCTION JOBS

REAL-RESUMES FOR MANUFACTURING JOBS

REAL-RESUMES FOR RESTAURANT, FOOD SERVICE & HOTEL JOBS

REAL-RESUMES FOR MEDIA, NEWSPAPER, BROADCASTING & PUBLIC AFFAIRS JOBS

REAL-RESUMES FOR RETAILING, MODELING, FASHION & BEAUTY JOBS

REAL-RESUMES FOR HUMAN RESOURCES & PERSONNEL JOBS

REAL-RESUMES FOR NURSING JOBS

REAL-RESUMES FOR AUTO INDUSTRY JOBS

REAL RESUMIX AND OTHER RESUMES FOR FEDERAL GOVERNMENT JOBS

REAL KSAS--KNOWLEDGE, SKILLS & ABILITIES--FOR GOVERNMENT JOBS

REAL BUSINESS PLANS AND MARKETING TOOLS

*Judeo-Christian Ethics Series:*

SECOND TIME AROUND

BACK IN TIME

WHAT THE BIBLE SAYS ABOUT...Words that can lead to success and happiness

A GENTLE BREEZE FROM GOSSAMER WINGS

BIBLE STORIES FROM THE OLD TESTAMENT

# Contents

# Real Business Plans & Marketing Tools

..including samples to use in starting, growing, marketing,
and selling your business

Anne McKinney, Editor

The goal of this book is to provide you with useful examples of tools to use in producing business plans and implementing effective marketing. Part One provides you with 17 different business plans which you can use as samples or "models" when you prepare your own business plan.

The 17 business plans you see in Part One actually worked. Whether you are a would-be entrepreneur or a business owner hoping to grow your business, you should find helpful examples of business plans in this book. Here's an overview of the types of organizations for which you will find business plans:

> an auto body shop
> athletes on tour
> medical business
> brew pub
> counseling service
> electrical service
> medical supply company
> convenience store franchisee
> hair salon
> insurance group
> janitorial supply business
> manufacturing company
> home-based mailing business
> medical business
> trucking company
> used car warranty business
> wholesale company
> pizza business

When you are in the process of preparing your business plan, you may have a pretty good idea of the facts and concept you wish to present. The business plans in this book will help you in making your final decisions about what to say and how to say it.

Business plan #1 is a document used to obtain financing to establish a new auto body shop through the purchase of an existing operation. This relatively simple business plan shows you how to present a request for financing, how to provide a concise description of the business, and how to communicate information about the market, personnel, and competition. You will also see financial projections for three years along with an executive summary.

# BUSINESS PLAN #1: Auto Body Shop

## PHILLIP'S AUTO REPAIR

### SUMMARY

I know that Phillip's Auto Repair Shop will come to be known as a very honest and reliable service center. I will offer services that most shops do not offer. All customers will be met with a smile and good service. My goal as a business is to give the customer a little more than they expect in terms of quality service and cost. As a new business I know that the first year will be hard but as a new business, most people will also want to try our service to compare the service they are already getting, and that will be all that we need and we will be able to prove that we offer quality service.

**AUTO BODY SHOP**

Here is the business plan for an auto repair shop which an entrepreneur wants to establish. This business plan was submitted to a bank in order to obtain a loan.

My location in 8741 Milburn Drive is very good location. Traffic flow is estimated at 12,000 to 14,000 cars per day. We will perform major and minor auto repairs. My personnel consists of two mechanics. I predict that within two to three years Phillip's Auto Repair Shop will be recognized as one of the best businesses in Springfield.

### REQUEST FOR FINANCING

Phillip's Auto Repair is requesting a loan for $30,000 to finance its new automotive repair business, which has an opening date slated for April 7, 2004.

### DESCRIPTION OF BUSINESS

I will be leasing with an option to buy an old, established business whose current owner would like to retire. The owner has cultivated a loyal clientele drawn to his business through his honesty and technical knowledge. My leasing terms will include use of the land, building, and all owned equipment and tools now located on the premises.

This business will be a total auto repair and service shop available for all types of vehicles. We will do brake jobs, tune-ups, rebuilding or replacing motors, transmissions, starters, alternators, valve jobs, oil changes, and lube jobs on all American cars, and most import cars. Days of operation are Monday through Friday 7:00 a.m. to 4:00 p.m., and a trained mechanic will be on duty who has two years specialized training from a technical community college along with several years of experience as a General Motors Mechanic at their plant. An important differentiating feature of my business is that all mechanics will be fully trained. Service costs will be competitive to most similar businesses in the Braxton County area. My research has shown that there is a definite need in this area for an auto shop that provides such service. I have an outstanding reputation as a reliable professional full of integrity, creativity, and vision, and believe Phillip's Auto Repair's established customers will like the "new blood" I'm bringing to the business. I plan to improve upon business profits by hiring excellent mechanics with excellent moral character.

My clientele will not only consist of the Milburn Drive neighborhood, but will also consist of military personnel stationed at Fort Leonard Wood, MO.

The "option-to-buy" lease states a price of $90,000 for land, building, equipment, and tools. The building has been rewired and a new heating system has recently been installed. The building has four vehicle bays and a large storage area. A large parking lot is adjacent to the building and all exterior and interior signage is already in place.

## LOCATION OF BUSINESS

Phillip's Auto Repair is located at 8741 Milburn Drive, Springfield, MO. The building and land are in fine condition and need no renovation. The neighborhood surrounding the business is stable and growing with many active small businesses in the area including a pawn shop, NAPA Auto Parts, Mega Market, Circle K Convenience Store, Gerald's Engine Repair, Allied Executive Care, Liberty Body Shop and Transmission Repair, a hair salon, and a fish market.

The shop is 2,267 sq. ft. and is done in block build. The lot size is 175 sq. ft. long and 95 ft. deep. The lease agreement is nine hundred dollars per month with a year-to-year agreement. I have "first rights" to buy the building and land. After one year, I intend to buy the place. I will maintain the building and grounds. As stated previously, traffic in the area tends to be high at 12,000 to 14,000 cars per day. I am close to Fort Leonard Wood, therefore very accessible to military professionals. The shop is very easy to find and Milburn Drive is a very well known road — it is like the main vein in your heart. Since Logan's Tires closed, we have been fortunate to get a great deal of their business.

## LICENSES AND PERMITS

The name Phillip's Auto Repair is registered with the Missouri and Braxton County Register of Deeds. Local zoning regulations will have little if any affect on the business. All licenses and permits are in order and copies of them are included in this proposal:

City License of Springfield — cost $5.00
County License, Missouri Department of Revenue - Braxton Taxes — Cost $50.00
State License of Braxton County and taxes — cost $20.00

## MANAGEMENT

I, Phillip McMillan, the manager and prospective owner of Phillip's Auto Repair exercise direct operational and management experience in auto repair and maintenance. I managed a profitable car wash for almost two years, worked as an Assistant Manager with AutoZone stores for six years, and operated a detail shop in Hillsboro, MO. I am in excellent health and am physically suited for the job.

I have 12 years of formal education, have worked as a mechanic for five and a half years, and have also worked at Advanced Auto Parts for two years as an Assistant Manager. As the manager, my job is to greet customers with a smile and let them know my job is to help them in their automotive needs. I personally will evaluate the problem and assign the right mechanic to the job. The chain of command will be my secretary and head mechanic in charge when I am not at the shop.

## PERSONNEL

Personnel will initially consist of three fully trained and qualified automotive mechanics. These employees are personally known to me and have a wide range of repair and maintenance skills, including rebuilding motors and transmissions, doing tune-ups and brake jobs, and replacing motors on all makes and models of vehicles.

Requirements for the job as a mechanic are to have at least 2 1/2 years of experience working on automobiles. Knowledge of how to do brake jobs, tune-ups, front-end work, rebuilding motors, and replacing transmissions is essential in order to work at Phillip's Auto Repair. The relationship between management and employees needs to be such that all must be competent and honest individuals.

# BUSINESS PLAN #1: Auto Body Shop

Wages will be 45% commission for mechanics with 55% going to the shop. Training will be done on an as-needed basis and will be done on new cars using new car books, and during night at Ozarks Technical Community College.

## THE MARKET

The market's present size and growth potential are almost unlimited in terms of this business. I project that I will handle between 15-18% of the Springfield automotive repair market. The demographics of my market segment will range from 18-65 year-old male and female car owners. As stated before, I expect a large number of military customers with incomes ranging from $17,000-$65,000 a year.

I have several "come again" promotions planned, including having a drawing every month for a $25 gift certificate to Phillip's Auto Repair. All customers who have patronized the shop during that month will have a chance to win.

Methods of acceptable payment will be cash or credit cards. I will accept no personal checks or "run a tab" for any customers.

The size of the market is very large in terms of population. With Milburn Drive and Fort Leonard Wood Army Base all being in close proximity, 38,000 to 45,000 registered vehicles travel in the area daily. The number passing directly by the shop is estimated to be between 12,000 and 14,850. I will be marketing to the consumer by means of advertising with signs, flyers, and through word-of-mouth advertising. We will advertise in the yellow pages; we will also post business cards at shopping centers, convenience stores, and at the AutoZone at Fort Leonardwood, MO. We will carry products such as motors and transmissions which will be priced very competitively.

My research has shown that signage in front of the business on a heavily trafficked road is possibly the best form of advertising. While complying with all city regulations regarding to signage, I will erect a very professional sign that puts the business's "best face forward" and which communicates a highly professional image to drive-by potential customers.

## COMPETITION

My "distinctive sales advantage" will be competitive prices and honest automotive advice and labor, in addition to conducting drawings and other promotions.

The quality of work performed by Phillip's Auto Repair will be of the highest caliber. I take great pride in my work and like to hear people say how good my work is. I can operate a Sun machine, do valve jobs, and troubleshoot most U.S. and foreign cars.

As previously stated, within a one-mile radius of my shop are Malcom's Body, NAPA Auto Parts, Gerald's Engine Shop, Liberty Body Shop, and Transmission Repair Shop. My hourly rate of $35 per hour is competitive in the area, but we will sell our motors and transmission at a lower-than-market price because I am a wholesale dealer with my closest competitors being Englemen's Auto and Neal's Performance Shop. Neal does very good work, but my costs for parts will be just a little bit cheaper because I can get motors and transmissions cheaper than he can — thus using lower costs to attract customers.

**AUTO BODY SHOP**
Notice the Executive Summary at the end of this business plan. Some business plans position the executive summary at the beginning of the business plan in the form of an introduction. Other business plans, such as this one, position the executive summary at the end of plan, where it functions as a summary.

Since Logan's Tire Shop has reopened we have been able to work together through his referring motor and transmission work which he is not equipped to handle.

## THREE-YEAR PROJECTION

I estimate the shop's income and expense figures for the first three years of operation according to the chart shown on the following page.

## EXECUTIVE SUMMARY

I believe our automotive repair shop, located at 8741 Milburn Drive, Springfield, MO, will come to be known as one of the most innovative and respected in the city. Phillip McMillan, Manager, and Carl Edinburg and Paul Swanson, Mechanics, will be offering services and products in conjunction with a professional customer service system that can usually only be found in much larger cities and at a much higher cost. Our goal is to give all customers more than they expect in terms of quality service at less than they might expect to pay. Word-of-mouth recommendation by satisfied customers will eventually become the business's best advertisement.

The sole owner/lease holder is Phillip McMillan, who is also requesting the loan in the amount of $30,000. If you look at APPENDIX A, you will see that the loan will easily be repaid by means of the projected monthly profit amount.

# BUSINESS PLAN #1: Auto Body Shop

**PHILLIP'S AUTO REPAIR**

**FINANCIAL PROJECTIONS**

| | | Year 1 | Year 2 | Year 3 |
|---|---|---|---|---|
| **Sales** | | | | |
| | Retail Products | $ 20,000 | $ 35,000 | $ 44,000 |
| | Labor Sales | 42,000 | 64,000 | 83,475 |
| | | | | |
| **Total Sales** | | $ 62,000 | $ 99,000 | $127,475 |
| | | | | |
| **Expenses** | | | | |
| | Advertising | $ 1,500 | $ 2,800 | $ 3,500 |
| | Bank Charges | 350 | 350 | 350 |
| | Insurance | 1,450 | 1,750 | 2,000 |
| | Miscellaneous | 1,000 | 1,150 | 1,200 |
| | Office Expenses | 800 | 1,200 | 3,500 |
| | Professional Fees | 300 | 300 | 300 |
| | Rent | 10,800 | 10,800 | 10,800 |
| | Repair/Maintenance | 200 | 300 | 400 |
| | Telephone | 875 | 1,000 | 1,000 |
| | Utilities | 2,580 | 2,900 | 3,100 |
| | | | | |
| **Total Expenses** | | $ 19,855 | $ 22,550 | $ 26,150 |
| | | | | |
| Profit from Operations | | $ 42,145 | $ 76,450 | $101,325 |
| | | | | |
| Other Expenses | | | | |
| | Equipment Lease | $ 1,200 | $ 2,900 | $ 4,500 |
| | Loan Payment | 3,600 | 3,600 | 3,600 |
| | Equity Line | 3,500 | 3,500 | 3,500 |
| | Employee Benefits | 0 | 3,400 | 3,575 |
| | | | | |
| **Total Other Expenses** | | $ 4,800 | $ 13,400 | $ 15,175 |
| | | | | |
| **Net Profit** | | $ 37,345 | $ 63,050 | $ 86,150 |

**AUTO BODY SHOP**

# BUSINESS PLANS #2, #3, #4, #5, and #6:
## Backing Athletes on Tour
## Medical Business Loan Request
## Loan Request for a Brew Pub
## Counseling Services Business
## Construction Loan Request

In this section, you will see a variety of business plans which illustrate varied techniques for using business loans to obtain financing.

In Business Plan #2, you will see a concept for a business plan which involved backing athletes on tour. If you are planning on developing a business which involves financing other professionals, you might find some interesting ideas in this plan. The plan was circulated to private investors in an effort to obtain financing from approximately 20 private individuals who wanted to invest in "local talent."

Business Plan #3 is a plan designed to obtain bank financing in the amount of $250,000 in order to purchase a successful medical business from the original financier and venture capitalist.

Business Plan #4 is a somewhat lengthier plan which was used to secure financing for a business start-up from a base of wealthy regional individuals. The business plan was very successful, and the financing was obtained which allowed a successful brew pub to be built.

Business Plan #5 illustrates a business plan which was used as a solicitation bid for a government contract. In this specialized business plan, the author had to demonstrate that the service business possessed key abilities which would allow the service to be delivered effectively and efficiently.

Business Plan #6 shows a business plan used by a construction business to embark on a major building project in order to boost its business capability.

# BUSINESS PLAN #2: Backing Athletes On Tour

Date

Exact Name of Person
Title or Position
Name of Company
Address (number and street)
Address (city, state, and zip)

**BACKING ATHLETES ON TOUR**

This is a sponsorship request for two successful tennis players. This letter and Estimated Expenses document were circulated to wealthy individuals and businesses in a community with the goal of obtaining "seed money" for two talented young tennis professionals.

Dear Exact Name of Sponsor: (or Dear Sir or Madam if answering a blind ad.)

We are requesting your financial support to help us represent Portland, OR as we seek to attain our goal of rising to the top of the international tennis tour.

We have both dedicated the last several years to refining the tennis talents with which we have been blessed. Although we have both had excellent success in singles, we feel that our best chance to attain a world ranking is in doubles. One advantage for us in doubles is that, unlike many top teams, we have had the same partner, namely each other, for over ten years. Secondly, we love playing the doubles game, as it allows us to set a team goal and share whatever success we have.

To attain the next level in the tennis ladder, we need your help. The upcoming USTA Satellites Circuit, which runs in six segments from March through November of this year, is our opportunity to gain points so that we can play the larger circuits. In particular, by the end of this year, we hope to have enough ATP points to play only in USTA Challengers tournaments, where the prize money is $50,000+ per event. Our immediate goal is to make the main draw of each tournament we play in. Our ultimate goal is to earn enough ATP points to attain a world ranking and play, and excel, in the U.S. Open and Wimbledon.

We plan to play singles and doubles in each event, and we are confident in our abilities to attain world rankings in both. However, we are committed to rising to the top together, as a team, and we feel that experience is the main thing, which separates us from the top doubles teams worldwide at this point.

We have compiled resumes of our singles and doubles results throughout our careers as well as an estimate of expenses which is exclusive of coaching expenses. Having our coach with us at the tournaments adds approximately $4,000 per segment to expenses, but greatly helps us maximize our results.

If you were to decide to sponsor us, we would want you to feel free to advertise that you are sponsors of ours. We assure you that we would take very seriously our responsibility of representing Portland in the most professional manner possible.

Sincerely,

Alexander M. Kahn

## Alex and Andrew Kahn: Estimated Expenses for USTA Satellite Tour

| | Segment 1 | Segment 2 | Segment 3 | Segment 4 | Segment 5 | Segment 6 |
|---|---|---|---|---|---|---|
| **Travel** | 652.00 | 1552.00 | 1463.00 | 1612.00 | 1618.00 | 1618.00 |
| **Lodging** | 1400.00 | 1400.00 | 1400.00 | 1400.00 | 1400.00 | 1400.00 |
| **Food** | 2240.00 | 2240.00 | 2240.00 | 2240.00 | 2240.00 | 2240.00 |
| **Entry Fees** | 40.00 | 40.00 | 40.00 | 40.00 | 40.00 | 40.00 |
| **Equipment:** | | | | | | |
| Racquets | 1200.00 | 0.00 | 0.00 | 0.00 | 0.00 | 0.00 |
| Strings | 256.00 | 256.00 | 256.00 | 256.00 | 256.00 | 256.00 |
| Grips | 100.00 | 100.00 | 100.00 | 100.00 | 100.00 | 100.00 |
| Shoes | 480.00 | 480.00 | 480.00 | 480.00 | 480.00 | 480.00 |
| Clothes | 1000.00 | 0.00 | 0.00 | 0.00 | 0.00 | 0.00 |
| **PLAYERS' SUBTOTAL:** | 7368.00 | 6068.00 | 5979.00 | 6128.00 | 6134.00 | 6134.00 |
| **Coaching:** | | | | | | |
| Travel | 326.00 | 776.00 | 731.50 | 806.00 | 809.00 | 809.00 |
| Lodging | 1400.00 | 1400.00 | 1400.00 | 1400.00 | 1400.00 | 1400.00 |
| Food | 1120.00 | 1120.00 | 1120.00 | 1120.00 | 1120.00 | 1120.00 |
| Salary | 3000.00 | 3000.00 | 3000.00 | 3000.00 | 3000.00 | 3000.00 |
| **COACHING SUBTOTAL:** | 5846.00 | 6296.00 | 6251.50 | 6326.00 | 6329.00 | 6329.00 |
| **TOTAL:** | 13214.00 | 12364.00 | 12230.00 | 12454.00 | 12463.00 | 12463.00 |

The above schedule is intended to illustrate tennis-related expenses which would reasonably be expected to be incurred during the six actual segments of the 2004 USTA Satellite Tour. There are four tournaments in each of the six segments.

# BUSINESS PLAN #3: Medical Business Loan Request

## THE CENTER FOR PODIATRY & SPORTS MEDICINE
### Dr. Michael D. Wright, D.P.M.
8540 Gristmill Road

Slidell, LA 78998

(888) 888-8888

August 28, 2003

CONFIDENTIAL BUSINESS PLAN PREPARED FOR

FIRST FEDERAL BANK

## I. Loan Request Summary

The purpose of this document is to request a business loan of $250,000 for the purpose of purchasing an existing and growing medical practice in Slidell, LA. The business was established in 2001 through the financial backing of a financier, and it is my desire to use the loan proceeds to purchase the business so that I can become its sole owner. The equity for this loan is the existing practice along with the fixed assets and accounts receivables. I am anticipating an interest rate of approximately 8%.

## II. Management Summary

As is revealed by the attached resume, the owner would be Dr. Michael D. Wright. I completed the Southern University School of Podiatric Medicine and then completed my residency from 1998-01 at the Podiatry Hospital of Slidell. The three-year Podiatric Surgical Residency program which I completed has equipped me with unique expertise which is in much demand not only in my market area but throughout the state. While I offer the capabilities of a physician and hold a Doctor of Podiatric Medicine, I am the only podiatrist within a nearly 200-mile radius qualified to perform surgery of the hind foot and ankle as well as trauma and reconstruction surgery. The surgical component of the business now constitutes approximately 15% to 20% of the business of the practice, and it is the segment which is expected to grow as my quality reputation expands geographically. There are no doctors in the Slidell area qualified to perform surgery of the hind foot and ankle as well as trauma and reconstructive surgery. Indeed, the doctor who is closest geographically who performs surgery is in Baton Rouge, LA. In addition to the surgery which I perform, I routinely see patients suffering from a wide variety of ailments which include sports injuries, heel pain, and complications due to diabetes, arthritis, and other diseases. Since establishing the practice in Slidell in 2001, I have established excellent relationships with doctors who have become strong referral sources including Doctors Yabolon, Augustine, Wyatt, and Hobbs, as well as other doctors in Slidell. I have also established an excellent relationship with the only other podiatrist in Slidell, who refers patients to me for surgery as well as for routine ailments, because demand for his services tends to exceed his capacity. I have also established a strong working relationship with Slidell Medical Center, where I perform most of my surgeries. The type of medical services I provide are typically covered by a wide variety of insurance including Medicaid, Medicare, private insurance, and many others. Since establishing the practice in 2001, I have taken great pains to ensure that the foundations of the business are solid. For example, The Center for Podiatry & Sports Medicine has a fully computerized accounting and bookkeeping system. In order to ensure correct and maximum allowable billing for all services provided, The Center for Podiatry & Sports Medicine has, nearly since its inception, utilized a third party billing service which specializes in podiatry practices. This has ensured the fastest possible cash flow and maximum profitability. In addition to my unique surgical expertise, one strength of the business is that the Pryor County area has been relatively underserved medically while the market is growing rapidly. I have established an outstanding reputation as a surgeon, doctor, and medical colleague in the community. I have an excellent office staff of two individuals who appear to be dedicated and loyal individuals. I am confident I can build on that good will and develop the practice into a booming and successful entity. Although I was born in New Hampshire, I have made Louisiana home and I am very happy in settling in this part of the country. I believe strongly that the state of Louisiana will experience rapid growth and Slidell is poised geographically to enjoy a rapid growth rate.

### III. Business Summary
The practice which I have established includes a practice through which I see patients on a daily basis. This includes daily monitoring of patients with patients being seen on Monday through Thursday with surgery on Friday. I am also on call and am known for my cheerful willingness to respond to emergencies, such as the urgent need to perform surgery on the foot or ankle when someone has been in a car accident. I have become known for my skill in performing reconstructive surgery of the foot and ankle. My strategy at all times is to provide the finest care so that I can grow the business by word of mouth because of my reputation as a superior doctor and highly skilled surgeon. In terms of short-term goals, my goal is to increase my number of surgeries, which is the high-ticket and high-profile aspect of my business. I want to become the leading authority in Louisiana and perhaps in the Southwest on the bones of the foot and ankle. The type of surgery I perform is among the most delicate type of surgery performed, and orthopedic surgeons — who can perform this type of surgery — seem quite delighted to refer patients to me because of the extremely delicate nature of the type of surgery which I perform. I have built the practice from scratch to its current point of more than $200,000 annually revenue on an annualized basis, and it is growing rapidly. In five years it is my goal to grow the business to a $400,000 practice with a high profit margin. One day, I might want to grow it even more by bringing a new podiatrist into my practice. I have a goal to grow The Center for Podiatry & Sports Medicine into a practice which has a regional, and perhaps even a statewide, reputation, but my short-term goal is to become established to the maximum degree possible in my local community.

### IV. Industry Summary
Since the business is a medical practice with surgical components and physical therapy, the demand for the services I provide is already strong with demand expected to be stronger in the future. Simultaneously, the market is growing. Although there really are no cyclical trends in medicine, I have found that profits are marginally weaker in the winter months, although the difference is slight. With the aging baby boom generation experiencing arthritis, diabetes, and numerous other ailments which tend to bring patients to podiatrists, I forecast a strong and growing demand for the services I provide.

### V. Market Summary
The Slidell community and the Chamber of Commerce have both welcomed me with open arms. The Slidell area is growing, but I also network aggressively with doctors in Baton Rouge who are viable sources of referral for surgery and medical care. The Slidell area has one other podiatrist, with whom I have an excellent relationship and who refers patients to me for medical treatment and surgery. My strategy is to develop a growing reputation as a skilled surgeon who is highly regarded by the general public as well as the medical community. I believe I am poised to expand on the quality reputation of The Center for Podiatry & Sports Medicine.

# BUSINESS PLAN #4: Loan Request for a Brew Pub

## MORRISON BREWING COMPANY

**BREW PUB**

Here is a business plan for a brewery operation which includes the industry structure and a market strategy. Request for financing: approximately $1.5 million.

# EXECUTIVE SUMMARY

## General Business Overview

Morrison Brewing Co. will be an upscale brewpub--a restaurant where varied styles of beer are craft-brewed on the premises and served with quality food at reasonable prices. Our goal is to locate in an upscale building where we can create the ambiance and character which matches the rich history of hand-crafted beers and authentic wholesome food which will be served. We will perform all necessary leasehold improvements in order to create a spacious, unique and comfortable atmosphere while ensuring the proper design and placement of the brewery.

We will open during the fourth quarter of 2003, and be open seven days a week for lunch and dinner. The driving theme of our business will be freshness and quality accompanied by superior service. We anticipate catering to patrons from every walk of life; people who appreciate a good meal with a pint of their favorite brew in a relaxed setting.

Morrison Brewing Co. will be located in one of the various shopping centers that have expressed interest in our project. We have met and will continue to meet with representatives from Allendale, Pinehaven Shopping Center, and Crowfield Plaza. The brewery will be a welcomed and attractive addition to any of these locations.

Morrison Brewing Co. will be characterized by the authentic old neighborhood pub brewery/restaurant design. The brewing equipment (copper-clad brewing kettle and mash tun, copper-clad fermenter tanks and serving tanks) will be highly visible from the restaurant area, and the bar area. We will feature a high quality sound system for after-dinner entertainment and several television sets in the bar area for special sporting events.

Morrison Brewing Co. will also keg and bottle their special brands of beer for retail sales. Morrison Brewing Co. will sell to other bars and restaurants as well as to convenience stores, supermarkets, and commissaries.

## Market Overview

In the mid-1980's the American consciousness was tapped by a startling realization: Beer is supposed to have flavor. Europeans have been savoring ale, porter, pilsner, and stout for centuries. But in the United States, such news was a revelation. Small breweries sprouted tentatively here and there. One by one, American beer drinkers sat down with unfamiliar brews from unknown sources - Anchor Steam, Redhook, Sierra Nevada, Bigfoot Ale. As they sipped, they were quietly converted. American "microbrews" became the beer aficionado's small stash of secret joy.

Ten years later, brewpubs and microbreweries have experienced explosive growth. Beer production at US brewpubs has risen by an average of 44% during the last five years. US craft brewers, (brewpubs, microbreweries, regional specialty brewers and contract brewers) produced nearly 1,669,982 barrels (51, 769,442 gallons) in 2001, reflecting a 40.4% increase over the previous year and nearly thirteen fold growth since 1993. This contrasts dramatically with production by the ten largest brewers which

# BUSINESS PLAN #4: Loan Request for a Brew Pub

experienced only 0.7% growth during 2001. The craft brewing industry has been, and will continue to be, the fastest growing segment of the US beer industry for many years.

Extensive market research indicates that the demographic profile of the Harrisburg area with the large number of military and the immediate surrounding communities is almost identical to our desired target audience — young to middle age, "white collar" population with high, median, and average household incomes. This target audience also includes several transient individuals that have spent time in foreign countries that have always served full-flavored beers. Our unique selection of brews will lead the potential German/Irish/English/Scottish beer drinker through our doors.

**Introduction to Management**

**William Addison** is *Chief Executive Officer* and *Co-Founder* of Morrison Brewing Co. Mr. Addison has several years experience in the food and beverage industry including positions at Harrisburg's Anheuser-Busch and Miller Products Distributors. Mr. Addison has worked the last nine years in sales and marketing in the paper industry. He received his Bachelor's degree in Psychology from La Salle University in 1997.

**Thomas Caldwell** is *Chief Operations Officer* and *Co-Founder* of Morrison Brewing Co. Mr. Caldwell has served as Store Manager and District Supervisor of Kroger Grocery Stores since 1998. Mr. Caldwell has opened and managed numerous locations from the ground up. He is experienced in personnel, payroll, inventory management, and vendor relations. Mr. Caldwell majored in Business at Bryant College.

**Everett Johnson** is *Vice President*, Restaurant Operations. Mr. Johnson has worked in the restaurant business since 1992 including being an Owner/Operator of Moon River Cafe since 1998. Mr. Johnson's experience includes kitchen operations, controlling food costs, personnel, and accounting. Mr. Johnson received a Bachelor's degree in Management from Marshall University in 1999.

**Lionel Ramon** is *Vice President*, Brewing Operations. Mr. Ramon has been brewing beer since 1994. Mr. Ramon is experienced in brewing ales and lagers utilizing a variety of specialty grains, honey, and fruits. Mr. Ramon is knowledgeable of malted barley varieties, application to beer style and grain milling. Mr. Ramon has served as Senior Systems Engineer for Satellite Ground Systems Development at Boeing since 1991. Mr. Ramon received his Bachelor's degree in Astronomy from Widener University in 1997.

**William Addison, Thomas Caldwell,** and **Everett Johnson** have all attended the Northeastern Brewers Academy. **Lionel Ramon** will attend the upcoming Fall session. This intensive 12-day course provides broad exposure to the science of brewing and the operation of a brewpub and microbrewery:
1. **Brewing Process:** Theory and Practice includes discussion and demonstration of all aspects of brewing science from malt milling through packaging.
2. **Product Formulation and Flavor Analysis:** Recipe design, appropriate use of ingredients and beer flavor defect identification.
3. **Quality Assurance:** Lab analysis techniques of $CO_2$, oxygen, and microbiological instruments.
4. **Beer Styles and History:** A discussion of the characteristics of all 59 recognized brewing styles.

5. **Equipment Selection and Requirements:** Choosing the proper space and facilities and sizing of brewery tanks and accessories.
6. **Leasing and Financing:** A discussion of raising capital and locating a suitable location for the brewery.
7. **Government Regulations and Agencies:** Includes major requirements of Federal, State and Local authorities.
8. **Flow of Operations:** A dissertation on the day to day management of the brewery/pub including hiring practices, training, and personnel management.
9. **Practical Business Management:** Covers what reporting is unique to the brewing business and practical choices for bookkeeping and inventory control.

## INTRODUCTION TO THE INDUSTRY

### Introduction

"Out of this world growth" was the title of the cover story contained in the November-December June 2002 issue of The Entrepreneur Magazine. The article reads ... "Sales of craft-brewed beers skyrocketed to more than 1.6 million barrels in 2001, a phenomenal increase of 40 percent. Once again, the domestic craft-brewing industry has rocked the beer world. Estimated total sales for this segment reached 1,670,000 barrels in 2001 - an increase of 40 percent over 2000 sales. This amount represents 0.9 percent of the estimated total consumption of beer in the United States, up from 0.6 percent in 2000. Top-tier brewing companies enjoy a banner year yet again, each with sales growth ranging between 47 and 83 percent. 'Critical mass' is a term many are using to describe the level of maturation currently enjoyed by this industry. The popularity of the beers of the above-mentioned companies - together with brands brewed by 10 regional specialty breweries (that started as micros), 131 microbreweries, 241 brewpubs and roughly 60 contract brewing companies in the US - has contributed to a critical mass of consumer acceptance for full-flavored beer. Whether it's called microbrew or craft-brew, full-flavored, brew with character, beer with class, beer like it used to be, European-style, or simply hand crafted beer, the new turn in the tide of American brewing history is unstoppable. City-by-city, county-by-county, state-by-state, and spanning all regions, local beer is back. All malt beer is back. Beer with the flavor and aroma of hops is back. The post-prohibition trend to homogenize, and by the 1970's, lighten the flavor profile of beer made good business sense for a few decades. Today, however, this trend appears to have faded. Just as large numbers of consumers recently have grown to expect more from the wine they enjoy or the coffee they drink and many other consumable products termed wholesome, hearty, all-natural and traditional style - more consumers are expecting more from the beer they drink ..."

The above article accurately summarizes the increasing momentum and size of the craft-brew industry. There are over 80 million beer drinkers in the United States who in 2002 spent over 50 billion dollars on their favorite malt beverage. People are more likely to reach for a beer than for any other drink when they choose to consume an alcoholic beverage.

# BUSINESS PLAN #4: Loan Request for a Brew Pub

## Industry Defined

Craft-brewing is a term used to define the hand-crafted brewing method that only a small segment of the US beer industry utilizes. This brewing method is usually very traditional, employing old European techniques, the finest ingredients, and no chemicals or preservatives. This process is relatively costly and tedious compared to that utilized by the larger brewers, but the final product is far superior. Unless explicitly stated otherwise, 'crafted-brew' includes brewpubs and microbrewery production, regional specialty brewery production and contract brewery company production as defined below.

**BREW PUB**
Why did these entrepreneurs decide to circulate their business plan to wealthy individuals instead of banks? They decided that banks would consider the start-up too risky and determined that they would be better off to try to raise the needed capital "$20,000 at a time" from wealthy local and regional individuals who would secure small equity positions in the new company.

Brewpub: In simple terms, a brewpub is a restaurant-brewery that sells at least 50% of its beer on premise. The beer is brewed for sale and consumption in the adjacent restaurant and/or bar. The beer is often dispensed directly from the brewery's storage tanks. In states where it is allowed, some pubs package their beer for carry out and off-site sales. Note: Brewpubs whose off-site sales grow to represent more than 50% of total sales are re-categorized as microbreweries.

Microbrewery: A brewery that produces less than 50,000 barrels of beer per year. Microbreweries sell to the public by one or more of the following methods: The traditional three-tier system (brewer to wholesaler to retailer to consumer); the two-tier system (brewer acting as wholesaler to retailer to consumer); and in some cases, directly to the consumer through carry outs or on-site tap-room sales.

Regional Specialty Brewery: A brewery with a capacity to brew between 50,000 and 1,000,000 barrels and offer a "specialty" or "micro" style beer as their flagship brand. Although it may distribute its beer only within a specific region, as used here the term refers to the brewery's size only.

Contract Brewing Company: A business that markets and sells beer brewed to its specifications by an already existing brewery. The existing brewery provides to the contract brewing company its space, equipment, and in most cases, personnel for brewing and packaging the contract brewing company's recipe. The contract brewing company is responsible for marketing, selling and distributing its beer to wholesalers and retailers.

In the late 1970's the three major US breweries began far more aggressive marketing campaigns in an effort to gain a nationwide market. Smaller, regional breweries could not compete or were bought out by the giants. Since the rule of mass marketing is to offend as few people as possible, brewers made beers blander and blander in order to maintain a wide appeal for their product.

In the early eighties, on the East coast, major importers noticed an increased demand for imported beers; products that retained some of the character that had been stripped from their domestic counterparts. On the West coast, meanwhile, the foundation of the microbrewery and brewpub explosion were being laid. Various breweries in Pennsylvania were attracting local clientele with full-bodied beers which contrasted sharply with domestic mass-produced beers. When coupled with the recent growing interest in fitness and healthier lifestyles, it is easy to see why the craft-brewing industry has exploded.

Today's consumer is demanding a more natural, healthier, product based more on actual substance than advertising hype; a product that symbolizes quality and recognizes not only that the consumer wants a choice, but is discerning in what he or she chooses to purchase. Thus has begun the latest development in the retail markets; a highly segmented market has become the norm, with retailers serving specialized audiences with superior quality products. There are homemade cookie shops and ice cream parlors, fresh pasta stores, espresso bars and now brewpubs.

## Dynamics

Why now? Where did brewpubs come from? Those of us who have developed more than a passing fancy for beer have asked these questions at one time or another. Is this a fad? It would seem not. Craft beer production grew by more than 40% in 1998 and 50% in 1999. Specialty brewed beer is here to stay, and sales figures suggest that the market has only just begun to be tapped. There is no doubt that the retail consumer market is changing. Anyone who ventures out, if only to the supermarket, must notice this change. People want quality products; natural, healthy items that they can feel good about using and eating and drinking. In the 1970's, people bought white bread. In the 1980's, they bought whole grain. People now buy boutique wines instead of jug wines. People choose expensive flavored bottled waters over tap water. One can see the same happening with coffee, ice cream, soft drinks, salsa, cheese and pasta - to name a few products. It is also happening with beer. Several events in the last twenty years have combined to create the demand for higher quality beer.

### SUCCESS RATES

## Openings & Closings

Brewpub growth alone has skyrocketed in the last six years, with production reaching 302,127 barrels (9,365,937 gallons) in 2001. The chart below illustrates this trend vividly and clearly shows that the failure rate for a brewpub is almost one fifth smaller than that for an ordinary new restaurant, 17% for the former and 80% for the latter.

| Year | Barrels | Number | Openings | Closings |
|------|---------|--------|----------|----------|
| 2001 | 302,127 | 347 | 106 | 5 |
| 2000 | 201,418 | 241 | 70 | 14 |
| 1999 | 146,792 | 186 | 39 | 7 |
| 1998 | 112,154 | 155 | 47 | 13 |
| 1997 | 88,112 | 124 | 34 | 9 |
| 1996 | 61,639 | 107 | 41 | 3 |
| 1995 | 33,589 | 69 | 44 | 4 |
| 1994 | 11,113 | 29 | 13 | 0 |
| 1993 | 7,803 | 16 | 10 | 2 |
| Totals | | | 404 | 57 |

**Competition and Pricing**

There are no brew pubs in Harrisburg. Our prices will be competitive with the successful bars and restaurants in our area. We expect to price our house beer competitively with the bottled beer offered in area bars. For example, a 16 oz. serving of our beer will be priced at $3.00, while less desirable bottled products cost $2.75 for a 12 oz. serving. Based on national brewpub data, we can expect 80-85% of our beverage sales to consist of our house beer, ensuring adequate volume to realize favorable profit margins.

**BREW PUB**

On these pages you will see an illustration of how to present facts about competition and pricing strategies.

Morrison Brewing Company will offer competitive pricing on our menu selections which will focus on fresh and wholesome salads, appetizers, sandwiches, a varied selection of entrees, and gourmet brick oven pizzas. The entrees will consist of a core of offerings that will remain on the menu and will be complemented by seasonal dishes and homemade soups. Our menu will focus on fresh, homemade dishes which will be complemented by our house brews. The average entree price (including all food items apart from appetizers) will be $8.50. We will be able to offer quality and freshness at reasonable prices so our customers feel confident that they are getting value for their money. Our overall pricing strategy will be based on:

1. Price of competitive products.
2. Price needed to be profitable.
3. Price sensitivity and its relationship to potential sales.

Pricing will be under continuous review by the company's CEO, COO, V.P. of Restaurant Operations, and consultants. Pricing and menu selections may be altered to respond to competition and other variables. Our menu selections will be priced similarly to comparable items at other area restaurants but we will strive to make our total product superior in every way.

## INDEX OF COMPETITORS

**Allentown**
- Manson Brewing Co. — Large Brewery

**Johnston**
- Pinehaven Brewing Co. — Microbrewery

**Lancaster**
- Blue Moon Grille — Brewpub

**Levittown**
- Golden Mill Brewery — Brewpub
- Hobson Brewery — Brewpub

**McKeesport**
- Sinclair Micro Brewery — Microbrewery
- Pink House Bakery Brewery — Brewpub
- Keesport Micro Brewery — Brewpub

**New Castle**
- Brandywine Brewery & Cafe — Microbrewery

**Norristown**
- Upstein Brewing Co. — Microbrewery

**Philadelphia**
- Ridgecrest Brewing Co. – Brewpub
- North Bound Brewery & Smokehouse — Brewpub
- Cameo Beer Co. — Microbrewery
- Ballard Pro Brewing Co. — Microbrewery

**Pittsburg**
- Millstone Brewing Co. — Microbrewery
- Chalet Restaurant & Brewery — Brewpub
- Pinehurst & Southern Pines — Microbrewery

**Pottstown**
- Eden Way Brewery And Pub — Brewpub/Microbrewery
- Shire Brewing Co. — Microbrewery
- Cobblestone Brewery — Brewpub

**Reading**
- Steak & Ale Brewery — Microbrewery

**West Chester**
- Red Gate Brewery — Brewpub
- Sky Line Co., Inc. — Microbrewery

**York**
- Sapphire Brewery Co. — Large Brewery

## THE BUSINESS PLAN

### Introduction and Philosophy

Morrison Brewing Company will be formed and operated under the guiding principles of product integrity, impeccable service and respect for the individual - both employees and customers. At the heart of the enterprise is a hands-on participative management style. We will strive to create a place that we ourselves would like to work for; a neighborhood atmosphere where one knows the product he or she is selling, knows their customers because they keep returning, and where the customer knows they are receiving a good value and enjoying a unique experience.

Our beers will be fresh, all natural, and of world class caliber. Our food will be tastefully prepared with only the freshest and seasonal ingredients whenever possible.

The management team will bring much significant experience to this venture in the areas of start-up, management, restaurant operations, brewing, marketing and human resources. These combined talents and energies coupled together with an experienced, enthusiastic and imaginative restaurant manager and an experienced and diverse consulting team will ensure success and prosperity.

Morrison Brewing Company will operate and be managed with creativity, insight, and hard work. This venture represents the culmination of many years of education and unique business experiences, and many months of intense examination of the marketplace in Harrisburg.

**Business Product Line**

**BREW PUB**

On this page
you will see a
discussion of
the company's
business
product line
and marketing
strategy.

Morrison Brewing Company will be open seven days a week, 363 days a year. We will open at 11:00 a.m. and close at 2:00 a.m. on Fridays and Saturdays, Sunday 11:00 a.m. - 12:00 a.m. All menu selections will be served from opening until 11:00 p.m., and we will offer a limited but appealing bar menu during all hours of operation. The menu will consist of a wide variety of appetizers, homemade soups and fresh salads, original style pizzas from our wood-fired pizza oven, hot and cold sandwiches, and a selection of entrees.

We will offer a minimum of four fresh, home-brewed beers at all times. A light beer will be on tap throughout the year with an amber ale variety or a pale ale variety. The textures and styles of our home-brews will reflect the current seasons; lighter beer during warmer months and heartier beers during cooler months. Other possible selections are described below.

**Amber Ale:** An American version of the English mild ale. Medium amber in color, complemented by a sweet, malty body ending with a floral hop finish.

**Pale Ale:** A deep gold patina in this beer belies its aggressively hopped character. Enhanced Cascade hops explode off the top and reappear in the aftertaste. The full malty taste is balanced with a dryness that complements lighter food.

**Wheat or Weisse:** One of the most refreshing beers made with a substantial portion of wheat in addition to the normal barley. A pale and sometimes cloudy beer deriving from Southern Germany.

**Porter:** A great introduction to the many darker styles of beers. A rich, velvet brown color and full flavor recommend this beer to be served with heartier dishes.

**Oatmeal Stout:** The granddaddy of beers, this style is almost a meal in itself and not for the faint of heart. Generous amounts of roast barley, oatmeal and specialty malts give this beer its spectacular head, deep black color and full body. A smoky, coffee flavor predominates and is best served as an aperitif or a fine after meal drink.

**Light Beer:** This style has a place even in the world of boutique brews. Ours will complement different menu selections and highlight the fact that a low alcohol beer can have color and taste.

**Seasonals:** We will offer beers that ring in the seasons and celebrate varied holidays. Possibilities include an Irish ale for St. Patrick's Day, a pumpkin porter for Halloween, a summer-fest beer to refresh and rejuvenate parched customers, a fall harvest beer to serve during the Oktoberfest, and the traditional English Wassail, a spiced beer that warms hearts and heads to celebrate the holiday season. Other possible products will include a wheat beer, fruit beers, lambics, cask conditioned real ales, and nonalcoholic beverages.

## Marketing

Market entry will initially be driven by the unique character and novelty of the brewpub concept in this area. Morrison Brewing Company will generate a majority clientele that has not yet had the opportunity to experience quality prepared food as well as finely made hand-crafted beer. An informal survey showed that many people are excited about the concept of a brewpub and would be eager to visit and take part in this unique experience.

Historically, brewpub openings have generated interest and coverage from the local and regional media. We will invite the major local and regional newspapers and magazines to our opening as well as their radio and television counterparts. Our premiere will be a newsworthy "opening" including generous samples of our beer and food as well as a few surprises which are currently fermenting.

We also plan to invite government officials, business leaders, suppliers, friends, family and the many people who have supported us from the beginning. Our opening will be a day to celebrate and commemorate the return of fresh, hand-crafted beer to our region.

The goals of our promotional efforts are to:
1. Maintain contact with our patrons.
2. Develop positive community relations.
3. Educate the public about fresh brewed beer.

We will sustain the energy and interest created at the opening by ensuring that the quality of the beer, food, atmosphere, and service is something that people will appreciate, publicize and return to enjoy. The initial flurry of articles on the brewpub will be due to the novelty of our concept. Follow-up articles will be the result of press releases and our own promotional efforts. In addition to maintaining an ongoing advertising presence through the local media, other promotional ideas include brewer's banquets, brewery tours, beer tastings and seminars, and brew-of-the-month club.

Positive press and media relations will be cultivated at all times by the principles. The image we wish to consistently portray is that of an enterprise of dedicated employees who are knowledgeable and enthusiastic about the beer, food and service that we provide to our patrons.

We will offer seasonal beers and menus to commemorate and celebrate the arrival of the seasons. Special events will also be tailored to correspond with the specific celebrations. We plan to include an Oktoberfest and Summerfest. After the opening, all subsequent "hoppenings" will be communicated by a newsletter sent to everyone on our mailing list.

Our efforts to become part of the community, will include cosponsoring local recreational activities. These types of events will publicize the brewpub, encourage healthy lifestyles and responsible behavior. We also believe such events will attenuate potential negative reactions from anti-alcohol groups.

We will also strive to form amiable relationships with the neighboring restaurants outside of our specific area in an effort to provide these restaurants with our fresh, local brews. We will be very discerning in this pursuit but we feel that this could benefit Morrison Brewing Company all the while increasing awareness of our tasty beers while bolstering sales. This will also help bring tourists in from surrounding cities to visit our brewery.

The customer base will be expanded by always sustaining the highest quality of beer, food, atmosphere and customer service. Market penetration will be sustained and driven by adhering to these basics and by creating a place and product that honors the history of microbrewing, while always remaining fresh and unique.

**BREW PUB**

This discussion of the company's service orientation and target audience is intended to inspire confidence and persuade potential investors that the business concept is strong.

## Service

SERVICE SERVICE SERVICE will be the catch phrase of Morrison Brewing Company. We recognize that maintaining a superior service platform is of paramount importance to the success of the company. Staff meetings which focus on service will be held on a bi-weekly basis. We will also emphasize company pride and loyalty. We are in the process of producing a comprehensive and stringent service manual that will detail the following service requirements and perspectives.

- Training: All staff members will undergo a demanding, thorough, and continuous training regiment.

- Attitude: Staff will be polite, outgoing, professional and attentive to our customer's demands at all times. The customer is always right!

- Execution: Food and beverage serving, seating by hostess, food preparation, table dress, taking orders, receiving payments, etc. will be performed consistently and professionally, utilizing exact procedures for each task. Service will be prompt and efficient.

- Knowledge: All servers, bartenders and managers will be very familiar with the preparation and content of all menu items, daily and seasonal specials, the various styles of our house-brewed beers, wines, and other beverages, and the history of the company.

- Cleanliness: The restaurant, bar, kitchen, bathrooms, utensils, glasses, staff, etc, will remain spotless at all times.

- Image: All visible staff members will maintain a professional yet relaxed appearance. Staff will wear sharp looking but comfortable uniforms and will be neat, handsome, mature, impeccably trained, courteous and smiling.

- Awareness: Staff will be perceptive of customers' wants and needs at all times.

- Interaction: Management will maintain constant interaction with customers in an effort to make them feel welcome and important. We will take note of customer's name, occupation, livelihood, beer of choice, etc.

- Safety: Stringent safety policies will be employed at all times.

**Target Audience**

Over the last ten years, there has been a distinct shift in the way Americans relate to food, almost a renaissance in the culinary arts. People now want to eat better and know what they are eating, and regional cuisines emphasize fresh and natural ingredients. There has been a dramatic shift from the excesses of the eighties to the value-added theme of the nineties.

The same trend is visible in beer consumption. Today's beer drinker is more sophisticated and finds himself or herself confronted with a wide assortment of beers to choose from. There are new regional, micro, and pub-brewed beers flooding the market in both draft and bottle forms. As with wine drinkers, beer drinkers are becoming increasingly sophisticated.

An in-depth analysis of the local demographics shows that our anticipated core audience will consist of groups of educated males and females (graduated or attending college) and the military population, with a secondary audience consisting of adults ages 25-54. We anticipate that our customers will primarily be a combination of singles and parents who work in the following fields: professional/managers, sales and precision/ craft, and the resident military. We believe our customers will cover a range of high, median, and average household incomes and will fall broadly into one of the following groups:

1. Destination Diners: Composed of a mature, affluent audience who dine our more than once a week and are looking for the new, the good and the trendy. We believe this group will pay a fair price for quality food and beer.

2. Beer Enthusiasts: Made up of home-brewers and beer connoisseurs who can identify and appreciate a quality brewed product and are also willing to pay for it. This group is loyal and will spread the word to friends and fellow enthusiasts. We believe the military population to make up the major portion of this group- informal surveys show that military personnel, with their wide experiences throughout the US and the world, prefer a quality hand-crafted brew to less desirable brands.

3. Walk-ins: This group is highly contingent on location and come in off the street or as they are driving by. We feel we can optimize on this group by placing the brewpub in a highly visible and convenient location.

4. Families: Moderate to high income families with young children who are attracted to a hospitable environment and who appreciate good value in their dining experience.

5. Tourists: Several hundred thousand tourists visit Morrison every year-once again, we include all new incoming military personnel in this group.

# BUSINESS PLAN #4: Loan Request for a Brew Pub

## Organization and Staffing

**Staff training:** Everyone involved in this project must be committed to the responsible consumption of our alcoholic beverages. Clearly, the majority of the 80 million adults who drink beer are responsible drinkers. The few individuals that abuse alcoholic beverages cast a dark shadow over the responsible drinkers and the entire industry. We will do everything in our power to ensure that our customers do not abuse our product.

**BREW PUB**

The business plan ends with a discussion of concepts related to organization and staffing, internal organization, and organizational design.

Staff education is the area over which we have most control. We will require all serving staff to participate in a training program designed to instruct servers to recognize underage drinkers, false ID's and customers that have had too much. Servers will also be reminded through posters and staff meetings that their livelihoods and ours depends on our patrons responsible consumption of our alcoholic beverages. Morrison Brewing Company will be involved with local and community programs such as "Designated Driver" and we will offer free nonalcoholic beverages to designated drivers.

**Drug free environment**: Morrison Brewing Co. will be a drug-free workplace. Drug abuse is one of the greatest challenges facing employers today. Drug abuse can result in absenteeism, loss of productivity, medical expenses, and workplace crime.

Morrison Brewing Co. is aware that we may risk loosing potential employees. However, we feel it is necessary to take that risk to ensure we have the best employees available. Federal companies (i.e. U.S. Army) require government contractors to be drug-free.

## Internal Organization

The goal of this organization structure is to keep it as flat and responsive as possible, while at the same time ensuring that everyone knows who they report to for guidance, support, and motivation.

The Chief Operating Officer will have overall day-to-day and strategic management responsibilities for the company, including personnel, purchasing and financial management. The Chief Executive Officer will maintain responsibility for marketing, public relations, advertising, new business development and strategic planning. The Restaurant Operations Manager and Brewing Operations Manager will report directly to the Chief Operating Officer.

This philosophy will further enhanced by a reward and compensation based on skill-based pay, bonuses, and flexible benefits. The specifics of the compensation system we finally design and implement will contingent on how we ultimately finance the business as well as input from our accountant and attorney.

Participative management, flexible compensation, and regular communication of goals, objectives and state of the business will be an integral part of ensuring that our employees are motivated and feel like they work in a positive environment. These actions will also spawn the type of atmosphere where employees are encouraged to be creative and committed to the company. Successful staffing, along with a quality product, great service and a comfortable and unique atmosphere, will ensure our success. The secret to good staffing includes recruiting, selection, training, and management.

**Recruiting:** Our recruiting efforts will focus on four sources:
- Best people from other establishments
- Word-of-mouth, friends and referrals
- Develop relationships with local Food Service, Restaurant Management, Cooking and Bartending schools to ensure quality referrals
- Advertisement in local papers

**Selection:** Every candidate for employment will interviewed by the Operations Manager as well as the appropriate Vice President of Operations. We will strongly suggest that each prospective employee talk to at least two current employees in order to understand the operating philosophy behind Morrison Brewing Company. This is a significant time investment but is more prudent than having to terminate some one who shouldn't have been hired in the first place. "Money can be saved on things but not on people." People are our best investment. Key characteristics to assess are: attitude, skills, previous experience, education, and future plans. The profile of our staff will reflect the profile of the customers we serve and the community in which we operate.

**Training:** Training will focus on four areas: Attitude, company philosophy, skills and external development. All employees will be cross trained so that they can assume three or four different positions in the brewpub.

**Management Philosophy:** The management philosophy can best be described as a combination of participative management based on a respect for the individual and responsibility to the organization. This approach reflects a healthy combination of an organization that gives as much as it expects. The responsibilities in a high involvement enterprise are equally shared by both owners and employees. The advantages of this participative approach can be summarized in the following way:
- Respect for the individual is paramount
- People want to be part of a team and be included in decisions that will affect their responsibilities in all aspects of the organization
- When employees participate, they are more satisfied and committed to the organization

## ARCHITECTURAL DESIGN

The sketch below illustrates a tentative look at the structure we desire for our brewpub/microbrewery. Ralph Tresvant, a registered P.A. Architect, sketched this design as well as the floor plans shown on the next two pages. The floor plans, includes seating for 250 plus, with a mezzanine for brewing equipment and office space.

# BUSINESS PLAN #5: Counseling Services Business

Solicitation and Bid for a Government Contract
KARL H. JUSTUS
RFP 659-16-94
SSN: 000-00-0000

**1. <u>Organizational Information</u>:**
**a. Describe in narrative form your organization's ability to provide required services in the State of Washington for eligible service members and veterans requesting these services. A detailed description of the organization's ability to support the required performance of this contract will be provided. This description should include the locations of the offices, staffing and managerial makeup of the organization. In summary, information should be provided which will demonstrate the offeror's understanding of how they intend to manage tasks called for under the contract.**

The organization providing these services — CCI, Career Consulting, Inc. — is operated by a respected professional who combines a distinguished military career with a master's degree education in the counseling/human services area as well as extensive recent experience in providing educational and vocational guidance counseling for the Veterans Administration. As the sole proprietor of CCI, I personally guarantee satisfaction with all services provided by CCI. A brief look at my background will reveal that I have the experience and qualifications to provide this "satisfaction guaranteed" service by CCI.

CCI's ability to provide these services is based on my ability personally to deliver these services. As a retired lieutenant colonel, I offer extensive knowledge of the military professional and of his/her needs as he/she transitions from military service into the civilian sector or into academic environments to strengthen his/her education. In my 25 years as an Army officer, I have provided extensive guidance and counseling to soldiers, and I have provided the service person with information of an educational and career nature along with self-information that facilitated decisions concerning education and career planning.

- Most recently, I have applied the concepts and techniques I acquired while earning my master's degree in counseling/human services as a contract Educational and Vocational Guidance Counselor for the Veterans Administration. While performing in that role for the past 15 months, I have performed activities which included administering testing and providing initial counseling interviews for Chapter 36 candidates. From May 1999 to October 2003 I completed more than 100 cases. I am currently under contract with the VA to provide initial testing and counseling services for Chapters 31, 35, and 36. The process which I conducted included counseling and interviewing veterans as well as conducting tests that assessed interests, aptitudes, and abilities to assist the individual in making informed career decisions. I spent a considerable amount of time interpreting counseling notes, explaining interest profiles, and helping the counselee/veteran develop a plan of action. In my most recent experience, I have demonstrated that I possess, and am able to apply in a counseling situation, my keen understanding of "pending" veterans' needs and what adjustments they will be exposed to after leaving military service.

- My 25-year career in the U.S. Army, during which time I rose to the rank of lieutenant colonel, provided me with certain kinds of "expert knowledge" that is needed in order to counsel eligible service members and veterans. In particular, I have gained expert knowledge of the military occupations ("military occupational specialties" or MOS's) and their applications in civilian life. I have made it a point during the past five years to immerse myself in reading magazines and periodicals which keep me apprised of trends and conditions in the job market. I also read newspapers from major metropolitan areas when I travel in order to gain insight into "who's hiring whom." I believe the U.S. economy is in a period of great fluctuation when many jobs traditionally available to retiring military professionals are in short supply, so I am avidly engaged in my spare time in obtaining whatever information I can about supply and demand situations so that I can be of maximum utility to military professionals planning a job search after departing from military service. Industries which I feel are "hot" at the present time and therefore viable targets for military professionals seeking employment include the transportation industry, the construction industry, and the environmental cleanup industry. I also have made it a point to perform some research into jobs available in government — local municipalities, state, and federal — because many military professionals seeking employment after military service have a preference for working in a government organization. Non-for-profit organizations such as the Red Cross, United Way, churches, and many other organizations also are hospitable homes for former military professionals, and I attempt to remain abreast of opportunities in not-for-profit organizations, too, in order to provide wise counsel and prudent guidance to the military professionals I counsel.

In addition to my expertise in the process of interviewing people, assessing their interests/aptitudes/abilities, and helping them develop plans to achieve their educational or employment goals, I offer proven abilities in the area of organizational effectiveness. In my 25 years of military service I became known as an exceptional manager of time and resources, and I have developed detailed plans which will permit me (CCI) to carry out the tasks involved in the process. I am known for my attention to detail and I have developed detailed plans which include the following:

- I have direct access on a daily basis to a private counseling office (please see Appendix A) located at a convenient site on Fort Lewis, WA. The office provides a comfortable, private, and professional environment in which to administer vocational and educational tests and conduct guidance counseling interviews. The office is located in the Army Career Alumni Program Building located on the corner of Bailey and Cumming streets on Fort Lewis. The map attached as Appendix A shows the location.

- I have direct access (one day a week) to a test facility that can accommodate 30 individuals for educational and vocational testing. The facility is located on McAllister Street in the Fort Lewis Main Post Area. Again, please see the map attached as Appendix A. This location as well as the one described above are conveniently located in an area which should be either well known or easy to find for military personnel.

- As the provider of these services myself, my main task will be to manage my time for maximum effectiveness, and I offer a reputation as a proven performer in time management. In the event that a need develops for additional staff, I am also a proven performer in recruiting, training, developing, managing, coaching, and evaluating employees. I have excelled in both "line" management jobs and in "staff" consulting and planning roles, and I have managed numerous personnel in those line and staff positions. Because I am not assuming that I will be hiring staff at the present time, however, I will not elaborate on my ability to recruit and train and manage a qualified staff of dedicated and motivated people.

# BUSINESS PLAN #5: Counseling Services Business

In summary, I believe that the key ingredients in expertly providing the services under this contract are (1) communication skills, both oral and written, (2) managerial effectiveness, and (3) specific expertise through education and experience. I offer outstanding skills as a writer and as an oral communicator; my managerial skills have been refined and tested in numerous "hotseat" positions as a military officer; and I offer the master's-level education along with practical counseling experience that this award seems to require. Finally, I offer a reputation for total honesty and reliability, and it would be a gratifying experience to assist fellow service members in achieving their educational and employment goals after serving their country as military professionals.

**COUNSELING SERVICES**

Solicitation Offer and Award
KARL H. JUSTUS
RFP 659-16-94
SSN: 000-00-0000

**2. Ability to Provide Initial Evaluation Services:**
**a. (1) Describe in narrative form your established program of services which will be evaluated in order to demonstrate the ability of your clinician(s) to provide evaluation services which comprehensively meet the requirements specified in the contract.**

The services I intend to provide are exceptionally strong in the area of providing evaluation. As is described in Section 1.a. of this Solicitation Offer and Award, the evaluation services have been finely synchronized into a well coordinated process. That process is briefly summarized below:

- Each client will be provided with educational and vocational testing. The clinician who will be administering those tests will be a professional who is expert in administering and evaluating a variety of educational and vocational tests, including those used most frequently by the VA in guidance counseling: the Differential Aptitude Tests (DAT) and the Kuder Preference Record (KPR).

- The test will be specially selected by me and administered by me. The test will be administered in an environment of comfort and privacy in a test facility that can accommodate up to 30 individuals. The facility is located on McAllister Street in the Fort Lewis Main Post Area.

- Once the test is concluded, the tests will be scored and the scores will be analyzed in order to determine interests, preferences, and other profiles which will be helpful to the individual being counseled with the goal of formulating employment or educational plans. Extensive analysis of the test will be performed by me.

- Although many counselors will determine plans of vocational/educational action based on the results of the tests administered, I intend to perform more individualized fact finding in order to provide thorough evaluation services. Before any planning is attempted, and before any goals are articulated of an employment or vocational nature, a personal interview will be conducted in order to gain information on the veteran's/serviceperson's/dependent's history. The intent of this personal one-on-one session will be to gather information to help profile his or her personality and current circumstances. It is my strong belief that, while testing instruments are helpful and often necessary in counseling, it is also important to gain, through oral communication, the counselee's perceptions of their current circumstances and of their future goals and objectives. An Interview Questionnaire which I have developed is intended to elicit information related to these and other areas:

> Personal history — family and marital status, support systems, finances
> Early interests/involvements and pre-military background
> Military occupational specialties
> Post military work experience
> Financial resources for extended educational involvements
> Disabilities/impairments that may affect educational or employment plans

- Performing syntheses of evaluations is an especially strong ability of mine, and I will be the provider of the services described in this award. After educational and vocational tests have been administered and evaluated, and after the counselor has conducted a personal interview to determine orally the client's personality characteristics and goals, a "partnership" will be formed between the counselor and the counselee in order to develop a Vocational/Educational Plan of Action.

- The Vocational/Educational Plan of Action that will be developed is at once a synthesis of all information and data obtained so far as well as a long-range plan targeting educational and employments goals. It may be that a "best case" and "most probable" and "worst case" will be developed so that options for future employment may be analyzed in light of variables in educational attainment. Alternatives will be addressed and tradeoff analysis will be performed of both educational and employment alternatives.

- The Vocational/Educational Plan of Action will clearly identify plans to overcome identified obstacles to planned educational goals and will attempt to formulate the plan of attack for overcoming those anticipated obstacles.

- The Vocational/Educational Plan of Action will incorporate in as much detail as possible the specific steps and tasks the individual will take to accomplish the goals and objectives identified. Where feasible a chronology will be developed. Specifics, details, micro-targets, mini-goals, milestones, and other itemized goal setting will be the heart of this Plan of Action.

# BUSINESS PLAN #6: Construction Loan Request

## J.J. Felix & Co.

General Contractor and Electrical Contractor

4815 Canady Pond Drive

Melbourne, FL  33433

(111) 111-1111 phone

Current Address:
P. O. Box 444, Tampa, FL  33484
Non-dedicated fax: (222) 222-2222

**GENERAL CONTRACTOR**

This is a business plan for an electrical contracting company formed in Florida.

### INDEX

# BUSINESS SUMMARY

Phase one: It is our business intention to embark upon a dramatic renovation project so that we may become more aggressive as a general contractor, especially in major industrial and commercial projects. The renovations will provide a more professional exterior while also permitting greatly enhanced capacity to take on larger jobs with higher profit margins.

Expanded facilities will permit us to bid on the most lucrative government contracts available at military bases in the South, since many government contracts specify that a company must have warehouse facilities of a certain size in order to bid on major projects.

With the objective of growth in mind, it is our intention to renovate the office/warehouse facility and associated general area near 4815 Canady Pond Drive. Our renovated professional facility will enable us to compete aggressively in the more lucrative commercial and industrial market. The facility will also enhance employee morale and will do much to ensure that we are an "employer of choice" within our local market.

Warehouse security is a "no-compromise" necessity. The state- of- the- art fire and burglar alarm systems we intend to install will allow for maximum security of inventory. Added warehouse capacity will also permit us to order needed items at the most economically advantageous rate. The modern facility will allow clientele to feel comfortable and will create an environment for productive negotiations.

We have discussed the matter with entrepreneurial associates and real estate appraisers who feel that the necessary cosmetic structural allowances and site preparations with associated rear parking area would introduce the possibility of the area's becoming a very lucrative office/industrial center.

The estimate for work to be performed in the renovation phase is $150,000.00.

Phase Two: The second phase of this project is to build a retirement community which will become a state-of-the-art living environment for senior citizens.

# BUSINESS PLAN #6: Construction Loan Request

**JAMES JACKSON FELIX**
4815 Canady Pond Drive, Melbourne, FL 33433
Mailing address: P.O. Box 444, Tampa, FL 33484
Bus: 333-3333 —— Home: 444-4444

---

**GENERAL CONTRACTOR**

Any time someone seeks a loan, from a traditional financing source such as a bank, or from a group of investors, the character and expertise of the individual requesting the loan are of primary importance. A part of this business plan is the resume of the individual who possesses the knowledge of the construction industry as well as the retirement community.

**LICENSURES**

Current Florida HA & Developmental Disabled Administrator License (02/03).
Current Florida General Contractor License (02/03).
Basic Emergency Medical Tech Course, Hillsborough Technical Community College, Tampa, FL (09/01-12/01).
Electrical Installation and Maintenance, Polk Community College, Winter Haven, FL (03/99-06/99).
Studied Business and Economics, University of South Florida, Tampa, FL (01/97-05/97).
Tampa Industrial Training Center, Tampa, FL (06/94-08/94).
Have completed continuing education credits for Electrical Contractor, and Bonding and Grounding classes to fulfill licensure requirements. Continue to take fifteen hours of continuing education annually to retain current license for Administrator of Health Facility.
Participated in numerous industry and trade association seminars and workshops dealing with the evergrowing needs of the health care industry.

**EXPERIENCE**

**ELECTRICAL CONTRACTING** (part-time). (01/03-present). Various jobs that required limited consideration. (See also attachment A labeled "Confidential").

**ASSOCIATE.** (12/01-01/03). Worked on various projects as an associate with a number of electrical contract companies including SCANA Electricity Co., South Florida Electricity, Co., and Piedmont Electricity Co., as time permitted in conjunction with the development of C.R.H. and the staff's support.

**ASSOCIATE DEVELOPER.** (09/99-12/01). Developed a retirement community along with other well known architects and engineers including Justin Hanover of Hanover & Associates and Pete Norsworthy PE.

**PROJECT MANAGER.** (03/97-09/99). While working with Kyle & Odom International, procured and maintained industrial power installations negotiating with engineering personnel of major oil refineries and a chemical processing plant concerning various alterations and new installations.

**SUPERVISOR.** (07/95-03/97). Supervised and installed electrical systems in two wings of an already constructed hospital (Melbourne Memorial) while working with E. L. Clapper Electric Company. Installed electrical system in a newly constructed hospital (Xavier Hospital) while working with Clarkston & Associates out of Melbourne, Florida.

**INDEPENDENT SUB-CONTRACTOR.** (06/94-07/95). Provided residential and commercial electrical contracting services performing mainly service and repair work for major corporations such as IBM and FL General Services Administration.

**ASSOCIATE ENGINEERING TECHNICIAN.** (10/92-06/94). Inspected servicing electrical utilities companies around the state along with complaint officer as part of the FL Utilities Commission; supported utility staff engineer with rate increases to present to the commission.

**ELECTRICIAN.** (12/91-10/92). Installed different electrical systems in an industrial waste water facility while employed with Elite Electrical Co., St. Petersburg, FL.

**ELECTRICIAN.** (08/89-12/91). While employed with Amberwood Electrical Co., Fort Pierce, FL installed a variety of electrical systems in an entire shopping center.

**CONSULTANTS**     The Fletcher Corporation, Tampa, FL.

**ASSOCIATES**     Associated General Contractors of America
(Tentative)     National Electrical Contractor's Association

# BUSINESS PLAN #6: Construction Loan Request

**Phase One: Physical Facilities: Construction Costs**
**Office and Warehouse Facility ( 50X25 )**

This scope of work and cost analysis is for the completed renovation of said location to the specifications of J.J. Felix, a small Electrical Contracting Firm. These renovations would satisfy any small scale distribution store or commercial garage or facilitations.

**GENERAL CONTRACTOR**

1. Roofing System: ( Demolition )
   A. Remove existing roofing system, all tin, and tar and material debris to be disposed of _____

2. Roofing System: ( Renovations )
   A. North elevation's graduation to be framed with 2" X 8" treated cap
      1. Blocks to be concrete-filled every eight (8) feet with 12" anchor bolts. _____
      2. 2" X 8" cap to be extended around the building _____
   B. South elevation's graduations to be leveled with 8" blocks to be concrete-filled every eight (8) feet with 12" anchor bolts
      _____
   C. Rear elevation to be framed with 2" X 4" studs from existing block wall
      1. (Preferably solid-block wall up to new truss system
   D. Truss system to be standard per specification with Sullivan's Supply Co. Representatives _____
   E. Plywood sheeting complete with asbestos shingles and aluminum storm drain in its entry _____
   F. Roof structuring to overlap existing bathroom wall (walls to remain if possible), new room structuring to join new overlapping roofing structure _____

TOTAL ROOF RENOVATION COST _____

3. Existing Structure's Renovations
   A. All existing openings to be filled in with masonry units (cinder blocks).
      1. Left front window to be replaced with masonry units and a 24" X 44" metal-clad window. _____
      2.. Existing garage door to be filled in with masonry units and a 24" X 44" metal-clad window. _____
      3. South front entrance to be a standard three foot (3') metal door and jam, primed and painted. _____
      4. South rear entrance to be standard garage doors (two 10' X 10'). _____
      5. Rear entrance to be reframed where necessary and new (42") metal door and jam installed (primed and painted) _____

TOTAL COST FOR STRUCTURE'S RENOVATION. _____

4. Interior Renovations are to be applicable to the specification of the general guidelines of facilitation of this structure.
   A. Ceiling work: five hundred (500) sq. ft. of 2' X 4' ceiling tile (Gen. Spec.) _____
   B. All walls bondexed and painted white _____
   C. Eighty (80) linear feet of 2" X 4" X 8' studded wall _____

D.     Four standard 30" regular interior doors hung     _____

E.     Floor System (prices include installation):

      1.     500 sq. ft. floor leveling compound     _____

      2.     18 sq. yds. graded comm. carpet     _____

      3.     4 sq. yd. 12" X 12" comm. tile     _____

      4.     Warehouse flr. cleaned and painted.     _____

**TOTAL INTERIOR RENOVATION COST**     _____

    5.     Heating and Air Conditioning System:     _____


**TOTAL COST OF HVA**     _____

    6.     Electrical System:

      A.     Lighting     _____

      B.     Switches     _____

      C.     Twenty-five (25) duplex receptacles     _____

      D.     Service equipment 200 amps (30 ckt's) Distribution

          panel in conference room     _____


**TOTAL FOR ELECTRICAL SYSTEM.**     _____

    7.     Security and Fire Alarm System

      A.     Three (3) smoke detectors.     _____

      B.     Two (2) five-pound ABC extinguishers     _____

      C.     All entrances to be announced     _____

      D.     Security system to be monitored by local dispatcher

          (City of Melbourne) Sawyer's Electric     _____


**TOTAL COST OF ALARM SYSTEM**     _____

    8.     Plumbing Repairs:

      A.     Existing laboratory facility to be removed and disposed of_____

      B.     New 20-gallon water heater (bthrm area)     _____

      C.     Install and furnish commode and sink     _____


**TOTAL COST OF PLUMBING ALTERATIONS**     _____

9.     Exterior Surfacing:

      A.     Painting     _____

      B.     Oscillation System     _____


**TOTAL SURFACING CONTRACT**     _____

    10.     Landscaping:

      A.     All trees and bushes to remove and dispose of     _____

      B.     It is the owner's contention and preference to do the necessary land

          scaping in the rear area of 4817 and 4815-B to accommodate the drive

          ways as well as the front yards of these locations.


**TOTAL LANDSCAPING COST**     _____

• All prices include labor and material unless otherwise specified.


**TOTAL JOB COST**     _____

**JOB/OVERHEAD 10%**     _____

**JOB PROFIT 10%^ OF COST & O/H**     _____

**COMPLETED JOB COST**     _____

# BUSINESS PLAN #6: Construction Loan Request

**Phase Two: Development of Retirement Community**

With respect to the proposed retirement community referred to as Addison Retirement Homes (A.R.H.), the ultimate intention of the facility is to become a state-of-the-art retirement community. It will be a thirty-bed group home with four to seven associated handicapped duplex apartments with community club house in a campus setting. This area with its proximity to the broader community would allow for a wholesome and graceful environment for the elderly in the community.

**GENERAL CONTRACTOR**

The retirement community has been a part of the American mindset now for the past twenty years, and we have created various visions of structural environments in which senior citizens may allow themselves the graceful opportunity of growing old. In this proposed community environment, we have provided for disabled individuals. Building a facility for the developmentally disabled is very similar to building a facility for senior citizens. Ultimately, the key to making this facility a success is staffing and administration.

We will seek governmental assistance in the administrative phase of this project. In the ten years that I have been associated with the rest home industry we've seen several satellite programs spun from the industry as viable alternatives. This is because of the structural environment of the rest home/nursing home setting.

# Projection of overhead expenses and profits

These projections anticipate annual overhead expenses and profits.

| | |
|---|---|
| $    450.00.......................................... | Mortgage |
|        250.00.......................................... | Utilities, ltg's, telephones, and advertisements |
|        158.00.......................................... | Office equipment |
|        200.00.......................................... | Insurance (facility) |
|        850.00.......................................... | Adm. Personnel |
|     1,908.00.......................................... | Monthly expenses |
|     1,538.00.......................................... | Mgr. Salary |
| | |
| $3,446.00.......................................... | Monthly overhead expenses *x12* |
| 41,352.00.......................................... | Annual overhead expenses |
| { 10% }.......................................... | Overhead expense applied to each job |
| | |
| $413,520.00.................................... | Given volume |
|    41,352.00.................................... | Annual overhead cost |
| | |
| $454,872.00.................................... | Required work volume to be secured annually |
|  *x10%* .......................................... | Anticipated profit margin applied to each job |
|   45,487.00.......................................... | Projected profit earnings |
| | |
| $454,872.00.................................... | Volume to maintain overhead |
|  +45,487.00.................................... | Anticipated PROFITS |
| | |
| $500,359.00.................................... | This figure reflects the total dollar value of work to be secured annually to maintain overhead costs as well as anticipated profit margins. |

All property hereafter mentioned as 4815 Canady Pond Drive owned totally by J.J. Felix and S.T. Quinn. Two independent deeds identifying these properties accompany this package: 4815 Canady Pond Drive, a 50'X25' cinder block building, and a proposed office and warehouse of J.J. Felix & Co.

# BUSINESS PLANS #7, #8, #9, and #10:
## Electrical Service Business Loan Request
## Medical Supply Company
## Franchise Application for a Convenience Store
## Hair Salon, Request for Financing

Many people want to read this book because they wish to see examples of business plans which were used to obtain loans.

Business plan #7 shows you a business plan which provides for the start-up of a business in the entrepreneur's spare time. This concise, relatively simple plan contains a simple balance sheet as well as a proposal for financing.

Business plan #8 is an executive summary pertaining to a medical supply company which had aspirations to become a multi-billion dollar company one day.

Business plan #9 is a lengthier plan which was successful in helping an individual obtain a franchise for a highly sought-after convenience store operation. The guidelines provided by the convenience store chain for potential franchisees was extensive and detailed, and this plan shows how one successful entrepreneur executed that plan.

Business plan #10 was used to obtain financing for a dynamic and progressive new hair salon.

# BUSINESS PLAN #7: Electrical Business Loan Request

## Yarboro Electrical Service Company

### Business Plan

I. **Form of Organization:** Sole proprietorship. To provide industrial installations, commercial and family dwellings with electrical installation and maintenance.

II. **Objectives:**
*Personal:* The development of a business which will become a full-time occupation for myself once I have retired from my current employer, just one year from now. I will work part-time while I establish the business.
*Business:* To organize a business for the primary purpose of profit and growth. The continued growth of the company will be insured through the reinvestment of all profits after set salary has been paid to myself.

III. **Desired Market**
Due to the continued growth of industry within the state of Illinois as well as in the Decatur area for a home base, all indicators point to a large demand for electrical contractors. There is still a growing pattern of single-family and multi-family units within the Decatur and Tatum county area. Existing units as to repair and maintenance would also be included in said market.

IV. **Competition**
Will include all electrical contractors within the state of Illinois. The competition most close at hand will be in the Decatur area where there are as many as 180 registered electrical contractors. Only 60 of these contractors are listed by the yellow pages. The companies registered in the yellow pages in Tatum County are from the eastern side of the county only.

V. **Market Stability**
Due to new construction and existing units within Decatur and Tatum County as well as the entire state of Illinois there is no limit to business to be generated. Many single-family dwellers are adding on additional rooms to their homes which will also need wiring. Daily homeowners have electrical problems that are too small for the larger electrical companies to realize a profit from.

VI. **Personnel**
The staff will include myself on a full-time basis with the help of one part-time helper. The helper is a close friend who is not interested in full-time employment. Other staff will be added according to need for each individual job. The market for such short-term helpers is plentiful due to numerous graduates from the Richland Community College who are looking for work. Many trained retired military persons live in the Decatur area that are seeking part-time employment.
*Physical Qualifications:* Have good general physical health being able to lift 50 pounds. All workers should be able to stoop, bend, and crawl. They must be able to work in small limited areas such as attics and crawl spaces which may have intense heat at times.
*Technical Qualifications:* The basics of electrical installation and repairs must be known. They should have necessary personal electrical tools. The use of electrical hand tools and bender must be known. Each helper must have a valid driver's license.

## VII. Location

The company will begin in an office that I will set up on my home. All heavy equipment used in installation will be stored in my garage. My wife will keep the books for me and take care of all correspondence.

## VIII. Zoning

There will be $350,000.00 liable insurance carried on my business. The city of Decatur requires that my company have a bond of $10,000.00. A Illinois Electrical Contractors license and permit will be held by the company.

## IX. Capital Needs

Capital needs include the following:

| | |
|---|---|
| Cash | 6,600.00 |
| Equipment Expense | 2,500.00 |
| Supplies Expense | 2,300.00 |
| Salaries Expense | 1,600.00 |
| Advertising Expense | 1,600.00 |
| Miscellaneous Expense | 1,000.00 |
| | 30,000.00 |

## X. Traffic

My customers will be gained through advertising (newspapers, flyers, and yellow pages) as well as satisfied customers and word of mouth.

### Supplemental Information

**1. Geographic Boundaries**

Business will be concentrated in the Decatur, Tatum County, Illinois areas.

**2. Source of Supplies and Equipment**

Supplies for the company will come from the numerous electrical supply distributors in the Tatum County, Illinois area. A limited amount of supplies will be stored at the business location. When jobs require additional supplies, they will be purchased as needed. With the expansion of the company growth in equipment will incur.

**3. Labor Pool**

The employees for the company will come predominately from Richland Community College graduates. All workers will begin on a part-time basis and as the business grows they will become full-time employees.

**4. Legal Requirement**

*Self (Owner):* An Illinois Electrical Contractor license, Illinois Privilege Permit. Bonding for Decatur City limits and trucker drivers class C license.
*Other Employees:* Truck driver licensed; qualified electricians.

**5. Promotion**

*Advertising:* The local phone book and newspaper will carry the company ad. Ads will be placed on an annual basis. *Other Promotions:* Flyer handouts and feedback, and word of mouth from satisfied customers.

**6. Optional Business Area of Expansion**

Illinois issues an unlimited Electrical Contractors License which will allow the company to expand into the states of Missouri, Kentucky, and Indiana. This will leave the door open for future expansion.

# BUSINESS PLAN #7: Electrical Business Loan Request

### Initial Requirements for First-Year Operations

**ELECTRICAL SERVICE COMPANY**

| | |
|---|---|
| **Cash:** | 6,600.00 |
| | |
| **Equipment:** | |
| 1 ea. truck 1/4 ton pickup (used) | 1,200.00 |
| Hand tools (electrical) | 300.00 |
| Benders (used) | 500.00 |
| Power tools (used) | 500.00 |
| | 9,100.00 |
| | |
| **Supplies:** | 2,300.00 |
| | 11,400.00 |
| | |
| **Salaries:** | 16,000.00 |
| | 27,400.00 |
| | |
| **Advertising:** | |
| Newspaper ads | 1,000.00 |
| Telephone Directory ads | 300.00 |
| Flyers, Publications, and Mailings | 300.00 |
| | 29,000.00 |
| | |
| **Miscellaneous:** | |
| Insurance and Bonding | 500.00 |
| Repairs, etc. | 500.00 |
| | |
| **Total Investment Required:** | **30,000.00** |

## Balance Sheet
December 1, 2002

**Assets:**

| | |
|---|---|
| Cash | $ 6,600.00 |
| Real Estate (Residential) | 80,000.00 |
| Land | 35,000.00 |
| Deposits (savings) | 20,000.00 |
| Vehicles: two (car - truck) | <u>25,000.00</u> |
| | **$166,600.00** |

**Liabilities:**

| | |
|---|---|
| Mortgage payable | 83,000.00 |

**Owner Capital:**

| | |
|---|---|
| Net Worth | 83,600.00 |
| **Total Liabilities and Capital** | **$166,600.00** |

# BUSINESS PLAN #8: Medical Supply Company

## EXECUTIVE SUMMARY

**EXECUTIVE SUMMARY** for a medical supply corporation in Georgia. This executive summary does not mention money or investment costs. It is simply intended to generate interest and stimulate discussion so that financial negotiations can be pursued at a later date.

U.S. expenditures on drugs and other medical nondurables approached $100 billion in 2002, and spending on medical devices such as wheelchairs, eyeglasses, and hearing aids was about $16 billion. Worldwide drug sales are rising at a rate of 8%-10% a year, and medical device sales at 7% a year. In the international marketplace, U.S. firms account for more than 40% of the $120 billion market for medical devices and more than 30% of the $265 billion pharmaceutical market. Medical products is indeed a huge and lucrative business.

Harrington Medical Technologies, Inc. (HMT, Inc.) is a Georgia corporation engaged in the research, design, engineering, clinical trial, field testing, manufacturing, marketing, sale, and distribution of primarily medical products. Our business is divided into four divisions.

**SUPPLY DIVISION:** Every so often a product or design philosophy comes along which revolutionizes an industry. As the innovator, pioneer, and leader in the area of medical supplies technology, we have the potential to absolutely transform the structure and methods of the medical supply industry worldwide. HMT's products can dramatically improve the quality of life for millions of patients throughout the world. The ingenuity, diversity, and marketability of our ideas and product lines have a unique history of growth.

HMT is much more than a stand-alone product company. We are a "system" company. We think in terms of systems and we design fully integrated systems to solve medical problems. We look at how the human body works, how biomedical and biomechanical systems function in the body, and how we can replicate them. We support the products we develop with defining medical and clinical models. Applying a computer analogy, we are both a "hardware" and a "software" company. Our medical models are the software which clinically support the hardware of all our medical devices.

In June 2002, a humanitarian mission to Haiti successfully deployed $1.5 million dollars worth of wheelchairs, glasses, hearing aids, and other much needed medical supplies. HMT's systems are the only functional devices which can be deployed cost-effectively in great quantity to the less fortunate people of this world, and as such, has already generated tremendous interest as a potential solution to many worldwide problems.

**MEDICAL DIVISION:** While our Supply Division is already generating sales and attracting national and international attention, we believe that our Medical Division could possess even greater worldwide market potential. Our Medical Division includes four groups:

- **Medical Equipment Group:** Two cutting edge medical device innovations will lead the success of the Medical Equipment Group.
  ***Human Spectrometer:*** We own exclusive manufacturing and marketing rights for a sophisticated physician-designed human spectrometer which accurately measures individual performance against individual potential. This is the first time in history that a device of this type has been constructed. Currently in the refinement and clinical testing phase, we are developing a relationship with a major international

university and technological institute to further explore the multiple application parameters of the device.

***Diagnostic X-ray Device:*** We are in the design stage of a revolutionary diagnostic x-ray device for brain cancer screening.

- **Clinical Group:** We develop biomedical and biomechanical models which support our technological designs and systems. We are currently defining the grant model and the research parameters for a jointly developed Harvard University's School of Medical Sciences grant with the Director of the Living Laboratory and the Medical University of Berlin, Germany. We have written a model for a clinical study on phantom pain and phantom sensation. Data will be compiled by a full clinical team as part of an upcoming major humanitarian mission to Colombia supported by HMT, Inc.

- **Pharmaceuticals Group:** We are in negotiations for exclusive licensing rights to a treatment protocol to combat several of the deadliest forms of cancer; the protocol is currently in the clinical trial stage.

- **Medical Supplies Group:** We currently have patents pending in the wound care area.

**TEXTILE DIVISION:** We have several copyrighted designs in the adaptive clothing field.

**CONSUMER DIVISION:** We have one consumer product patent pending and other products in the design stage.

This Executive Summary should not be construed in any way as a solicitation to invest. It is intended solely as an overview of our philosophy, values, goals, and objectives. Questions should be directed to HMT at 888-888-8888.

# PLAN #9: Franchise application, convenience store

Date

Exact Name of Person
Title or Position
Name of Company
Address (number and street)
Address (city, state, and ZIP)

**FRANCHISE**

This is a business plan for a Circle K convenience store. The convenience store provides extensive paperwork which gives details about the business plan which must be submitted in order to apply for a franchise. This individual was successful in obtaining a franchise.

Dear Exact Name of Person (or Dear Sir or Madam if answering a blind ad):

Attached is my business plan for Circle K. After reviewing my plan, you will, I am sure, realize that the potential for such a business is good.

To start my venture, I will need a loan of $85,000. I am sure you will also agree that my military background and management knowledge will ensure the success of this venture.

If you have any questions, please do not hesitate to call me. Thank you for your consideration. I look forward to hearing from you shortly.

Sincerely,


Wesley Hamilton

BUSINESS PLAN

## I. PRIORITIES

The Circle K Store will offer high quality take-out foods, beverages, candies, dairy products, specialty items, and nonfood merchandise at moderate prices compared to the convenience retailing market. In order be successful in operating a Circle K, I believe the following five priorities are critical:

- **Management control:** First in importance, I believe, is the necessity for the owner-operator to exert strong control over personnel and finances. My background is ideally suited to this priority, as I have distinguished myself as a leader and manager as a noncommissioned officer in the U.S. Army. I have become adept at using automated technology to account for inventory and equipment, and I have also become skilled at managing personnel and motivating them to achieve maximum efficiency. It is my belief that the four following priorities are a subset of managerial competence and managerial control.

- **Extended hours:** The owner recognizes that extended hour convenience stores emphasize convenience to the customer and provide high quality takeout foods and nonfood merchandise. This is a priority, and it takes a well-oiled machine to achieve this priority. Consumers must be able to count on the Circle K being open at all times at the advertised hours so that the convenience factor—a great motivating reason for frequenting the Circle K—is something the consumer can rely on.

- **Local service and local image:** It is anticipated that the great majority of customers who will patronize the establishment will be from local neighborhoods and individuals using the heavily traveled Ellison Road, Highway 56, and Butler Street. These customers are mostly individuals traveling east and west bound on Ellison Road going to and from work in a heavily populated area. I believe it is important that the local Circle K be perceived of as a "good citizen" in the community. The Circle K tends to become a mainstay and a well-known site in the community. It must be maintained in a clean and respectable fashion at all times so that it is always an attraction and never an eyesore.

- **Employee training:** Although I do not underestimate the difficulties of staffing and retaining good personnel at the lower-level wage scale which must be paid within a Circle K structure, I am excited about the challenge of recruiting and training good quality employees. I am an experienced trainer and motivator, and I will aggressively tackle the challenge of finding the best employees and training them to do their jobs in an outstanding fashion with **"Outstanding Customer Service At All Times"** as our first priority. I intend to attempt to attract quality individuals from the local neighborhood to work within the quality organization I intend to build, as I feel that many people could derive job satisfaction from having a job they enjoy at close proximity to their home.

- **Quality stock selection and skillful inventory control:** In a relatively small store, I believe it is of critical importance to make sure that the consumer finds the merchandise he or she is looking for when they come to shop. For that reason, I intend to perform extensive research of other area convenience stores

# PLAN #9: Franchise application, convenience store

to assess their inventory selection policies, and I will also thrive on the training provided by the Circle K Corporation. However, I feel there is no substitute for listening to the customer, and for that reason I intend to maintain a "consumer suggestion box" near the front cash register so that consumers can always make suggestions about items they would like to see carried in the store, changes in policy or hours they would like to see, or other alterations which consumers feel would make their neighborhood Circle K more convenient for them.

"Convenience" is the name of the game, I believe in the convenience retailing business, so I intend to keep my thumb on the pulse of the consumer and make sure that consumers know they can make their ideas, suggestions, and problems known to management at any time!

## II. CUSTOMER RELATIONS

As stated previously, **"Outstanding Customer Service At All Times"** will be the motto of the Circle K I manage, and I feel it is customer service which will keep a customer coming back time and time again when he has the choice of patronizing other similar establishments. The great majority of customers will come from the neighborhood areas, main thoroughfares, and nearby shopping centers. The store will attract lunchtime customers, early shoppers, weekend, and holiday customers and customers who may need only a few items.

- The primary marketing objective for the Circle K is to gain maximum market share of the area neighborhoods as well as the travelers going both west and east on Ellison Road. These travelers are primarily area employees and those driving long distances, and their primary vehicle is the automobile. It is expected that the average number of passengers per vehicle will be two. There will be some seasonality to the business in view of the much heavier traffic that is expected on the interstate during the winter months. However, our main concentration will be on becoming a positive influence in the community and in "courting" the "locals" who will be the "bread and butter" of our business.

- A second marketing objective will be to gain repeat business from those who patronize the Circle K for the first time as well as to gain customers through word of mouth advertising from first-time users. This will be done by serving high quality products in pleasant surroundings and a clean comfortable atmosphere.

**A.    I plan to provide the service in my store which will meet the needs and wants of customers through a strong employee training and development program.** Because of my background as a manager and trainer in the U.S. Army, I am professionally equipped to training employees to aim for the highest standards of customer service, and I will at all times model the behavior which I expect my employees to demonstrate.

**B.    While advancing ahead of my peers to leadership positions in military service, I have become aware of the importance of effective communications.** I will train employees in the "big picture" of customer service as well as in the minute details of handling instore traffic. For example, research has shown that people who smile at others are perceived of as more intelligent than those who do not smile. I will make the details of customer service—such as making eye contact, and providing "service with a smile"—standard ingredients and "the common denominator" of my store's customer service policy. Employees relate to customers through body language as well as through verbal communication, and I will make sure that employees know that their future advance and bonuses are dependent on their maintaining outstanding customer service. One thing the military has taught me, however, is that people are not always born knowing the right thing to do; they have to be trained and often retrained. I will relentlessly train and retrain my employees to achieve the highest standards of effective communication. Furthermore, as stated previously, I will maintain a Customer Suggestion Box and will encourage customers to communicate with management about any store policies or personnel which led to an unusual amount of satisfaction or dissatisfaction.

C. **First appearance is critically important in merchandising, and one of the first priorities appearance-wise is to maintain an outstanding sanitary rating and the highest standards of cleanliness.** "Cleanliness is next to godliness," they say, and while in military service I have been trained to achieve exceptionally high standards of orderliness and cleanliness. A neat, clean store would not only be a pleasure for an customer to visit but it would be a pleasure for an employee to work in such a place. So I believe the first key to presenting a good store image is to maintain the highest standards of cleanliness and orderliness.

## III. STORE STAFFING AND SCHEDULING

In the area of store staffing and scheduling—a critical ingredient of success—I feel I am exceptionally well qualified to establish and manage a business which depends upon quality staffing and scheduling of employees. Although I do not underestimate the difficulties of staffing and retaining good personnel at the lower-level wage scale which must be paid within a Circle K structure, I am excited about the challenge of recruiting and training good quality employees. I am an experienced trainer and motivator, and I will aggressively tackle the challenge of finding the best employees and training them to do their jobs in an outstanding fashion with **"Outstanding Customer Service At All Times"** as our first priority.

I intend to attempt to attract quality individuals from the local neighborhood to work within the quality organization I intend to build, as I feel that many people could derive job satisfaction from having a job they enjoy at close proximity to their home. Studies have shown that, when people are asked about what motivates them at work, they do not mention money first, but they say that they need enough equipment to get their job done, and they say that they want to feel appreciated. With those research findings in mind, and with my 10 years of experience as a middle manager in the U.S. Army constantly training and managing employees, I am confident that I can attract and retain the most qualified employees who will be a credit to the Circle K corporation as well as to the local community.

The competition to my Circle K store will come from the local Ellison Road Shopping Center which has four eating establishments which are located near the Circle K, and I believe we can compete aggressively with our competitors because of the professional store staffing and scheduling policies which I will implement and control.

# PLAN #9: Franchise application, convenience store

### IV. STORE BUDGET

Please see projected store budget.

### V. PERSONAL STATEMENT OF INCOME AND EXPENSES

It is the objective to operate the business with a minimal first year loss and have an operating profit by the first quarter of the second year of operation. The principal will pay himself a minimum salary so as to not imperil the cash flow of the business. Please see attached sheets for detailed discussion of my personal statement of income and expenses.

### VI. CONCLUSION

In conclusion, I believe I am well qualified to enter into a franchise relationship with Circle K, and I believe I possess many qualifications which will make me an effective franchisee. My 10 years of military service as a middle manager has helped me gain experience in managing and motivating people as well as in solving problems, making decisions, utilizing automated systems for accountability and control, and serving customers. I see the proposed franchise relationship as a mutually beneficial one in which I am trained to do things "the Circle K way" and then I in turn become "the voice and face" of the Circle K corporation to the common man in the street who visits the store. I believe Circle K must be very careful indeed about choosing its franchisees because it is we franchisees who shape the consumer's opinions of the overall organization. As a franchisee, it would be my goal to make a career out of my relationship with Circle K, and I believe the Circle K corporation would do well to seek franchisees who have a very long-term orientation such as I do. My outstanding personal character, my 10 years of management experience in supervising people and organizing activities, and my strong personal qualities of initiative and perseverance all make me an outstanding choice for a Circle K franchisee, and I believe strongly that Circle K should franchise this store to me because of the outstanding bottom-line results and impressive customer satisfaction levels which would be produced through my commitment and management skill.

### VI. WHO AM I?

In order to introduce myself and my strong qualifications for becoming a franchisee, wish to provide a brief summary of my background through the enclosed resume. Furthermore, I am providing a couple of "testimonials" regarding my character and skills in the form of two letters of recommendation and reference which are also shown in this section.

### VII. MAP OF THE AREA SHOWING THE DESIRED LOCATION OF CIRCLE K

The town boasts several institutions of higher learning and, indeed, the site of the Circle K which I propose is nestled within the University of Colorado grounds. The business would be located near Dowling Street. The business would be in an upscale, fashionable neighborhood with a clientele accustomed to requiring the services of an excellent convenience store.

The competition to my Circle K store will come from the local Ellison Road Shopping Center which has four eating establishments which are located near the Circle K, and I believe we can compete aggressively with our competitors because of the professional store staffing and scheduling policies which I will implement and control.

## POSTSCRIPT: PERTINENT FACTS ABOUT GOLDEN:

Expected to see its population grow to 40,817 in the year 2004, Golden is in Central Colorado about 110 miles southwest of Denver; 70 miles west of Greely. It is in Gilpin County, which is bordered by Brookvale, Evergreen, Morrison, Indian Hills, and Englewood. The city of Golden covers 10.8 square miles.

The city is considered an upscale area with a wide variety of cultural and social activities available. The climate of Golden, CO is modified continental with mild winters and humid summers, with average temperatures of 37 degrees December through February and 75 degrees June through August.

Because the site of the Circle K is within the community of the University of Colorado, I anticipate being able to draw from the pool of students as part of my labor supply.

### STORE BUDGET

After evaluating the past performances, I have investigated each item line-by-line and determined that historical growth has occurred at 16 percent over the last 12 months. However, for purposes of this analysis, the growth rate was held to 3 percent. The actual year-to-year growth rate varies in accordance with decline and flow of the local economy. The 2000-02 year shows an actual moderate increase in sale and gross profit dollars.

### SALES

While sales levels have risen moderately, much can be attributed to the change in management. Initially the original franchisee was rather successful. The predecessor was not as successful in the development of the business Historical growth has shown a continued and steady 3 percent increase in merchandise sales each year. I have based my projections on the assumption that the trend will continue.

### GROSS PROFIT PERCENT AND DOLLARS

For the past 12 months of 2001 the gross profit percent and dollars were 16 percent higher than the comparable months of 2000. My projections are based on inventory controls. I have based my projections on achieving a 3 percent increase.

### PAYROLL AND PAYROLL ITEMS

The payroll and payroll taxes will not vary sufficiently from season to season. It will not necessarily impact the payroll. The payroll will normally be the same during slow months. If I wish to maintain the same gross profit margin, I must cut hours.

**Example:** Let's assume the months of May, June, and July average sales of $90,000.00. Let's also assume that the months of October, November, and December average sales of $80,000. Based on the average sales, there is a 12 percent decrease in merchandise sales during the slower period. It will be necessary to curtail the number of personnel hours and not the payroll. Assuming that there are 265 total hours per month, one must curtail 12 percent of hours.

# PLAN #9: Franchise application, convenience store

## INVENTORY VARIATION

I anticipate that I will be able to sustain a minimum gross profit margin of 39 percent. I will seek to sustain this level through management of the inventory sourcing. The establishment of the opening inventory levels is a key issue which a new franchisee faces. The franchisee must balance the need for the broad selection of products with the capital needed to pay for the inventory. Careful attention must be paid to the selection of the products as cash flow will be restricted if too much start-up capital is incorrectly spent on slower moving products.

The computerized inventory tracking system will support this strategy by allowing me to monitor inventory levels, track sales levels, and project the need to reorder stock on a daily basis.

## FINANCING SOUGHT

I am seeking to secure financing of an $85,000 loan. The $85,000 loan would be for seven years and the money will be repaid from the proceeds of the Circle K located on 9374 Ellison Road. The $85,000 will be spent on beginning inventory, franchise fee, good will fee, cash register fund, licenses, permits, bonds, and working capital for the first three months.

I anticipate that I will be able to sustain a minimum gross profit margin of 30% to 35%. I will seek to maintain this level through management of the inventory. I will contribute $70,000 cash during the start-up phase.

The working capital will enable the franchise to meet current expenses, offset any possible negative cash flow in the beginning, and ensure growth of the business.

## APPLICATION AND EXPECTED EFFECT ON BUSINESS LOAN

The $85,000 loan will be used as follows:

| Use of Funds | $ |
| --- | --- |
| Initial Franchise Fee | $50,000 |
| Down Payment on Opening Inventory | $18,000 |
| Good Will Payment | $60,000 |
| Cash Register Fund | $ 1,000 |
| Licenses, Permits, and Bonds | $ 1,000 |
| Working capital (reserved, not disbursed) for the first three months: | $10,000 |
| | 140,000 |
| Minimum cash on hand | $15,000 |
| Total Use of Funds | 155,000 |
| Personal Contribution | 70,000 |
| LOAN NEEDED | $85,000 |

# FINANCIAL PROJECTIONS

The following projections are based on past performances:

- Most conservative projection of $1,046,282/year in sales is based on 364 days/year.
- Most optimistic projection of $1,015,808/year in sales is based on 364 days/year.
- Labor costs are based on prevailing wages for necessary employees. Hours and duties based on similar operation. Current government tax rates and insurance quotes are the basis for the payroll taxes and benefit package.
- Growth in sales is figured to sustain 2% - 3% per year.

## LOAN REPAYMENT

A loan was requested for $85,000 with a monthly payment plan of $1,367.57. The amortization is 7 years. The interest rate requested is 9.0%. The first payment should be due 60 days from closing to allow Purchaser to be certified by Circle K as a Franchisee and take possession of the Circle K convenience store.

# BUSINESS PLAN #10: Hair Salon, Request for Financing

## REQUEST FOR FINANCING
### *NEW IMAGE, INC.*

New Image, Inc. is requesting a loan for $65,000 to finance its new salon, which has an opening date slated for March 15, 2004.

## SALON SIZE AND TYPE

**HAIR SALON, REQUEST FOR FINANCING** for a full-service organization which includes a spa located in Kentucky. Amount of financing sought: $65,000.

The salon is designed to accommodate 12 to 24 hairstylists at full capacity. The salon will open with two to five stylists, and should reach full-stylist status within two to five years after opening. The salon will occupy a spacious 3,000 square-foot freestanding building in a high-traffic area with very much exposure at the corner of Wilshire Drive and Roxdale Boulevard, across from the Howard Johnson Hotel. The salon is in the middle of a small cove of restaurants and shares the community parking area. It is easily accessible for the clients of Howard Johnson. The location is leased from Dr. Phillip Evanston, Piermont Medical Center, Frankfort, KY.

Other salons located within a three-mile radius are single-person salons and booth rentals. We do not view these salons as direct competition; in fact, we see them as an asset in that clients will now have the option for an updated full-service salon with a strong business structure that is quality service oriented. Many of these salons have not been renovated in several years and are in poor condition. The stylists have had few training updates and many customers are only receiving basic haircare services. We feel the proposed salon both creates a need and fills a void in the community where haircare options and spa services are concerned.

The primary goal of the salon is to provide men, women, and children of all ages with a full-service haircare package (including shampoo, conditioning, haircutting, and chemical services) plus other salon services (makeup, skin care, body waxing, body treatments, massage, manicures and/or pedicures). All salon services are designed to meet the needs of fashion-conscious individuals desiring a complete line of quality services at moderate prices.

## SALON PRICING STRUCTURE

The salon services will be moderately priced, with haircuts ranging from $15 to $28, depending on the pay rate of the particular stylist (see EMPLOYEE PAY/BENEFIT PACKAGE). Chemical services will range from $45 to $80 for color services — depending on the type of service done and time needed to complete it. Other salon services are based on a per application cost, i.e. one skin care/makeup session will range in cost from $25 to $50 and one full-body massage $45.

## THREE-YEAR PROJECTIONS

According to the preceding SALON PRICING STRUCTURE, we estimate the salon's income and expense figures for the first three years of operation according to the chart shown as APPENDIX A.

## EMPLOYEE PAY/BENEFIT PACKAGE

| | |
|---|---|
| Services Sales up to $600/week | $4.25-$4.50/hour |
| Services Sales from $600-$700/week | $4.50-$5.50/hour |
| Services Sales from $700-$800/week | $5.50-$6.75/hour |
| Services Sales from $800-$900/week | $6.75-$8.00/hour |
| Services Sales over $900/week | $8.00-$9.25/hour |

Staff is eligible for one week paid vacation after one year of service, two weeks after three years of service. Paid holidays are New Year's Day, Memorial Day, July 4th, Labor Day, Thanksgiving Day, and Christmas Day. Health insurance and a retirement program will go into effect one year after date of employment, the cost of which will be shared between employees and the salon.

## THE STATE OF THE INDUSTRY

In a time when a large portion of the population is becoming more and more concerned with health and appearance combined with an increase in dual income families, the salon industry finds itself faced with unique possibilities. The health-conscious working male and female population requires salons that fit their image and lifestyle. Customers are demanding services and products that allow them to look equally good at board meetings and on the tennis court, in group advertising meetings and at the gym, at the theater and at the beach. These dual income families require extended hours, a variety of services, and the convenience of purchasing all body and beauty care items and services in one location. The majority of these families are willing to pay moderate to high prices but expect quality service.

Our salon is aware of the unique needs of today's customers. The salon is designed to meet these needs with evening and weekend hours, an extensive service menu, a variety of professional haircare products, and quality staff to bring it all together.

## DEMOGRAPHICS

The salon will be located in a city with a population of 75,700 and a county with a population of 279,995, contained within approximately 417.7 square miles. The median household buying income is $26,590 for Franklin County. Ninety percent (90%) of the existing clientele of our business has an effective buying income of $27,000 to more than $50,000 a year. The median age of our clientele is 37 years old, with the average age of the population falling in the 22 to 62-year group. Average years of schooling completed is 16.

Population experts estimate increases in both total population and income over the next 10 years. The salon is geared to appeal to customers in the 22 to 62-year age group with a sophisticated and upbeat decor plan. The services and products that will be available are designed to satisfy the most discriminating older customer as well as cater to the younger clients and their ever changing fashion needs (see STAFF TRAINING).

There are numerous large companies in the area that each employ over 500 persons. They include Franklin County Medical Center, U-Haul Moving and Storage Company, and HONDA, just to name four. Franklin County and many other medical groups are located within less than a half-mile radius of the salon. The Howard Johnson Hotel is right next to the salon location. We expect to promote the salon to all these organizations through special offers and incentives.

## STAFF TRAINING

The first persons to be hired will be the salon apprentices. Information provided to the salon industry proves that a stylist may double her service income by the use of an effectively trained apprentice. The owner has training experience with both large and small groups and has the ability to effectively evaluate the staff and communicate their weaknesses to them. As the trainer/manager, the owner will work directly as part of the management group so that the entire salon is updated regularly on the current trends, techniques, and product uses available.

All staff members will undergo an intensive four-week training period prior to the grand opening, and will be on "probation" for the first 60 days after the grand opening. During that time they will undergo further training in customer handling (as per the customer handling system recommended by the salon), technical training, and retail sales training. At the end of 90 days, all staff members will either be fully prepared to meet any and all needs of salon customers or they will be given further training or replaced at the discretion of the management team. The ultimate goal of training must be to increase the likelihood that the customer will be satisfied enough with services received to not only return, but to recommend the salon to friends.

## MANAGEMENT

The salon owners will take on the duties as managers and salon trainers and, as sales increase, a receptionist will be hired. All staff members will be given job descriptions prior to beginning work. The salon policy and procedure manual will be reviewed with the group on the first day of employment. Corrective action procedures as well as daily salon procedures that are the responsibility of each employee will also be reviewed and the employee will be asked to sign a form stating that the information has been reviewed and understood.

## ADVERTISING AND GRAND OPENING

We expect to utilize an intensive and ongoing advertising plan that will include gift-with-purchase, multiple purchase packages, referral and frequent visit packages, and more for our customers. By working with our distributors, we believe we can put together promotions that are effective in bringing in new customers without having to discount prices. We will be utilizing a Merchandising, Advertising, and Promotions Kit (MAP KIT) which contains many camera-ready ads, station banners, and point-of-purchase materials. We expect to maintain an aggressive marketing plan which will include at least 12 promotions annually and will coincide with in-salon training, contests, and employee incentive programs designed to enhance the promotions.

Grand Opening advertising will go into effect three to four weeks after the salon has opened. Our research tells us that the most effective grand opening plans include gifts for the customer, a drawing, and special values for returning customers. We plan a drawing for a weekend getaway to the La Vida Spa. We will take out an ad in the local paper promoting the drawing and do direct mailings and have flyers made to be hand-delivered (by employees) around the community to large businesses. Secondary prizes will include various free services and miscellaneous haircare tools and products. Grand Opening week will also include discount days such as Men's Day, Women's Day, Senior's Day, and Children's Day, at which time anyone fitting the necessary criteria for the day will receive a 10% discount on all salon products and services.

## OWNER PROFILE

With 14 years in the industry, owner/manager Carol Manigault will bring strong customer-service experience and staff leadership to the salon. She has been chosen as a technical educator with the Lancome Corporation during her career, as well as attending numerous advanced training classes to fine-tune her craft.

Her partner and spouse, Harris Broswell, has worked with their business for the last six years and will add strength in both sales and management functions of the salon.

We feel our desire for and dedication to quality in service will be a welcome addition for all community members. We expect the same standard of service from our staff members and we will place a major focus on employee training, which we will promote through consistent and innovative advertising campaigns.

## SUMMARY

We believe our proposed salon will come to be known as one of the most innovative and respected in the city. We will be offering services and products in conjunction with a professional customer handling system that can usually only be found in much larger cities at a much higher cost. Our goal is to give all customers more than they expect in terms of quality service at less than they might expect to pay.

Our training and operational systems are modeled after the most effective in the industry. High-quality systems and computerization will allow the salon to run at maximum efficiency and we project strong growth figures in the upcoming years.

# BUSINESS PLAN #10: Hair Salon, Request for Financing

APPENDIX A

|  | YEAR 1 | YEAR 2 | YEAR 3 |
|---|---|---|---|
| Sales |  |  |  |
| Haircare | $115,000 | $138,000 | $165,600 |
| Retail Products | 63,000 | 75,600 | 90,720 |
| Spa Services | 25,000 | 30,000 | 36,000 |
|  |  |  |  |
| Total Sales | $203,000 | $243,600 | $292,320 |
|  |  |  |  |
| Cost of Goods Sold |  |  |  |
| Stylist Salaries | $ 39,200 | $ 48,800 | $ 58,400 |
| Administrative Salaries | 14,000 | 14,000 | 14,000 |
| Payroll Taxes | 10,640 | 12,560 | 14,480 |
| Supplies - Backbar | 11,200 | 13,440 | 16,128 |
| Merchandise Retail | 31,500 | 37,800 | 45,360 |
|  |  |  |  |
| Total Cost of Goods Sold | $106,540 | $126,600 | $148,368 |
|  |  |  |  |
| Gross Profit | $ 96,460 | $117,000 | $143,952 |
| Gross Profit Percentage | 47.52% | 48.02% | 49.24% |
|  |  |  |  |
| Operating Expenses |  |  |  |
| Advertising | $ 6,000 | $ 7,000 | $ 8,000 |
| Bank Charges | 600 | 600 | 600 |
| Cash Over/Short | 120 | 175 | 225 |
| Dues and Subscriptions | 275 | 325 | 400 |
| Business Insurance | 1,700 | 1,800 | 1,900 |
| Employee Benefits | 0 | 3,140 | 3,620 |
| Miscellaneous | 1,000 | 2,000 | 3,000 |
| Office Expenses | 3,000 | 3,500 | 4,000 |
| Professional Fees | 300 | 300 | 300 |
| Rent | 10,000 | 12,800 | 15,600 |
| Repairs/Maintenance | 200 | 300 | 400 |
| Telephone | 2,100 | 2,300 | 2,400 |
| Training | 2,000 | 2,000 | 3,000 |
| Utilities | 6,000 | 7,000 | 8,000 |
|  |  |  |  |
| Total Operating Expenses | $ 33,295 | $ 43,240 | $ 50,445 |
|  |  |  |  |
| Profit from Operations | $ 63,165 | $ 73,760 | $ 93,507 |
|  |  |  |  |
| Other Expenses |  |  |  |
| Equipment Lease | $ 9,517 | $ 9,517 | $ 9,517 |
| Loan Payment | 19,620 | 19,620 | 19,620 |
| Equity Line | 4,524 | 4,524 | 4,524 |
|  |  |  |  |
| Total Other Expenses | $ 33,661 | $ 33,661 | $ 33,661 |
|  |  |  |  |
| Net Profit | $ 29,504 | $ 40,099 | $ 59,846 |

**HAIR SALON EXECUTIVE SUMMARY**

# BUSINESS PLAN #11
# Insurance Group Plan

You have already seen that the business plans in this book vary in length. Business plan #11 is one of the lengthier plans in this book. It goes into great detail on the industry background, current trends, other ways of doing business in the industry, and other matters. If you are looking to develop a comprehensive business, this could be a valuable model. Some of the sections in this business plan are these:

Industry overview and analysis
U.S. health industry overview
Insurance provider market
Regulations
Trends
Insurance Demand
Competitive Insurance Demand
Strategy
Target Markets
Development
Operations
Administrative Service Agreements
Management
Key Success Factors

# BUSINESS PLAN #11: Insurance Group Plan

### VAN ROBINSON INSURANCE GROUP, INC.
### CONFIDENTIAL BUSINESS PLAN

**INSURANCE COMPANY**

This is a business plan for a company that offers health, dental, liability and supplemental insurance.

This Confidential Plan (the "Plan") and its appendices are furnished to you by Van Robinson Insurance Group, Inc. (the "Company") on a confidential basis. The information contained in this Business Plan has been prepared by Robinson. This Plan, however, is not intended to provide the primary basis for any decision about, or recommendation that any person participate in, a transaction with Van Robinson Insurance Group.

The Business Plan has been prepared in three separate parts for ease of reading:
(i) Executive Summary,
(ii) Business Plan and
(iii) Financial Analysis and Projections
regarding the future prospects of Robinson. All three sections of the Business Plan should be read in their entirety for a complete understanding of the Company, its business and prospects.

The information concerning Robinson's insurance business and prospects set forth in the Business Plan is derived from publicly available information as well as material furnished by Robinson and its management. All references to projected or anticipated results are based on financial projections prepared by Robinson's management. The financial projections and forecasts included herein are based on numerous assumptions made by management, and no assurances can be given that any such assumptions and the resulting projections and forecasts will prove to be accurate. All forecasts and proforma financial information are included for illustrative purposes only. It is impossible to predict future operating results of Robinson with certainty, and no representation or warranty is made that any particular financial results can or will be achieved. No representations can be expressed or implied as to the attainability of any such forecast.

Robinson reserves the right to request the return of the Plan at any time. Any reproduction or distribution of the Plan, in whole or in part, or the disclosure of any of its contents, is prohibited without the expressed prior written consent of Robinson. The recipient will promptly return this Plan and all material received in connection herewith without retaining any copies should Robinson request such action.

Insurance Officers of Robinson are available to answer questions concerning the company and will, upon request, make available such other information as might reasonably be requested. This Plan is a working document and changes will be incorporated as necessary to refine the plan. Updates are reflected by the date of change on modified pages. Readers are encouraged to review all three sections of the Business Plan and forward any questions and comments to: Van Robinson Insurance Group, Inc., 6430 Wellington Avenue, Suite 206, Charleston, South Carolina 29409, ATTN: Joseph O'Connell, or call us at 123-456-7890.

## I.     INDUSTRY OVERVIEW AND ANALYSIS

Over the last several years, the insurance coverage industry has been in the process of significant evolution and reform. The scope of services needed by the integrated insurance industry has expanded to include the negotiation of managed insurance, coverage and self-funded contracts, the creation and operation of sophisticated information systems, and a turn-key management service for managing agency offices. Robinson believes that this climate of change presents a significant opportunity to expand market share and profitability of the business.

## A.    U.S. HEALTH INSURANCE INDUSTRY

National insurance spending currently exceeds $1.5 trillion, with approximately $400 billion directly attributable to medical, dental, physician liability, and supplemental insurance policies. At this level, insurance coverage expenditures represent more than 13.6% of the gross domestic product ("GDP"). The Insurance Provider Financing Administration forecasts that national coverage spending in 2001 was approximately $1 trillion, with approximately $310 billion directly attributable to agency services. Insurance agency expenditures continue to be the largest sector in the insurance coverage industry with costs of approximately $400 billion, representing 40% of all provider expenditures. The Medicaid and Medicare programs, which provide coverage services for approximately 31 million and 35 million individuals in the United States, respectively, are estimated to each have accounted for over $200 billion of Federal expenditures in 2001. Despite industry-wide cost containment pressures, the Board of National Insurance Providers ("NIP") expects that the industry will continue to grow 12% to 15% per year both in absolute dollars and as a percentage of GDP and projects that by the year end 2000, expenditures in the United States could increase to as much as $1.4 trillion or 15% of GDP. These estimates assume that continued cost containment measures will be more than offset by demands resulting from current demographic trends, such as the aging of the population, growth in income, general inflation and new technology.

Health insurance in the United States historically has been delivered through a fragmented system of providers, including individual or small groups of primary care physicians and specialists. According to the American Medical Association (AMA), approximately 625,000 physicians are actively involved in patient care in the United States. A study by the AMA estimates that there are over 86,000 physicians practicing in 3,600 multi-specialty group practices (three or more physicians) and over 82,000 physicians practicing in 12,700 single specialty group practices in the United States. All of these factors contribute to the increased cost of insurance coverage.

## B.    INSURANCE PROVIDER MARKET

### Group Practice Insurance

The concept of group practice is not new, providing the basis for such leading nonprofit organizations as the P.A. Joel Clinic and the Carolina Medical Clinic. The environment in which they operate is what makes the new generation of group practices different. The growth of managed coverage and capitated plans, the resource-based relative value scale (RBVRS) payment system, and a growing demand for complex outpatient services are the driving forces behind the growth of physician groups. A study by the American Medical Association (AMA) estimates that there are 16,576 group practices (defined as three or more formally organized physicians) in the United States, with a mean number of 11.5 physicians per group. The number of physicians in the groups ranges from three to more than 3,000 with 189 groups reporting 100 or more physicians. However, most groups tend to be small, with 45 percent having three or four

# BUSINESS PLAN #11: Insurance Group Plan

physicians. Multi-specialty insurance groups tend to be larger than single specialty groups, and their average size is 24.6. The proportion of non-federal physicians in group practices grew from 10.6 percent to 33 percent.

**FIGURE 1**
**INSURANCE GROUP MANAGEMENT**
(Dollars in Billions)

| Growth Rate | 2002 | 2004 |
|---|---|---|
| **INSURANCE COMPANY** Total Health Insurance Expenditures | $904 | $1,500 |
| 7.5% | | |
| Percentage of Expenditures for Physician Services | 18.5% | 18.5% |
| Physician Service Expenditures | $167.2 | $277.5 |
| 7.5% | | |
| Percentage of Non-Federal Physicians | | |
| (Insurance Group Providers) | 33.0% | 56.0% |
| Insurance Group Revenues | $55.2 | $155.4 |
| 15.9% | | |
| Mean Percentage Net Practice Revenues | 43.0% | 41.0% |
| Revenues Net of Compensation | $23.7 | $63.7 |
| 15.2% | | |
| Retained by Physicians | | |
| Percentage Investor and Physician Owned Groups | 50.8% | 43.5% |
| Total Investor Owned Market | $12.1 | $27.2 |
| 12.6% | | |
| Insurance Investment Revenues | $0.46 | $8.6 |
| 52.1% | | |

## C. HOSPITAL AND INSURANCE INTEGRATION

Hospitals and insurance companies are two traditional business partner choices. No data exist regarding the absolute number of these arrangements. Available statistics place groups into broad categories, i.e., 75.6% are professional corporations, 15.0% are partnerships, 3.4% are associations, and 1.2% are investor-owned. Figure 2 shows the distribution of ownership reported by the AMA. This data implies that most groups are still physician-owned, and that penetration by hospitals, insurers, and investor-owned management services organizations is still quite low.

**FIGURE 2**

**DISTRIBUTION OF GROUPS BY LEGAL FORM OF ORGANIZATION**

| Legal Form of Organization | Percentage |
|---|---|
| Professional Corporation | 75.6 |
| Investor-Owned for Profit Corporation | 1.2 |
| Partnership | 15.0 |
| Association | 3.4 |
| Other | 4.8 |

**PIP Regulations**

HCFA has issued final regulations (the "PIP Regulations") covering the use of physician incentive plans ("PIPs") by HMOs, various insurance coverage agencies, and other managed care contractors and subcontractors ("Organizations"), potentially including Van Robinson Insurance Group. Any Organization that contracts with a physician group that places the individual physician members of the group at substantial financial risk for the provision of services (e.g., if a primary care group takes risk but subcontracts with a specialty group to provide certain services) must satisfy certain disclosure, survey, and stop-loss requirements. Under the PIP regulations, insurance payments of any kind, direct or indirect, to induce providers to reduce or limit covered or medically necessary services ("Prohibited Payments") are prohibited. Further, where there are no Prohibited Payments but there is risk sharing among participating providers related to utilization of services by their patients, the regulations contain three groups of requirements: (i) requirements for physician incentive plans that place physicians at "substantial financial risk;" (ii) disclosure requirements for all Organizations with PIPs; and (iii) requirements related to subcontracting arrangements. In the case of substantial financial risk (defined in the regulations according to several methods, but essentially risk in excess of 25% of the maximum insurance payments anticipated under a plan with less than 25,000 covered lives) organizations must: (i) conduct enrollee surveys, and (ii) ensure that all providers have specified stop-loss protection. The violation of the requirements of the PIP regulations may result in a variety of sanctions, including suspension of enrollment of new Medicaid or Medicare members, or a civil monetary penalty of $25,000 for each determination of noncompliance. In addition, because of the increasing public concerns regarding PIPs, the PIP regulations may become the model for the industry as a whole. The new regulations could have an effect on the ability of Robinson to effectively reduce the costs of providing services by limiting the amount of risk that may be imposed upon physicians.

## D.  TRENDS

The health insurance industry in the United States has been placed in constant motion by the government and private sectors as never seen before, driven by politicians, employers, insurance companies, health maintenance organizations, hospitals, physicians, nurses, and vendors to these organizations. Politicians are driving toward change due to the budgeting process and the downturn in economic recovery. These drivers are forcing the other players in the insurance industry to strategize in order to maintain as much self-determination as possible. As shown in South Carolina, Tennessee, and Georgia, these states are forging ahead with their own legislative laws hoping for later Federal waivers from Medicare programs. Employers are becoming leaner and are attempting to reduce insurance costs to improve their company's bottom line. HMOs are consolidating in order to create competitive delivery systems to fit in the managed care world. Hospitals and physicians, together or independently, are forming foundations, PHOs, management service organizations, as well as other competitive strategies. Physicians, the gatekeepers, are forming the same groups in addition to clinics without walls, IIAs, and networks. The vendors are attempting to find their role with technology enhancements and new products, with cost efficiency.

Businesses, with non-insurance investors, attempted to bring business principles and ownership to previously sanctified grounds by acquiring the assets of insurance providers. In short, because of the market forces, large and small-scale consolidations

# BUSINESS PLAN #10: Insurance Group Plan

are occurring in nearly all segments of the insurance industry. Hospitals are currently retooling, since in past years, they kept primary care physicians at the bottom half of the decision-making chain. Specialists have placed these hospitals in competitively weak positions by spurning the advances of HMOs and managed care organizations. The hospitals' purchasing of high-tech, underutilized technology has created inpatient services that may be relocated to outpatient settings. Large insurance carriers are looking to purchase physician and hospital delivery systems in order to maintain and improve market share. These same insurance carriers will also bring their capital to the marketplace by erecting managed service organizations. These companies will control segments of the market where hospitals and physicians have been dormant.

**INSURANCE COMPANY**

Evolution in health insurance reform has taken on many faces, impacting the force of managed care, the form it has taken, and the organization of forms of physician groups. In addition, the economy of America will also force the delivery of health insurance to change in the coming years.

Managed care has in the past few years become the most utilized form of health insurance. Over 55% of all persons having health insurance have some form of managed care plan, be it an HMO (22%), a PPO (25%), or a POS plan (8%). Of the 45% of health insurance that is still indemnity-related, only 4% of the plans have no pre-certification requirement for hospital admission, down from 22% as recently as ten years ago.

The growth of managed care has led to a shift to new arrangements over the past few years, with more of the expansion taking the form of preferred provider organizations, point-of-service plans, and independent practice associations. In addition, market demand has led to greater development of integrated delivery systems, as well as specialized products such as managed care "carve-outs" that handle broad categories of diseases or treatments and "carve-ins" that contract with well-known providers for specific treatments. HMO growth has been away from the staff model (down 35%) and toward models of HMO networks offering more autonomy for the physicians (up 70%).

The health insurance industry has predicted rapid growth in group agencies over the next five years. As these changes impact the form in which physicians practice, the population's aging will impact the manner of their practice. The size of the elderly population, the segment with the largest per capita usage of various health insurance services, is increasing more rapidly than the rest of the population largely as a result of demographic trends and advances in medical technology that have increased life expectancies. The rapid aging of the U.S. population also has resulted in a greater incidence of disease and disability. In the United States, the general population has aged dramatically since the beginning of the century. In 1900, only 4% of the population was 65 or over; by the year 2020, with the aging of the "Baby Boom" generation, the over-65 segment is expected to account for 17.7% of the population. The high prevalence of chronic conditions among the elderly and the functional limitations that result generate a large demand for diagnostic, therapeutic, rehabilitative, and supportive services. According to the U.S. Bureau of the Census, the American Hospital Association, and HHS, persons in the United States aged 65 and older, while comprising only 13% of the population in 1993, accounted for 35% of the hospital admissions, 46% of hospital inpatient days, and 39% of health insurance expenditures.

# The Evolution of Managed Care with Insurance Coverage

Robinson believes that portions of the United States are on the verge of a fourth stage of evolution in the development of managing health insurance and insurance.

Phase One included reducing costs by developing purchasing power. With a critical mass of enrollees and control of the patient, managed care companies exacted volume discounts. In the early years of managed care, negotiating discounts with physicians, hospitals, and other providers was a key driver in reducing insurance costs. Volume discounts (or reducing unit prices) became a less significant driver in controlling costs, and controlling utilization (or volume) came to the fore.

Phase Two involved the reduction of costs by curtailing inappropriate utilization of specialists and other high-cost providers. In this phase, managed care organizations allowed services by specialists and other providers only if a primary care physician referred the care given. Managed care companies depended on the primary care physician to act as a gatekeeper, assuring only appropriate utilization to flow through the system. Volume discounts and the gatekeeper concept allowed HMOs to price products lower to attract enrollees. However, the restrictive features that drove costs down also limited enrollment growth potential; a large portion of the population demanded freedom of choice and free access to the system.

Phase Three is the driving of enrollment by adding an indemnity feature. Although managed care had developed an effective supply-side of the insurance equation, the demand side was seeding unrestricted access to providers. To meet demand, managed care companies developed the point-of-service plan, which is a hybrid of HMO and indemnity coverage. In a POS plan, members choose a PCP (primary care physician) and if they use the HMO system, out-of-pocket expenses are limited to a $5-$10 physician fee and $5-$10 charge per prescription. In the HMO system, enrollees do not have to file forms and there are no co-payments. If at any time, however, the enrollee chooses to visit a specialist or other high-cost provider without a referral from his/her PCP, he/she receives indemnity-type coverage. (This type of indemnity coverage customarily consists of the beneficiary paying the first $1,000 out-of-pocket costs or meeting the deductible. Then, the beneficiary is reimbursed 70-80% of his/her out-of-pocket costs.) When using the indemnity option, an enrollee must fill out insurance claim forms. POS products have been the main driver in the enrollment growth of many large HMOs. With a product to expand enrollment growth, managed care companies sought means to further control costs.

Phase Four will be the reduction of costs by medical management. Managed coverage companies are developing a new, powerful tool that will provide a third layer to controlling costs: medical (or disease) management. Contrary to limiting access to specialists, medical management programs depend on effective use of specialists to improve the care (and reduce the cost) of people with high-cost diseases and conditions. This new concept revolves around the fact that 5% of the population consumes 60% of the insurance claim dollars. Medical management centers on more effectively caring for that 5% of the population and depends on sophisticated information systems as well as comprehensive clinical systems. Managed care companies exploit this potential. Robinson believes that clinical management will be the main driver in reducing costs over the next five years and that the companies that are in the best position to capitalize on the potential that disease management offers will be successful.

### E.    INSURANCE DEMAND

As the health insurance industry evolves, the demand for business partnerships with physicians has increased for several reasons.

**INSURANCE COMPANY**

Managed care is pushing doctors to join together and with business partners. Managed care has dramatically changed the business environment for physicians. HMOs have now forced physicians to negotiate discounts and capitation arrangements before treating patients. As a result, the physicians must estimate how sick the potential patient population will be. Essentially, this requires patient information that the physicians usually do not have; even if they did have it, they would not have time to analyze it. Hence, they fear that HMOs may be providing them with unfairly low capitation rates and volume discounts. Moreover, physicians fear that they could lose their patient base to an HMO if they cannot negotiate group contracts. Physicians are also concerned that they may eventually become dependent. Physician practice management firms relieve physicians of the administrative burdens related to negotiating group contracts and give them more power in negotiating contracts with HMOs. They also allow physicians more say in clinical matters, which gives them more control over care delivery and a greater feeling of autonomy.

Physicians would rather align together with a business manager than with an insurance company, hospital, or HMO. Physicians see insurance companies and HMOs as adversaries that have always focused on minimizing costs, with less regard for the quality of patient care. Hospitals still seem to rely too much on length of stay management rather than ensuring appropriate health care, while providing mediocre management. Also, joining these organizations may limit doctors' ability to see patients that are represented by other hospitals or payors. Physician practice management actively supports quality care and allows relationships with multiple hospitals and payors. Over the long term, doctors should recognize this, thus giving business-oriented partners the upper hand in the ability to sign additional practice management contracts.

Insurance providers like to use large physician groups. Multi-specialty insurance groups can handle large patient volume, making it easier for managed care insurance providers than for single or small group physician practices to negotiate, bill, and monitor patients. In addition, since health care is a local service, a business-oriented physician partnership that has 25-100 primary care physicians with a high-quality reputation can be a dominant group. This gives the group pricing leverage with payors, even though the payors may be large, regional companies with millions of enrollees.

### II.    COMPETITIVE INSURANCE ANALYSIS

The business of providing insurance-related services is competitive. Robinson Insurance Group is aware of other companies actively pursuing a strategy of affiliating with physicians and dentists, some of whom are larger and have greater financial resources than Robinson. Robinson assumes that additional companies with similar objectives will be organized in the future. Potential financial sources of competition include hospital and alternate site management companies, larger, nationally known, multi-specialty medical groups, dental groups, and others. Several of Robinson's largest competitors are described below.

## A. BACKGROUND, GOALS AND OBJECTIVES

The formation of Van Robinson Insurance Group was driven by the marketplace maturing to a point where the HMO industry was prepared to outsource the provision of medical care to a network, and the physicians comprising the network were prepared to consolidate their efforts to take advantage of this shift in the marketplace. Robinson's basic business premise is to help create an insurance network business structure so that this entity could become the centerpiece for contracting, development of information systems, education of physicians and the provision of practice management services.

As a multifaceted insurance provider, this e-business entity and a management service organization, Robinson is structured to organize and manage insurance agents, physician practices and networks that contract with HMOs and other insurance providers. They provide funding and information to physician and related insurance services to enrollees as well. Robinson provides primary and specialty services to prepaid managed care enrollees and fee-for-service patients through a network of physicians. The company's objective is to provide cost-effective, high quality insurance coverage for an increasing number of applicable enrollees served by physician within the Robinson Network. Robinson believes new enrollees and provider relationships are possible because of its ability to manage the cost of insurance premiums without sacrificing quality.

Robinson consolidated and aggregated the health insurance clients, contracts, projects, employees and assets of several insurance agency businesses located in the Charleston and all throughout the Southeastern part of South Carolina through the acquisition of certain assets of such companies. Kellar Consulting Inc. developed the majority of the physicians and professional corporation projects now part of Robinson over the last 26-year period.

Robinson's management has been serving the health, dental, and physician liability insurance market for over 30 years and possesses an intimate knowledge of the marketing skills and dynamics of how to successfully serve this client base. Over this period of time, the scope of services needed by the integrated health and dental insurance industry has expanded to include the negotiation of managed care and insurance contracts, the creation and operation of sophisticated information systems, and a turnkey management service for physician offices.

## B. STRATEGY

Since the health insurance industry is in an evolutionary period, the plans and strategies described in the following sections are evolutionary and subject to change.

Robinson's mission is to develop regionally prominent, integrated health insurance delivery networks that provide high quality, cost-effective insurance coverage throughout Southeastern South Carolina, Western Tennessee and Northern Georgia markets. Its financial goals are to (i) achieve returns through value added participation and active oversight of the networks, (ii) capitalize on the health insurance information provided by and to Robinson Network, (iii) capitalize on the development of chronic disease management in given specialties, (iv) capitalize on the continued growth of the insurance market in general and the physician services market in particular, and (v) reduce overall insurance costs by expanding the availability of business and information oriented for physicians.

# BUSINESS PLAN #11: Insurance Group Plan

By enabling physicians to develop and efficiently manage insurance payments and network activities, Robinson seeks to assist physicians in facilitating risk-based managed insurance contracts, developing and implementing disease management programs and monitoring and controlling health care outcomes and costs. The key elements of Robinson's strategy to accomplish its mission and fulfill its goals are to (i) establish long-term contractual alliances with physicians, (ii) develop integrated health insurance systems through strategic alliances with other insurance providers, (iii) pursue large scale managed contracts, (iv) develop and maintain a leadership position in management information systems, (v) foster physician autonomy in selected geographic markets that offer concentrations of physicians seeking Robinson's services, and (vi) provide cost effective insurance coverage.

To date, Robinson has focused upon developing its presence in Southeastern South Carolina, Western Tennessee, and Northern Georgia. Robinson believes that once it has developed a large base of affiliated physicians its strategy will enable Robinson to generate increased demand for the services and capabilities of its affiliated physicians, treat patients in lower cost settings and negotiate favorable managed insurance contracts. Robinson intends to achieve growth through the recruitment of additional physicians, the expansion of agent-physician relationships and the development of contractual or strategic relationships with providers of supplemental insurance services.

## 1.    Develop Long-term Alliances with Physicians

The core of Robinson's proposed integrated health insurance delivery system is its affiliation with groups of physicians and dentists and other supplemental providers who enter into long-term management agreements with Robinson. Robinson assumes responsibility for the nonmedical aspects of an affiliated professional's practice (including claims administration, and billing, credentialing, and recruitment) and focuses its efforts on seeking to increase revenues and improve operation margins, implementing management information systems and negotiating managed insurance contracts. The physicians and dentists remain responsible for, among other things, the clinical, professional and ethical aspects of their practices. By affiliating with Robinson, physicians and dentists have increased opportunity to access capital, continue to participate in the profitability of their individual practices.

Robinson affiliates with physicians and dentists by entering into long-term management agreements with the affiliated practices, by managing IIAs and by providing contract management services to physicians in primary and specialty care networks. By affiliating with leading physicians, dentists and physician groups in a given neighborhood or community, Robinson can secure a large patient base, ensure appropriate, quality treatment and maintain patient satisfaction. Additionally, as Robinson affiliates with professionals in certain insurance markets, it makes available to these physicians and dentists medical support services. By integrating the affiliated health, dental, and physician coverage, Robinson is able to develop a continuum of insurance coverage within its target markets. Robinson believes that its affiliations with additional physicians and dentists through managed networks will enable it to increase its market share.

Robinson seeks to affiliate with physicians and dentists in solo or group practices by entering into contractual arrangements to assume the practice management aspects of the managed insurance. Upon affiliation, Robinson seeks to provide the physicians and dentists with, among other things, increased opportunity to access capital, management experience, improved information systems and increased opportunity to participate in favorable managed insurance contracts. Robinson's structure allows physicians and dentists to continue to practice in their existing locations with no disruption to patient flow patterns while providing access to coordinated supplemental insurance services. By affiliating with Robinson, physicians and dentists, through the services agreements between the affiliated groups and Robinson, continue to participate in the profitability of their individual practices.

Robinson seeks to achieve operating efficiencies through the consolidation of the administrative functions of physician and dental practices. By consolidating overhead, including billing, collections, accounting and payroll, Robinson believes that it can realize operating efficiencies. In addition, by rendering support and management functions, Robinson enables its affiliated physicians and dentists to spend more of their time with patients, thereby improving patient care and enhancing revenue.

## 2.    Develop Integrated Insurance Networks Through Strategic Alliances

Robinson believes that strategic insurance alliances with physicians, dentists, hospitals and health plans improve the delivery of managed health insurance coverage.

In addition, through its third-party administration (TPA) services, Robinson processes numerous insurance claims for medical and dental services for certain of its strategic affiliates. Employers often purchase TPA services which are bundled with utilization review services and selected PPO networks in an effort to apply managed techniques to their self-funded plans. Under its TPA arrangements, Robinson will not generally bear any insurance cost risk and, accordingly, is not paid an underwriting premium. Instead, Robinson's TPA arrangements typically will provide for the payment of administrative fees that generally vary by the number of members covered. A certain number of these policy contracts may contain performance guarantees as to timeliness and accuracy and certain other features which can place premium compensation under such contracts at risk.

In conjunction with its network affiliation strategy, Robinson seeks to build integrated networks of dental, health, and physicians liability, and supplemental coverage in its targeted markets. Robinson typically affiliates with core physician or dental practices. Robinson then seeks to affiliate with additional insurance providers such as hospitals, supplemental facilities and providers of other medical support services. Through the implementation of this strategy, Robinson seeks to provide a comprehensive range of health insurance coverage within a given region, thereby enhancing its ability to enter into contractual arrangements with numerous health, dental, physician liability, and supplemental insurance organizations.

Robinson has proposed to include several business partners within the Van Robinson Insurance Group that will ensure its propensity to be a more dynamic organization as insurance coverage evolves into an industry that produces optimal insurance premiums with outcomes at a cost that will not prohibit entry at any level. This evolution will require extensive integration of the varied components of health insurance to remain on the "cutting edge" of effective delivery. By the involvement of value added organizations, Robinson may continually explore new methods of providing insurance coverage to ensure itself of a cost effective, high quality product that invariably will endure through many variables that invades the industry.

# BUSINESS PLAN #11: Insurance Group Plan

The movement toward managed coverage in every aspect of the insurance industry shouldn't be viewed as the end of all strategies, nor will it be. There continually will, and must be new mechanisms that will further the quality of medicine as it exists today. As the varied insurance purchasers ratchet medical costs down, there will be the necessity to find new and more effective methodologies to ensure a given population's health status. These can only be identified through a concerted initiative of the principle deliverers of insurance coverage, the physicians and the other partners who have knowledge, expertise and incentive to create such a delivery organization.

**INSURANCE COMPANY**

Robinson has identified as initial but certainly not all inclusive, value-added partners, a major pharmaceutical company, a physician driven information system company, medical supply and equipment companies and a consortium of hospital and health research and education organizations. Robinson believes these entities represent the most capable partners to forge a relationship with the physicians affiliated with Robinson. With these prototypes, it is believed that the organization will establish itself as an entity capable of competing in a managed insurance coverage arena, while fixing an eye towards experimentation and creativity of future initiatives that will set the course of the health insurance evolution and initiative. There can be no assurance, however, that Robinson will be able to develop relationships with such entities.

Finally Robinson does not believe this list to be static but rather dynamic as other partners may be mutually identified. Organizations representing the insurance industry, medical specialty areas, medical supply companies, laboratories, and others may emerge as sound contributors to the evolving organization.

3.    **Pursue Large-Scale Managed Insurance Coverage Contracts**

Robinson intends to continue to aggressively pursue managed insurance coverage business. Robinson believes that by providing comprehensive geographic coverage in each market, Robinson Network will be strongly positioned to be offered managed coverage contracts in the area, which may allow it to rapidly expand its patient base. In addition, as managed coverage penetration increases, Robinson's ability to improve productivity, manage complex reimbursement methodologies, measure patient satisfaction and outcomes of coverage protection, and integrate information from multiple sources should serve it well. As Robinson continues to grow both internally and through new affiliations, management believes that Robinson Network will be positioned to compete effectively for large group managed coverage business.

Within each local area, Robinson seeks to provide an appropriate balance of physician liability, health, dental, and other supplemental insurance programs to attract managed coverage providers and payors. Depending upon the particular market, Robinson may develop specialty recruitment networks which can be used to procure managed coverage contracts pursuant to which Robinson's affiliated physicians are responsible for providing all or a portion of specific health coverage services to a particular patient population, or Robinson may develop a broader array of services designed to enhance its ability to attract comprehensive managed coverage contracts. In addition, Robinson manages the contracts of specialty care physicians with managed coverage companies in order to facilitate the delivery of services in specialty health coverage networks.

Robinson's target marketplace has made significant advancements to the point where managed coverage companies are now willing to enter into negotiations of contracts for integrated coverage delivery systems similar to those that Robinson develops and manages. The magnitude and continuance of this trend in the marketplace has and will continue to be dependent on the readiness of the insurance carriers to accept a redefinition of their role in the insurance industry, as they move toward a more financial role and away from the role of insurance sales. To this extent, management believes that Robinson is in an opportune position to capitalize on this industry transition.

Robinson has signed ten contracts with various managed coverage organizations for the provision of services for health, hospital, dental, vision and pharmacy services. These contracts provide for capitated payments for services, predetermined fee schedules for services, and contracted amounts for certain insurance coverage services. Robinson receives a percentage of the revenue from these contracts as a negotiation and management fee, and also performs administrative services to fulfill the contractual terms.

## 4.    Develop and Maintain a Leadership Position in Information Systems

Robinson believes that information technology is critical to the growth of integrated insurance delivery systems and that the availability of detailed clinical data is fundamental to quality control and cost containment. Robinson develops and maintains sophisticated management information systems that collect and analyze clinical and administrative data. These systems allow Robinson to control overhead expenses, maximize reimbursement and provide utilization management more effectively. Robinson evaluates the administrative and clinical functions of affiliated practices and re-engineers these functions as appropriate in conjunction with the implementation of Robinson's management information systems to maximize the benefits of those systems.

In addition to providing administrative management services to physician and dental organizations, Robinson seeks to differentiate itself by assisting physicians in managing certain aspects of the clinical operation of their practices. Robinson believes that its integrated management services and clinical information systems will enhance the ability of physician group practices and networks to implement disease management programs and to manage practice under risk-based contracts. It is anticipated that these management programs will be delivered through linked practices and networks of specialists under management or development by Robinson who will provide integrated, high-quality coverage for patients based on clinical care guidelines developed by the physician networks. Robinson anticipates that the physicians within these practices and networks will be linked together by Robinson's clinical information systems.

## 5.    Preserve Autonomy Through Select Geographic Markets

While Robinson provides insurance management expertise to a newly affiliated group, it believes that each physician and dental group presents unique management issues and therefore is best served by decentralized management. Robinson generally retains the group's existing administrative staff, adding additional management personnel as the group expands. Each group's physicians and dentists continue to maintain full professional control of the practice's account. Robinson establishes for each local market a policy council, comprised equally of physicians or dentists and Robinson representatives, to determine the strategic and operational policies.

Each of Robinson's health, dental, and physician liability groups and IIAs will operate in a very different market and focuses on the particular needs of each local community to gain market share and improve profitability. As to the needs of the local market, Robinson will rely in large part upon the marketing plans developed by local management, in consultation with physicians, dentists, employers and other members of the local communities. This localization reduces Robinson's need for expensive market research analysis. The ability to maintain a high level of market share locally is a sustainable barrier to discourage further market entry by insurance providers and payors.

**INSURANCE COMPANY**

## 6. Providing Cost-Effective Health Insurance Coverage

Robinson organizes its managed insurance coverage networks around given management specialties to create an environment conducive to the development of specific policy management techniques. Robinson believes that a successful system should be balanced between primary care physicians and specialists to provide efficient coordination and utilization of the appropriate levels of coverage, and Robinson intends to seek to develop this balance in the physician groups with which it affiliates. Of the 5000 physicians currently affiliated with Robinson, approximately one-half are engaged are engaged in specialist practice are in need of effective delivery systems of coverage. Robinson believes the industry trend toward integrated delivery systems will result in an increasing demand for primary care physicians because a higher degree of coordination of risk sharing and care. Insurance coverage will be required than that which can be achieved in a system controlled by specialists. Robinson's strategy is to have the primary care physician serve as the central manager in the patient system and to develop effective coordination between specialists and primary care physicians within its network.

Robinson believes that the management of insurance coverage costs provides significant opportunities. Special populations, including the elderly, the disabled and those with debilitating chronic or high-cost, complex diseases represent a minority of the population but account for a disproportionately high percentage of the health insurance coverage costs in the United States. Robinson believes that a significant portion of these costs can be avoided with effective case management and proper use of information systems, coordinated with the use of the full continuum of health insurance coverage. At present, a relatively small percentage of these patients are enrolled under capitated contracts. However, Robinson believes that the cost pressures that fostered the development of managed coverage for other segments of the population should have an even more significant impact on the rapid development of managed coverage for such patients. Through affiliation with physicians and academic experts who specialize in medical conditions that disproportionately affect these population segments, effective use of case management techniques designed specifically for such populations, and management information systems, Robinson believes that its affiliated physicians should be able to manage cost effectively the risks of providing insurance coverage to these populations on a capitated basis.

## C. TARGET MARKETS

Robinson's primary focus has initially been Southeastern South Carolina, Western Tennessee, and Northern Georgia. Robinson believes its business model is replicable and will allow it to compete in other areas as well. Robinson's development goals emphasize the affiliation of high-profile practices, both primary and specialty insurance coverage, to meet the needs of patients and payors, adjusted according to the dynamics of individual markets. Robinson focuses on developing and maintaining a comprehensive, integrated insurance coverage network in each market to which it commits its resources. Robinson targets markets by considering the following factors:

- *Population Size and Distribution.* Robinson believes that the ideal catchment area has a population base of at least 100,000 to 200,000. A population base of this size will support a primary insurance coverage physician base of twenty-five. Additionally, a network of twenty-five primary care physicians, negotiating as a unified group, will command the attention of managed insurance coverage organizations, specialists and hospitals.

- *Physician Practice Density, Specialty Composition, Saturation, and Average Group Size.* Robinson will develop an understanding of the physician population. As stated above, at least twenty-five primary care physicians are ideal in forming a local network. The mixture of primary care physicians to specialists within the network should be approximately 50:50. The existing pool of physicians must be able to support this goal. Attitudes toward manage health and dental coverage and group practice will be surveyed to ensure that local physicians are able to accept the imminent changes in work habits that network formation will bring.

- *Local Competitors in the Physician Acquisition and Management Business.* Robinson will survey other efforts to unite local physicians. Markets with active efforts by established or growing physician practice management companies may affect positively or negatively the opportunities to recruit quality physicians into Robinson Network.

- *Level of Managed Insurance Coverage Penetration.* Market forces, as created by managed insurance coverage organizations, often create an air of urgency with regards to physicians organizing into local groups and networks. Geographic areas with high levels of managed coverage penetration may already have experienced efforts in physician merger and consolidation. The threat of increased managed coverage activity or early stages of managed insurance coverage enrollment present the highest level of opportunity to develop an affiliated network. Markets with physician payor mixes of 50% or less managed coverage contracting will offer the best opportunities for network development.

- *Local Industry and Economy.* Efforts on the part of local employers to embrace managed insurance coverage organizations will directly affect the growth of such organizations. Financial stability of local employers must also be considered as a large layoff or plant closure may have a significant negative effect on the local economy.

- *Population Demographics (age, income, gender).* Population age and its economies as related to that age group offer Robinson insight as to the stability, growth and long term needs of the catchment area. Robinson's ability to project these needs should be measured. An age and income analysis will also serve in long-term product development.

- *Market and Network Growth Potential.* A primary care physician base of twenty-five, serving a population base of 100,000 to 200,000 presents an attractive market. Robinson will also consider the ability of the local network to expand in relation to the networks ability to maintain market share.

- *Geographic Barriers, (population's ability to commute).* Robinson will consider any geographic barriers that prevent the local population from commuting to utilize physicians involved in the network. Geographic barriers also increase the prosperity for point of service plans thus increases Robinson's need for geographic expansion.

- *Numbers and Stability of Hospitals.* The local region containing at least two hospitals increases competition between those hospitals, competition that involves the formation of MSOs, PHOs and other models to recruit physicians. Alliances to those hospitals may fracture physician leaders or prevent the smooth development of an affiliated network.

- *Physicians' Relationship with Hospitals.* Formation of a local physician owned network would require at least minimal support of the area hospitals. Robinson will survey the physicians' relationship with area hospitals, along with direct meetings with the hospitals surveying areas of mutual understanding.

- *Uninsured Population.* A large uninsured population is indicative of a struggling local economy. Robinson will consider these factors prior to commencing any effort to establish a physicians' network.

- *Existence of Alternative Delivery Services (home health services, outpatient services).* Robinson's savings models are based on the assumption that many forms of less expensive delivery mechanisms are available. Robinson will survey the availability and quality of alternative delivery services. These services must include rehabilitation facilities, home health/visiting nurse services, home infusion services, durable medical equipment suppliers and long-term care facilities.

The specific markets currently targeted by Robinson are described below:

Charleston, South Carolina - Independent physicians practicing in groups or in solo practice represent the greatest marketing opportunity as the physician practice management service will propel the sale of information systems and the retention of Robinson for managed insurance coverage services and contract negotiation projects. The Southeastern South Carolina market consists of over 7,500 physicians of which approximately 5,000 are in independent practice. The remaining 2,500 physicians are employed by several hospital systems or insurers in a staff model type of physician organization. While these 2,500 physicians are being served by the hospital MSOs, Robinson's ability to provide services to this group is not entirely precluded. The 5,000 independent physicians nevertheless, are the clear near term marketing opportunity in Southeastern South Carolina. Of this group, it is estimated that less than 2% have contracted for MSO services with a corporate partner such as Robinson.

## D.   DEVELOPMENT

Development of each physician network follows a structured process, guided by Robinson. The process involves recruiting physician leaders in the targeted market, organizing the physicians, structuring alliances with other health, dental, physician liability, and supplemental insurance providers, negotiating managed coverage contracts, and guiding the entire process of organizing the individual entities into a functioning network. This process results in the development of both an infrastructure for the network and a culture for the newly formed entity.

Robinson's physician recruitment begins by attracting physician leaders within the specialties of family practice, internal medicine, pediatrics and/or obstetrics. Attracting physician leaders is critical to the development of the network. Physicians receive a presentation that not only serves as an educational presentation for the group leaders, but also serves as a forum to receive their input with regards to how the physicians will develop into a formal group. Participants must be in agreement with Robinson as to the type of services needed whether it be health, dental, physician liability, or supplemental insurance. The physicians to be recruited, the structure and timing of developing the network, and the need for and type of strategic alliances are all factors considered with developing Robinson's basic strategy.

Robinson's marketing strategy is to increase the size, number and locations of medical practices to which it provides its services. Robinson's strategy is also to broaden the types of insurance options that it provides, to develop a client base of primary care and specialty practices and to implement growth strategies for its existing and new clients. Robinson expects to promote growth of the patient and revenue basis by assisting its clients in the development of multi-specialty coverage practices and opening of additional offices and implementing an aggressive program of affiliating with other insurance coverage options. A major focus of Robinson's near term marketing efforts will be the identification of appropriate target markets within the southeastern South Carolina area. This will make effective use of Robinson's management services.

Robinson's marketing efforts to establish relationships with new clients for its full range of insurance management services are conducted by employees under the direction of the Vice President of Managed Coverage Options. Marketing activities that meet the size, quality and operating parameters set by Robinson. Robinson's marketing staff also helps existing clients analyze opportunities for expanding the services they offer and expanding into new geographic areas either through opening new offices or acquiring existing insurance coverage packages. Strategies are also developed for increasing the patient volume of existing clients, including identifying to clients attorneys handling workers' compensation and no-fault insurance claims and arranging meetings with such attorney to make them aware of all possibilities as a Robinson client. The marketing staff also oversees and facilitates the exchange of information with attorneys and insurance companies that are sources of new patients for Robinson's clients.

Robinson believes it can increase its market share in the medical management services industry by providing its clients with significant competitive advantages and by relieving them of the complex, burdensome and time-consuming nonmedical aspects of their businesses. Robinson believes that relieving agency personnel of these obligations may enhance productivity, efficiency and profitability and the growth potential of the client and thus also enhance the ability of such agents to serve their clients. Robinson also believes that a fully integrated medical office for the diagnosis and treatment of injuries provides significant advantages to patients and third-party payors. By providing a full array of medical and testing services in one facility, a medical practice will serve the patient more effectively and efficiently and also alleviate the injured patient's burden of traveling from one location to another. The centralization of comprehensive services also facilitates administrative and regulatory reporting to third-party payors.

# BUSINESS PLAN #11: Insurance Group Plan

### E.   OPERATIONS

Upon affiliation, Robinson assumes management responsibility for the practices, allowing physicians to focus on practicing medicine and developing medical guidelines. Robinson performs all insurance business functions of the physician's practice, centralizing many functions such as billing, collections, accounts payable, payroll and human resources, purchasing, lease administration, property management, and telecommunications. Each of these systems will be integrated to achieve maximum cost savings and efficiencies.

**INSURANCE COMPANY**

Robinson works with the affiliated physicians in targeting and recruiting additional physicians into the affiliated physician networks. Robinson may also assist in the development and capitalization of new and expanded supplemental services. Robinson recognizes and develops opportunities to provide services throughout a market by positioning its practice locations to service an entire geographic market. This approach improves patient convenience and responds to demographic coverage criteria essential to payors. The specific operations of Robinson are described below.

### 1.   Managed Insurance Coverage

Robinson believes that managed insurance coverage will continue to play an important role in the delivery of and payment for health, dental, physician liability, and supplemental insurance services. In particular, Robinson believes that the most efficient way to deliver high quality, cost effective insurance coverage is by utilizing primary care physicians to manage the patient care, including the utilization of specialty care physicians and supplemental coverage services. Robinson believes that as the importance of primary care physicians' role is recognized, more HMO's will embrace the management of services through these physicians. Additionally, as primary care physicians expand their role in the delivery of medical care, Robinson believes that these physicians will require the assistance of practice management companies, such as Robinson to help them manage their operations and contractual relationships. Upon affiliation, Robinson will immediately begin managed coverage contracting activities designed to increase practice revenues and market share, identify additional network affiliations, and analyze all operational aspects of the practices. After evaluation of these factors, Robinson and the affiliated physicians develop and implement additional strategies, including: (i) practice specific contracting designed to increase access to managed coverage patients, (ii) development of global priced products which establish a single price for all medical costs of a designated procedure, (iii) specialty carve outs with single specialty networks, such as orthopedics, ophthalmology, and obstetrics/gynecology, that service as exclusive providers, and (iv) perhaps over time full risk capitation by contracting with a payor to provide all physician services and, in some cases, hospital and other facility services for a fixed price.

### 2.   Insurance Coverage Contracts and Payors

Robinson will arrange for insurance coverage contracts between payors and the physicians, other insurance providers, or Professional Corporations within Robinson Network. These contracts generally will provide for terms of one to three years, with automatic renewal periods, terminable upon prior notice (generally between 30 and 180 days) by either party. These insurance contracts will obligate the Professional Corporations to deliver covered medical benefits and to coordinate all inpatient and outpatient care for enrollees. Under most of these arrangements, the Professional Corporation will receive a capitation payment for each Payor enrollee who selects a primary care physician who is employed by or affiliated with such Professional Corporation.

In negotiating or renewing insurance payor/provider contracts, Robinson will consider a number of specific factors that affect capitation rates, the risk pool and breadth of covered benefits. These factors include, but are not limited to, the demographic risk profile of the enrollee pool, prior financial experience, availability of stoploss protection and an understanding of the fee-for-service equivalent charges. In undertaking this process, Robinson will analyze pertinent data to assess the providers' contractual and economic opportunity and exposure, and then conduct the negotiations on behalf of the physician, physician group or other providers.

3.    **Insurance Contracts with Providers**

Robinson Network, through the Professional Corporations, subsidiaries and payors, contracts with a variety of providers, including primary and specialty care physicians, hospitals and other supplemental providers. These agreements generally have terms up to three years, are automatically renewable and are terminable by either party upon at least 90 days prior notice. A primary care physician's affiliation and compensation arrangement with a Professional Corporation or subsidiary may take one of several forms. The physician may be (i) an individual or a member of a group practice or an IIA which (a) insurance contracts with Robinson and a Professional Corporation for Robinson's services and receives capitation payments based on the number of enrollees and premiums and is entitled to additional compensation based upon efficiency in utilizing the services of insurance providers, subject to other factors including but not limited to compliance with contractual quality standards, or (b) enters into an arrangement with Robinson and one of its Professional Corporations; or (ii) an individual or group practice of physicians which sells to a Professional Corporation the assets of its practice and receives as compensation for employment a base salary and productivity bonus, of receives a percentage of net collections of the practice determined in accordance with applicable law. The physician or group, which sells its practice, still practices medicine in the same location. While such physician or group is employed and paid by a Professional Corporation or subsidiary, Robinson provides many administrative services to such physician or group.

Specialty care providers contract with a Professional Corporation or subsidiary to provide medical services to enrollees and are compensated on a discounted fee-for-service or capitated basis. Hospital and affiliated medical facilities contract with a Professional Corporation or subsidiary and Payors to provide both inpatient and outpatient services to enrollees on a fee-for-service, per diem or capitated basis, which are discounted from customary charges.

4.    **Management Information System**

Robinson will utilize integrated information systems to enhance its strategic development plans and its day-to-day management of operations. Robinson will configure its systems to give affiliated physicians and their staff efficient and rapid access to complex clinical data. Robinson also believes that the availability of timely information on utilization patterns improves physician decision-making effectiveness. This data also plays an integral role in the physician utilization control process by enabling the medical directors and utilization control to monitor case management decisions, evaluate patient outcomes and monitor coverage utilization trends. In addition, Robinson's management information systems will perform various administrative functions, including appointment scheduling, insurance verification, billing, accounts payable and receivable, out of network referrals and verification, financial reporting and all third-party claims processing.

**INSURANCE COMPANY**

Members of the network will access the management information systems from their individual offices, thereby eliminating communication barriers often found in managed care environments. The real time information system will allow for an opportunity to eradicate the static production of outdated clinical protocols and referral sources associated with paper manuals and directories.

Robinson recognizes the need to centralize the insurance coverage data being generated by the individual physicians in the network. Robinson has determined a successful performance measurement/improvement program to include the following:

- The organization's strategic initiatives and mission determine needs
- Focuses on high-leverage areas: high-volume, high-risk, or problem prone areas
- Contains a systematic method of performance improvement that assures rapid, ongoing, sustained improvement
- Can easily monitor performance
- Based on industry best practices
- Is supported by leadership
- Is data driven

Many organizations believe a physician is responsible for clinical results, the finance department guides and directs fiscal expenditures, and administration assures patient satisfaction. This compartmentalized 'silo' approach does not acknowledge that various insurance coverage organizations are inherently systems, in which any change in one department affects all players. It is this concept that demonstrates the importance of an enterprise-wide information system. The ability to store every piece of information that the organization encounters and easily manipulate that data to produce a variety of statistics is the key feature behind any successful insurance organization of present.

Robinson has designed its Information System to meet the communication, business and clinical needs of practicing physicians, hospitals, payors and employers. Robinson utilizes e-business application service provider (ASP) solutions in the design of the Information System to minimize insurance coverage costs to physician practices and maximize the ability for them to share data across the care spectrum. This technology allows physicians to access the Information System remotely; thereby eliminating cumbersome servers, hardware and sophisticated information technology personnel from the physician office. Instead, each office is supplied with state of the art communication devices that allows for instant access to the central data repository, the Internet, Robinson's Intranet, business tools such as the billing system, electronic patient records and on-line purchasing.

Robinson has partnered with the pharmaceutical industry to distribute workstations to the network at no cost to the individual physicians. Robinson can; therefore, quickly disseminate this technology.

Robinson has established centralized computing capabilities to enable effective access to information and communication capabilities required to improve effective insurance coverage services and reduced costs. The services delivered through this centralized capability include:

- Data warehousing and visualization
- Quality insurance management, utilization management, and coverage outcome reporting
- Insurance policy order entry and results reporting
- Professional referrals
- Electronic mail
- Internet access
- Electronic access to standard reference literature
- Transcription services
- Managed Insurance Coverage services

### 5.   Insurance Claims Administration and Billing Service

Robinson possesses complete medical bill review and insurance claims processing capabilities. These capabilities include determining enrollee eligibility, identifying appropriate benefits, issuing payments to providers, processing hospital and outpatient facility charges for the payment of insurance claims and providing and analyzing encounter data. As a service to certain Professional Corporations, Robinson will perform fee-for-service billing and collections. The billing staff will register fee-for-service patients, send monthly statements and pursue collection.

### 6.   Insurance Coverage Management

Insurance coverage management involves the coordination of a variety of services, including health, physician liability, and supplemental insurance including the coverage of durable medical equipment. This approach is designed to provide a continuum of quality insurance coverage throughout an extended period.

### 7.   Physician Credentialing and Recruitment

As a service to Payors and the Professional Corporations, Robinson will verify that the credentials of physicians in Robinson meet the minimum requirements specified in payor/provider insurance contracts. In addition, Robinson may assist the Professional Corporations in the recruitment of highly competent physicians and other insurance coverage providers who share in the philosophy of prepaid managed insurance coverage. All of the physicians will be licensed to practice medicine in the state where they practice medical services and will generally be either board certified or board eligible.

### 8.   Managerial and Financial Controls

Robinson will apply comprehensive managerial and financial controls in order to enhance profitability. Practice managers and directors will be trained in methods for analyzing and improving utilization, payor/provider mix ratios, reimbursement and overhead controls. Robinson also will implement procedures designed to ensure that information relevant to improving results of operations is gathered and evaluated in a timely manner. To further improve operating efficiencies, Robinson will centralize certain functions, such as payroll, accounts payable and financial statement compilation, marketing and billing.

Specific controls will address reimbursement, financial, labor costs, accounts payable and other areas of practice management.

**9.    Educational Programs**

Robinson will use an educational program that provides a forum for the dissemination of information to individuals who are working towards the goal of designing a system that provides the appropriate insurance coverage. Each network physician will address needs for education and training programs for member insurance and financial management, information systems technologies supporting insurance coverage programs, specific disease management methodologies for common illnesses, and processes and techniques supporting the development of practice guidelines.

**10.   Facilities**

To the extent that it is unnecessary to control locations, Robinson will lease office space for its corporate functions.

**11.   Personnel**

Robinson is committed to a decentralized management style in which business and clinical decisions affecting the local physicians network will be made locally. Therefore employment policies will encourage as few non-local personnel as possible in the local physician network. Key leadership positions in the local IIA may however be hired and trained by Robinson. Policy guidelines will be undertaken and compliance ensured by Robinson personnel. Advances in technology allow Robinson the opportunity to centralize into the corporate office the general accounting, finance, and operational analysis from information that will be processed at the local physician network.

**12.   Insurance**

To manage the risk associated with the management of Robinson, Robinson will undertake to secure general risk business insurance covering, general liability, directors and officers' liability, property damage, and business interruption.

**13.   Third-Party Administration Services**

Through its TPA services, Robinson process insurance claims for medical, dental, liability coverage and supplemental coverage of employer-sponsored, self-funded plans and reimburses the provider or member according to the terms of each plan. Employers often purchase TPA services that are bundled with UR services and selected PPO networks in an effort to apply managed coverage techniques to their self-funded plans. Under its TPA arrangements, Robinson will not generally bear any health insurance cost risk and, accordingly, is not paid an underwriting premium. Instead, Robinson's TPA arrangements typically will provide for the payment of administrative fees that generally vary by the number of members covered. Certain of these insurance contracts may contain performance guarantees as to timelines and accuracy and certain other features which can place compensation under such contracts at risk.

### 14. Physician Liability Insurance

Physician Liability Insurance provides coverage for physician involved in liable suits of a malpractice nature. Robinson provides will provide this service to all eligible physicians in the Southeastern South Carolina, Western Tennessee and Northern Georgia markets.

## F.   ADMINISTRATIVE SERVICE AGREEMENTS

Robinson will enter into administrative services agreements with the physicians, Professional Corporations and other insurance providers which will delegate to Robinson certain administrative, management and support functions which are required by physicians in Administrative Services Agreements, Robinson will provide practice management services. The Professional Corporations and the providers which contract with Robinson will be solely and exclusively in control of and responsible for all aspects of the practice of medicine and the delivery of medical services including, but not limited to, diagnosis, treatment, surgery and therapy.

As compensation for services rendered to the Professional Corporations by Robinson under the Administrative Services Agreements, Robinson will receive a management fee, which will consist of a percentage of the practice's revenue or a set monthly fee.

Robinson's relationships with its subsidiaries, affiliated professional corporations (the "Professional Corporations"), other providers of medical services, and Payors (collectively, the "Robinson Network") offer physicians the opportunity to participate more effectively in managed coverage programs by organizing physician groups within geographic areas to contract with Payors. Robinson improves physician practice operations by assuming administrative functions necessary in a managed insurance coverage environment. These functions include insurance claims administration, utilization management of medical services, payor/provider contract negotiations, and the operation of management information systems. Robinson believes that its network management model is appealing to independent physicians because it allows the physicians to retain control of their own practices while gaining access to more patients through participation in a managed insurance coverage program.

## G.   MANAGEMENT

The principle officers of Robinson have been serving the Southeastern South Carolina health, dental, physician liability, and supplemental insurance markets for over 30 years and possess an intimate knowledge of the marketing skills and dynamics of how to successfully serve this client base. Over this period of time, the scope of services needed by the integrated insurance industry has expanded to include the negotiation of managed care and insurance contracts, the creation and operation of sophisticated information systems, and a turn-key management service for managing physician offices. Robinson has the resources, personnel, knowledge and marketing plan to address this new era of managed insurance coverage. Management believes that this climate presents a significant opportunity to expand market share and profitability of the business.

### Operations

Network Development and Management is an area that represents the core business of Robinson. Effective execution of the strategic and tactical plans of this division will contribute to the ultimate success of Robinson's sustainable competitive advantage. Responsibilities will include the development of the local physician networks and IIAs, market analysis, physician marketing, and full implementation of the Development Plan. As local IIAs become effective, this group will assume responsibility for the oversight of the local IIAs. Included in this function is the establishment of policies and procedures, ensuring compliance and monitoring progress and growth. Both the development and management component of this operating group will require detailed and innovative analysis of the financial and operating potential, implementation and progress in meeting tactical and strategic goals for local physician networks (including outcome analysis and productivity reviews). The basis for this has been established in the prospective financial model created as part of this Business Plan, which will serve as the initial benchmark against which Robinson's progress can be judged. The President will be responsible for maintaining and augmenting this model's function.

### Managed Care Operations

Robinson's ability to contract with insurance payors/providers at the local and regional level will contribute to Robinson's financial success. The managed insurance operations group will also assist the local IIAs to develop, implement, measure and improve policy and guidelines and ensure compliance with respect to business operations of Van Robinson Insurance Group.

### Directors and Officers

Shareholders of Robinson elect Directors for three-year terms who serve until their successors have been elected and qualified. Officers serve at the pleasure of the Board of Directors. Robinson will be actively seeking qualified individuals to serve on the Board. The Board will be made up of persons from inside and outside of Robinson. The following is a partial outline of the characteristics desired for potential Board members:

- One member to be a physician having long tenure in the health care industry, strong business orientation and expertise as a senior level health care executive with possible national exposure.
- One member to have a nationally recognized background in health or dental insurance laws.
- One member to have strong national background and recognition in insurance coverage, product design and marketing.
- One or two members to have backgrounds as senior executives in national companies involved in information technology and insurance coverage and information systems.
- The balance of the Directors will be made up of individuals with strong business backgrounds (insurance not a requirement), preferably representing Robinson's value-added partners.

Robinson believes that its sustainable competitive advantage can be enhanced by augmenting its Board and advisors with individuals who are foremost among experts within the health, dental, physician liability, and supplemental insurance industry.

The directors and officers must have a shared vision and culture of innovation and leadership.

## Principal Shareholders

The principal shareholders of Robinson, and the amount of stock owned by each, it set forth in the following table:

| Name and Address | Common Stock | Percent |
|---|---|---|
| Thomas B. Kellar c/o Robinson | 600,000 | 98% |
| Other officers of Robinson | 3,200 | 0.5% |
| Individuals | 10,000 | 1.5% |

As of July 31, 2002, there were 613,200 shares of common stock outstanding.

## III.  BUSINESS ANALYSIS-KEY SUCCESS FACTORS

### Competitive Market Forces

The managed insurance coverage industry is highly competitive and is subject to continuing changes in how services are provided and how providers are selected and paid. Increased enrollment in prepaid premiums because of health insurance reform or for other reasons, increased participation by physicians in group practices and other factors may attract new entrants into the management service segment of the managed insurance coverage industry and result in increased competition for Robinson. Certain of Robinson's competitors are significantly larger and better capitalized, provide a wider variety of services, may have greater experience in providing insurance management services and may have longer established relationships with payors. Accordingly, Robinson may not be able to increase the number of providers affiliated with Robinson, negotiate contracts with new payors on behalf of the Professional Corporations or renegotiate favorable contracts with current payors.

Robinson's strategy of concentrating on developing strategic alliances with physicians and other insurance providers, rather than acquiring them, its state of the art information systems, and its emphasis on more local markets, should give it a competitive advantage in these areas, however.

# BUSINESS PLAN #11: Insurance Group Plan

### The Components of Van Robinson Insurance Group
### As Joint Venture Opportunities

| Charleston Medical Market<br><br>Segment/Joint Venture | Regional<br>Joint Venture<br>Investment | National<br>Joint Venture<br>Investment |
|---|---|---|
| **Managed Insurance Services** | | |
| Practice Management | | |
| • Robinson Management Services | $ 400,000 | |
| • Robinson Financial Services | 200,000 | |
| • Robinson Insurance Technologies | 0 | $ 400,000 |
| | | |
| Contract Insurance Sales | | |
| • Robinson Health | 0 | 500,000 |
| • Robinson Dental | 100,000 | |
| • Robinson Pharmaceutical | 200,000 | |
| | | |
| **Insurance Coverage Services** | | |
| • Robinson Pharmaceutical Programs | 200,000 | |
| • Robinson Dental Insurance | 800,000 | |
| • Robinson Health Administrators | 200,000 | 600,000 |
| • Robinson Supplemental Insurance | 200,000 | |
| • Robinson Physician Liability Services | 200,000 | |
| • Robinson Work Related Services | 200,000 | |
| • Robinson Insurance Fairs | 400,000 | |
| • Robinson Insurance Group | 200,000 | |
| | | |
| Contract Insurance Sales | | |
| • Robinson Insurance Group Services | 200,000 | _____ |
| | $3,500,000 | $1,500,000 |

## Other Information

•    The investment equates in part to an organization fee payable by the Joint Venture back to Van Robinson Insurance Group for having organized the Joint Venture. The remaining part of the investment will stay in the Joint Venture company for working capital purposes.

•    Each Joint Venture, once created, will be self-sustaining with Van Robinson Insurance Group providing sales, marketing and administrative services necessary to sustain the operations of the entity. Each Joint Venture, however, can make autonomous decisions.

•    The Joint Venture will be the exclusive entity for specified functions that Van Robinson Insurance Group would participate in and can conduct business on a national level.

•    Van Robinson Insurance Group and the Joint Venture partners will negotiate revenue splits, responsibilities etc. on a case-by-case basis.

# BUSINESS PLAN #12: Insurance Company

Here you see an example of another business plan which is designed to set up an insurance organization. You can compare features of this more concise business plan with the one immediately preceding it.

## GRIFFIN & ASSOCIATES INSURANCE COMPANY

**INVESTOR OVERVIEW**

This is a business plan discussing the products and services needed for a successful insurance company in Arizona

Griffin & Associates Insurance Company, brings together the diverse interests of the insurance marketplace: physicians, other insurance professionals, insurance companies, hospitals and patients. Griffin & Associates Insurance Company organizes and manages physician practices and physician-managed networks. The chief advantage to the provider network member is their ability to practice medicine free from most of the usual pressures of the managed insurance coverage environment. As Griffin & Associates continues to expand the network and refines our consulting/administrative capabilities, we will be propelled into a role as a major provider of integrated solutions to the self-funded marketplace in Phoenix, Arizona. We've recently added chronic disease management and employee wellness programs to our offerings. Through our rapidly expanding network base, combined with a variety of partner arrangements, we create dynamic options for payors and self-funded employers on the demand side of the industry. On the supply side, Griffin & Associates is committed to grow revenue through the expansion of our practice management contracts and the addition of future contracts.

### 1. The National Market

The insurance industry receives over $1.5 trillion in revenue from private industry, government Medicare and Medicaid programs, and private self-insured payors. This amount is divided almost equally among physicians and dentists, hospitals, and other insurance professional services, including pharmacy, nursing homes, and outpatient services. Nationwide, there are over 1,000,000 professionals providing medical care.

In addition to the more than $1 trillion of direct insurance coverage cost, over $300 billion is spent administering the process of insurance coverage. This $300 billion in revenue is received by insurance companies and third party administrators for handling claims payments, utilization management, financial reporting and health plan design. The insurance market is growing at a rate of 7 percent a year, and is projected to be a $2.0 trillion market within ten years.

### 2. Products and Services

Griffin & Associates provides the following products and services to companies that finance the demand for insurance and/or supply services:

- Design, development, and management of practitioner networks, which are then contracted to local and national Managed Insurance Coverage Organizations (MICOs), such as Preferred Provider Organizations, Health Maintenance Organizations, large employers, workers' compensation carriers, Third Party Administrators, Insurance Companies, and government entities. This business line includes contracts to generate nearly $8 million in gross revenue annually. This is a growth business that will increase in direct proportion to the expansion of the network itself.
- Provides assistance to third party administrators, insurance companies, both indemnity and casualty, and other claim payers in the development and management of employee benefit plans. The network's ability to manage claim costs is especially valuable in the area of self-funding, as large employers in Phoenix are presented with attractive options to the current dominant MICO

in this market. With market capital, we will accelerate our market network expansion activities, adding practitioners in Northern Arizona, and then continuing our expansion across the state. Ultimately, the cost-effective results achieved by Griffin & Associates' network model will provide opportunities for all payors to compete on an equal basis in the marketplace.

- Provides administrative services on an outsource basis to any insurance claim payer that assumes the risk and responsibility of providing medical benefits. These opportunities can include health, workers' compensation, or automobile liability-related medical claims. Services can include network management, delegated credentialing, and other horizontally integrated outsource arrangements.
- Provides information technology services to the physicians, dentists, and other insurance coverage professionals who function within the supply side of the service. These information technology services can also be delivered to the insurance companies, TPAs, government, and hospital sectors supply side.
- Financial and business administrative functions are marketed to the physician community to streamline their business processes. These services include billing and cash flow management, information processing, electronic medical records and information technology deployment.
- Marketing and business development services are offered to existing physician practice management clients. The fees for these services are based on a percentage of the physician's revenue or a set monthly fee.

## 3. Customers

### Demand Side
We identify our customers based on their position within the circle as follows:
- Currently, employers are our single largest block of customers, because they provide and pay for benefits for their employees. Their expenditures support the entire structure of today's insurance system.
- Managed Insurance Coverage Organizations administer benefit plans for employers and, in attempting to control claim costs, recognize and support managed network structures similar to those Griffin & Associates has developed. These customers include all payors of insurance related claims.
- Public sector entities, such as Medicare and Medicaid, will benefit greatly from our services because these sectors have seen cost overruns, and many payors have withdrawn from these markets. Our concept of non-risk outsourcing of services allows us to generate revenue from payors who are intent on finding cost-effective delivery methods.

### Supply Side
- Physician groups represent our major supply side customers. Their needs parallel the development of our services due to the nearly 25 years we have been providing them with business management services. We anticipate a growing need for IT services and the business connectivity that will be engendered by our e-business development. In addition, there will be a growing market for business and financial management, as well as management of the contractual process with the demand side.
- Physician groups are also important in the development of the insurance networks with which we then contract. Their full value will be realized as we develop gain-sharing arrangements with large MICOs to drive costs lower, and

as we generate additional revenues through contract management.

- We also negotiate contracts with payors on behalf of dentists and other insurance professionals for the delivery of cost-effective services.
- Hospitals are customers for network management services. Additionally, there is a large market opportunity here in purchasing efficiencies, as well in the area of IT services and financial management.

### 4. Economics

The financial opportunity for Griffin & Associates revolves around forming and contracting with insurance provider networks, and providing administrative services to payors. Revenue from these services is earned from the total flow of medical costs at a rate of 6% of the plan's medical cost. Net operating revenues equal approximately 65% of the income for these services. IT, financial, marketing and administrative services comprise Griffin & Associates's additional revenue stream. We provide these services on a contract basis to individual companies, normally at a percentage of their revenue. Net operating revenue for these services approximates 25% of our billing.

### 5. People

Our management team includes senior-level professionals who possess extensive business management and growth skills in every area of the current and future business environment, except a senior-level IT business development officer. We anticipate filling that position in advance of the projected roll out of our practice support products.

The management team has developed business contracts that will generate gross revenue of over $4.7 million annually. Current strategic plans call for gross revenue growth to exceed $40 million in five years.

### 6. Strategic Objectives-Insurance Management Services

Griffin & Associates first asserted itself as a managed insurance coverage company in mid-1999, using its network of approximately 1,400 practitioners to attract large national Managed Insurance Coverage Organizations that were interested in marketing their products in Phoenix. These insurance claims payors received significant health claims costs savings, enabling them to access lower fee contracts we negotiated with these physicians. Through our services, Managed Insurance Coverage Organizations also enjoyed significant savings on costs associated with developing and managing their own networks, including expenses involved with credentialing providers.

### Execution

Griffin & Associates began closing on contracts with a number of national Preferred Provider Organizations (PPOs). Combined, they represent more than 100,000 health members using the Griffin & Associates Network in Phoenix. These PPOs are:
- Multiplan
- CCN
- Evolutions Health Systems
- QRS
- FOCUS
- USA Managed Insurance Coverage Organization

This growth has positioned us as a major player in the Northern Arizona marketplace, enabling us to negotiate contracts from a position of significant strength. This positioning continues to increase our value to our existing clients, and generate new sales.

Another beneficial aspect of our aggressive management is that a number of early contracts have been reassessed, resulting in more business and better arrangements. The following are some examples:

- FOCUS and QRS, two major Workers' Compensation networks, have added our hospital network.
- USA Health Network is re-examining their business direction in Arizona, and will add another eight counties to their marketing area. They will also work with Griffin & Associates to direct more of their current members through our network.

## Network-Based Growth Strategies

In order to maximize revenue from the effective delivery of care, Griffin & Associates has two network-based growth strategies. The first is to increase business from current clients. The second strategy is to add additional clients.

## Increased Business from Current Clients

- Each National PPO has lives outside our current network coverage area. To grow this business opportunity, we will expand our physician base throughout Phoenix and Northern Arizona. At the same time, we are asking our current clients to use us as their "Regional Network Administrator". In this capacity, we act on their behalf, contracting with practitioners in areas where they either already have business, or plan to expand. This means that fewer companies will actively work at the local level to contract with physicians, and will turn to us to perform this function for them. In essence:

- We gain by representing more members, giving us better fee arrangements

- We expand our number of directly contracted physicians, thus increasing our revenue from all customers:
    - We currently have 5,500 practitioners.
    - We will add another 2,500 practitioners.
    - We add additional value to prospects by giving them a better network than they now access.

- We will expand the network throughout Arizona into Phoenix, Arizona, and rural areas dictated by the location of client members, as well as by emerging growth opportunities. We already have the agreement of National PPO clients to use our network on a provider-by-provider basis.

- We are developing/enhancing additional products for our clients, as follows:
    - Our hospital network is not being universally used by our National PPOs. We are increasing our number of facilities to encourage utilization.
    - Coverage network savings are comparable to our physician network results, and we are focusing on adding these services for each client.

**Adding Additional Clients**

Since our core competencies relate to network development and management, we will develop new clients through two basic areas of the insurance business.

The first is the insured market, represented by various Insurance Companies and the National PPOs that contract with them. We are fully engaged in this market, and since our PPO contracts represent nearly every large insurer in the country, we are well on the way to being the network of choice for insured benefit plans.

**INVESTOR OVERVIEW**

The second area is the self-funded market, which we will address as follows:
- We are currently targeting nearly 100 Third Party Administrators as potential clients for our network services. At this time, all of these TPAs use our major competitors' networks.

- We plan to contact every large employer in Northern Arizona, and to offer them an alternative to their current coverage program. In order to succeed in this major strategic initiative, we need the following services, at minimum:
  - A competent Third Party Administrator and an Insurance Claim Adjudicator with EDI/Internet capabilities.
  - A cost-competitive Stop Loss Insurer.
  - Effective Utilization Management/Case Management Programs.
  - Disease Management Programs.
  - Insurance Service Agreements.

**7. Status of Company Operations**

Network and Health Plan Management Services:
- 25 medical network access contracts have been signed which are projected to generate $550,000 of net revenue.
- Griffin & Associates' net revenue for these contracts will be attained in 2003.
- The provider network continues to develop and expand. There are now 5,000 physicians, 200 dentists, and 50 hospitals in our network. The Phoenix network will grow to 7,000 physicians, 500 dentists, and 60 hospitals over the next 18 months.

**8. Company Needs**

Griffin & Associates needs cash to successfully execute our sales plan, which encompasses IT, financial services, administrative services, and other products. We need to hire a senior level IT business development officer, and eight sales management positions need to be developed over the next twelve months as sales continue to expand. Although sales positions are 100% commission-driven, we must still meet certain start up expenses and training costs. In addition, Griffin & Associates needs cash to pay down accounts payable and certain note obligations incurred during the network development and IT service development stages. Both of the network and IT service areas are sufficiently developed and are fully operational. Future development costs of our products and services will be paid through operational cash flow.

# BUSINESS PLAN #13: Janitorial Supply Company

This business plan has the purpose of securing a loan of $75,000 to purchase an existing janitorial supply company. The plan was successful in obtaining the financing, and the janitorial supply company which resulted is today a thriving business. You will find these and other sections included in this business plan:

Licenses and Permits
Executive Summary
Personnel
Market
Competition
Major Supplies
List of Business Assets
Five-Year Projections

# BUSINESS PLAN #13: Janitorial Supply Business

## WHITAKER JANITORIAL SUPPLIES

**JANITORIAL SUPPLY SERVICE**

Here is a business plan for an organization that sells various cleaning equipment and supplies

We will be selling various cleaners and cleaning equipment both in-home and commercial in type and strength. (See APPENDIX for detailed item list.) Our business will be a retailer with a "flavor" of wholesale image. Our attraction will be free delivery and personal service and attention, with rapid turnaround time from order to delivery.

The market we intend to serve are businesses and professionals both in town and outer rural areas.

With telephone, WATTS line, fax, ordering, and personal contact ordering, we expect to improve our market share another 10% from 15% to 25%.

Other points which will make our business special to the consumers are computer invoicing and billing, along with information on uses and dangers on our products, along with an unconditional guaranteed satisfaction, total refund, or replacement.

Making our customers satisfied will be "job one." Our plan is to know the personal history of all family members and key personnel if possible. There will be birthday cards, anniversary cards, Christmas cards, and congratulatory notes, not only to direct contact or owners, but to all employers and their family members.

The changes we will make should generate much new life in our business.

The first of many positive improvements will be to computerize the running of the business. In that, we will have accounts receivable/payable, inventory, billing information, and key item sells by customer, order cycles, monthly reports, or financials (such as cash flow), pertinent customer information, specific sell trends, and customer information such as type of business, address, owners, employee names, addresses, birthdate, children, ages, and anniversaries.

We also plan to begin looking for a new business site, more strategic increased walk-in traffic, larger floor area for displaying, and closer to the high traffic area of town (Collier Road close to bypass, Highway 73, or "on" the bypass itself).

The price formula is $10,000 by equipment fixtures and vehicles, $59,000 in physical inventory, $25,000 in accounts receivable, and $5,000 in goodwill, for a total of $95,000.

### LICENSE AND PERMITS

Whitaker Janitorial Supplies is currently registered with the Wisconsin Secretary of State and is incorporated. Our plans are to reincorporate under the same name (have permission of owners to do so). We will also obtain the La Crosse County business license through the La Crosse County Registrar of Deeds.

# EXECUTIVE SUMMARY

There are many good reasons for a business plan: set monetary goals, sales goals, profits, general company direction, and lender information. I hope that this plan does all.

During the past two months I have spent working on this plan, I have been forced to discover a lot of questions I needed to know the answers to and even the questions themselves. Even though it has been tedious at times, I have grown a great deal from my endeavors here.

It is my hope that you, the lender, will appreciate the fact that my plan is simple and direct.

This plan is to put down in words the direction I will be taking with the company in the coming years. The marketing strategies, sales, expenses, profits, profit margins, other expenses, personnel needs, and payroll projections.

I plan to incorporate the business in the next six months and will be President of the corporation. The company will be "Whitaker Janitorial Supplies and More."

The company will be successful for a number of reasons. Two of the most important bare my character and credibility. Thirdly, a solid plan which will be monitored and adjusted to ensure the necessary changes are made when needed. Fourthly, years of background and experience (See RESUME). Fifthly, updating how we do business, computerization of accounts, improving ordering methods (utilizing the 80/20 rule), future relocation, better organization, and very important, committed to success whatever it takes.

I, Melvin Brett Stephens, am requesting a "LOB" loan in the amount of $75,000, to purchase Whitaker Janitorial Supplies Company, Inc. At an interest rate of 10.125%, repayable in monthly installments over five years.

I will "put up" $20,000.00 of my own money and have $5,000 in the bank for any unforeseen monetary needs. The owners will carry a note for $5,000 for one year, payable June 2004. With this, I offer $59,000 in company inventory, $25,000 in accounts receivable, $10,000 in fixtures and equipment assets, and my personal guarantee.

This loan will not only help me secure a lifelong goal and a means for my personal dreams, but will secure jobs in the community, maintain tax base, and be an investment in the future if the community which we all are a part of.

Further, I cannot end without writing a statement made to me by my grandfather when I was a young boy. He simply said, "Son, always remember this: a man who is willing to roll up his sleeves seldom loses his shirt." This has been my guide in every endeavor I have ever undertaken, and has carried me through both the easy and hard times in my career. I will not forego my lifelong work ethic now. I will succeed.

# BUSINESS PLAN #13: Janitorial Supply Business

## MANAGEMENT

My education will be an asset to our business. With an Associate of Science degree in Business, I completed courses in Business Management, Business Math, and Marketing and Motivation, along with over 25 self-help tape courses and seminars, I will be prepared to effectively handle opportunities as they present themselves to me. Physically, I am trim and fit. Very seldom have a cold very rarely and am almost never out of work because of illnesses.

**JANITORIAL SUPPLY SERVICE**

My product knowledge and experience in selling the products, and overall sales experience, should lend itself to be invaluable assets to our success. The organization structure will be as follows: Myself, Melvin Brett Stevens, President of corporation; Connie Alechia Williams, Vice-President; Office Manager, and Receiving and Delivery Manager.

I will be doing 90% of direct sales calls and cold calls in addition to delivery work. Sarah, our Office Manager, will handle walk-in sales, bookkeeping responsibilities, and invoicing. Shipping and Receiving Manager will handle 90% of the receiving and 85% of the delivery responsibilities.

The wages will be set as follows for the first year:

M.B. Stevens — $10,600          Sarah — $16,800          John — $10,900

We have retained Scott Sanford, CPA, as the corporation accountant and Anthony Borris as the corporation lawyer.

## PERSONNEL

The staff, other than the owners, will stay as is, with the exception of an additional part-time office and part-time delivery person. These positions will be added during the second year as sales demand it. Training will be minimal with the exception of updating staff to be able to work with the information and forms of the planned computer installation in the first months. The cost here should be minimal as the training and support for computerization will be provided by the computer company, along with ongoing training and support.

## MARKET

Our market area is currently the fourth largest by population in Wisconsin and is expected to have solid growth in the future. The influx of the manufacturing companies locally and the request for a new distribution center will continue to constitute growth and stability in our trade area.

Our market percent is currently about 30% of like business sales in the market and we are planning to increase that by 5% to 35% over the next 18 months.

Our market is very diverse in that all ages, sexes, occupations, lifestyles, incomes, and locations are included in our customers. But we will target small businesses and business professionals, such as medical offices, dentists, funeral homes, janitorial services, car washes, maid services, insurance offices, machine shops, independent automotive parts, car dealerships, banks, churches, rest homes, glass companies, diet centers, real estate offices, and other such businesses.

We will keep and attract our market segment with quality products, unconditionally guaranteed customer satisfaction, personal service, and free delivery.

The company's mission statement will be, "Satisfied customers are not just our goal, it is the only reason we will be here tomorrow."

## COMPETITION

The main direct competition to us is "Taylor Commercial Cleaning." They have not existed nearly as long in the area as we have. "Taylor Commercial Cleaning" is owned by Franklin L. Gregory and managed by hire. Their main selling point is price.

We will be owner-operated and motivated, and concentrate on products, and service.

## MAJOR SUPPLIERS

Hollingsworth Mop Company
Montgomery, AL

Trellman Manufacturing
Spokane, WA

Hilliard Broom Company
Richmond, VA

Kilmer Works
Harrisburg, PA

Tri-State Manufacturing
Atlanta, GA

Temple Supply Company
Ozart, AL

Zackerman Company
Savannah, GA

Briar, Incorporated
Manning, SC

Johnson Paper Company
Los Angeles, CA

Hinkamp, Incorporation
Seattle, WA

Concord Manufacturing, Inc.
Portland, OR

Piedmont Corporation
Charleston, SC

Ivarsson Laboratories
Miami, FL

Einsen-Dale, Inc.
New Orleans, LA

Hughes Manufacturing
Lawton, OK

Navarro Broom Company
Pittsburgh, PA

Edinburgh Cleaning Co.
Los Vegas, NV

Heritage Paper Plan
Portland, OR

Lehmer Janitorial Inc.
Bossier City, LA

# BUSINESS PLAN #13: Janitorial Supply Business

**JANITORIAL SUPPLY
SERVICE**

Inventory
Accounts Receivable
Utility Deposits
Telephone Numbers
Whitaker Janitorial Supplies Name
1995 Ford Explorer
1998 Mercury Grand Marquis
3 Executive desks
3 Swivel Chairs
1 Gas Heater
2 Air conditioners
1 Victor Adding Machine
1 Texas Instrument Adding Machine, TI-8210
1 Texas Instrument Adding Machine, TI-5219
1 Four-Drawer Filing Cabinet
1 Accounts Receivable Cabinet on Wheels
1 Counter W/Storage in Bottom
2 Office Shelving Units
2 3' X 12' Platform Displays
1 Four-Tier Shelving Unit
2 12' Display Units
3 Roll Matting Racks
1 Six-Tier Aerosol Display
1 Three-Tier Mop Display
1 8' Carpet Mat Display
5 Peg Board Wall Units
18 Wholesale Shelving Units
2 Hand Trucks
1 Hydraulic Drum Lifts
1 Work Desk
1 Drum Rack
2 Set Skate Wheel Conveyer

# FIVE-YEAR PROJECTION

I estimate the shop's income and expense figures for the first five years of operation according to APPENDIX A.

## APPENDIX A

|  | YEAR 1 | YEAR 2 | YEAR 3 | YEAR 4 | YEAR 5 |
|---|---|---|---|---|---|
| **Cash Receipts** | | | | | |
| Sales | $305,000 | $315,000 | $324,000 | $324,000 | $330,000 |
| Less-Increase in A/R | <2,000> | <2,000> | <2,000> | <2,000> | <2,000> |
| Net Cash Receipts | 303,000 | 313,000 | 316,000 | 322,000 | 328,000 |
| | | | | | |
| **Cash Disbursements** | | | | | |
| Cost of Goods Sold | $198,250 | $204,750 | $203,520 | 207,360 | 207,900 |
| Add-Increase Inventory | 5,000 | 4,000 | 3,000 | 2,000 | 2,000 |
| Less-Increase in A/P | <3,400> | <3,000> | <2,250> | <2,250> | <2,000> |
| Total Cash Expended for Merchandise | $199,850 | $205,750 | $207,110 | $207,110 | $207,900 |
| | | | | | |
| Salary - Officer | $ 10,600 | $ 12,600 | $ 14,000 | $17,600 | $ 21,600 |
| Salaries - Other | 25,800 | 27,600 | 29,400 | 31,200 | 33,000 |
| Sales Commissions | 0 | 0 | 0 | 0 | 0 |
| | | | | | |
| Other Expenses | $ 38,388 | $ 39,540 | $ 40,726 | $ 41,948 | $ 43,206 |
| | | | | | |
| **Capital Expenditures** | | | | | |
| Trade for New Delivery Van | $ 0 | $ 6,000 | $ 0 | $ 0 | $ 0 |
| Computer System | 3,000 | 0 | 0 | 0 | 0 |
| | | | | | |
| Debt Service | $ 17,848 | $ 17,848 | $ 17,848 | $ 17,848 | $ 17,848 |
| | | | | | |
| Total Cash Disbursements | $ 99,636 | $107,588 | $106,574 | $112,596 | $119,654 |
| | | | | | |
| Net Cash Flow | $<7,514> | $<4,338> | $<9,656> | $<6,294> | $<4,446> |
| | | | | | |
| Cumulative Cash Flow | $ 7,514 | $ 7,852 | $ 13,508 | $ 15,802 | $ 16,248 |

# BUSINESS PLAN #14:
# Loan Request,
# Manufacturing Company

This business plan was intended to obtain financing for an expansion of a relatively large manufacturing business. You will see components which include the following:

Overview
The company
Strong market position
Management stability and commitment
Restructuring
Summary of asset sale
Cash flow of asset sale
Overview of request for financing
Detailed loan request
Company history
Product information
Summary of the production process
Schedule of manpower
Analysis of the competition
General comments
Management: officers and senior managers
Profit and loss
Project income statement/cash flows

# BUSINESS PLAN #14: Loan Request, Manufacturing Co.

## TIDWELL & MCNEIL VULCANIZING COMPANY (TMV)

### EXECUTIVE SUMMARY

**OVERVIEW**

Tidwell & McNeil Vulcanizing Company (TMV) is headquartered in Lawton, Oklahoma, just southwest of Oklahoma City, Oklahoma, and is owned by the McNeil family (50%) and by the Tidwell family (50%).

**THE COMPANY**

TMV began operating in March 1997. The Company was the result of an asset purchase of the Hydraulic Division of the Louisiana Vulcanizing Corporation (LVC). The assets purchased consisted of three strategically located manufacturing plants in Oklahoma, Texas, and Louisiana.

The Louisiana Vulcanizing Corporation (LVC) was a wholly owned subsidiary of Centura, which continues to operate its synthetic rubber business at a nearby facility.

**STRONG MARKET POSITION**

TMV generates sales via service vulcanizing for miscellaneous synthetic rubber, conveyor belts and polyurethane products. While TMV has three principal competitors in its service vulcanizing business, its strategic plant locations provide freight and service advantages that make it the dominant vulcanizing company in the Southwestern region. In its vulcanized rubber manufacturing services, Tidwell & McNeil Vulcanizing has no meaningful competition due to the cost and quality advantages resulting from its unique, proprietary manufacturing process. Additionally, no other competitor has an inventory of vulcanized or conveyor belting materials available for resale. Unlike the competition, TMV can guarantee same day shipping of any item in its extensive inventory. TMV is the only high temperature vulcanizer in the Southwest region with an established outside sales force and is the largest in the Southwest. The Company has far exceeded its three competitors due to its reputation for quality, capacity, and service. Having multiple plant locations gives customers the confidence that a vulcanizing job will be completed on a timely basis.

**MANAGEMENT STABILITY AND COMMITMENT**

Mr. McNeil worked with LVC for over 20 years before the asset purchase. Mr. Tidwell managed the former LVC's operations for over 12 years and is currently President of TMV.

**RESTRUCTURING**

Management has determined that the time has come to expand the vulcanizing business by adding an additional facility. Management also desires to enter into a new conveyor belt product line — idlers. Conveyor idlers are new to TMV — but not to management. Conveyor idlers were a product of LVC since 1985 and are a major product of Centura, the parent company of LVC. Management was in direct control of the idler product until 1997, when management signed a five-year non-compete agreement which expired on April 15, 2002. The vulcanizing facilities were always run as an operating division separate from the conveyor application division.

*Management feels that it is key to the success of both products (vulcanizing and conveyor belts) that they be separated in the future.*

Management intends to produce conveyor idlers in the TMV Legal Entity. The conveyor idler production will be located at the Irving, Texas TMV production facility. The largest potential vulcanized conveyor idler customer (Centura) has a second plant located nearby.

**LOAN REQUEST**
For a vulcanizing corporation located in Oklahoma

A new entity has been formed to manage the vulcanizing business. The new entity is the South West Industries (SWI). SWI will purchase all of the inventory and receivables of TMV.

Millhide Management, LLC will purchase from TMV all of the equipment located at the Louisiana plant. Millhide will lease this equipment to SWI.

Vanderhorst Management, LLC will purchase from TMV all of the equipment located at the Oklahoma plant. Vanderhorst will lease this equipment to SWI.

SWI will assume the land leases for Vanderhorst and Millhide on December 20, 2004.

A second, newly constructed company, Beringer, has also been formed. Beringer will construct a new vulcanizing plant near Shreveport, LA. This construction has begun and the building will be erected during the summer of 2004. The plant will be in operation by mid 2004. Management determined that Shreveport was the best location for a new plant because of the growth in Louisiana and the concentration of business on the I-43, I-10 interstate highways. Management also determined that a 50' kettle is necessary to service the changing market and that it was not practical to enlarge the Lawton plant to accommodate the larger kettle. We protect our OK market, and open up the Louisiana market, by building a large, strategically located facility in Shreveport. SWI will lease the new facility from Beringer.

SWI will lease the Lawton facility from TMV for one year. This will give SWI time to be operating the new Shreveport facility. There will be no service vulcanizing at the Lawton facility after June 1, 2004. TMV will start the production and marketing of vulcanized conveyor idlers on August 31, 2005. This activity will take place at the Lawton facility.

TMV and SWI will be managed as separate companies.

# BUSINESS PLAN #14: Loan Request, Manufacturing Co.

## SUMMARY OF ASSET SALE

### PURCHASE PRICE PAID BY SWI

| | | |
|---|---|---:|
| 1. | Accounts Receivables | $1,625,236 |
| 2. | Cash | 35,000 |
| 3. | Inventory | 1,037,975 |
| 4. | Prepaids | 71,400 |

**LOAN REQUEST**

| | |
|---|---:|
| TOTAL: | $2,769,611 |

### PURCHASE PRICE PAID BY MILLHIDE AND VANDERHORST

| | | |
|---|---|---:|
| 1. | Equipment | 491,303 |

| | |
|---|---:|
| **TOTAL PURCHASE PRICE** | $3,260,914 |

### SOURCE OF FUNDS/PURCHASE PRICE

| | | |
|---|---|---:|
| 1. | Millhide and Vanderhorst Equipment Loan | 686,000 |
| 2. | Payables assumed | 1,188,846 |
| 3. | SWI Line of Credit | 1,176,080 |
| 4. | SWI Loan to TMV | 210,000 |

| |
|---:|
| $3,260,914 |

## CASH FLOW OF ASSET SALE

| | *CASH OUT* | *CASH IN* |
|---|---:|---:|
| **TMV:** | | |
| 1. Pay existing Fidelity Bankers | (436,596) | |
| 2. Pay existing Centura loan | (671,686) | |
| 3. Pay existing Coldwell Bankers | (755,202) | |
| 4. Cash from SWI | | 1,863,484 |
| | 1,863,484 | 1,863,484 |
| **SWI, Millhide, Vanderhorst:** | | |
| 1. New equipment loan Millhide/Vanderhorst | | 686,000 |
| 2. New working capital loan SWI | | 1,177,486 |
| 3. Cash to TMV | 1,863,484 | |
| | 1,863,484 | 1,863,484 |

This loan will not be paid until the due date (12/04). The proceeds will be kept in escrow and the payments and final payments will be made from escrow.

Real Business Plans & Marketing Tools

# OVERVIEW OF REQUEST FOR FINANCING

**South West Industries**
- A working capital loan financing 80% of receivables and 40% of inventory.
- The initial loan amount will be $1,176,068 on August 31, 2003.

**Beringer**
- A 3-year fixed loan of $1,000,000 which will be used to complete the new vulcanizing facility.

**Millhide Management Company, LLC**
- A total Millhide and Vanderhorst 3-year fixed loan of $686,000 which will be used to purchase the equipment of TMV located at the Louisiana plant.

**Vanderhorst Management Company, LLC**
- A total Millhide and Vanderhorst 3-year fixed loan of $686,000 which will be used to purchase the equipment of TMV located at the Oklahoma plant.

# BUSINESS PLAN #14: Loan Request, Manufacturing Co.

**DETAILED LOAN REQUEST**

I. South West Industries
  A. SWI Working Line of Credit
     1.  Line           $1,750,000
     2.  Interest Rate  Not to exceed 3/4% over prime
     3.  Term           1 year
     4.  Processing fee Not to exceed 1/2% per year
     5.  Security       Inventory and receivables

**LOAN REQUEST**  *Guarantors*: Jackson McNeil and Kalvin Tidwell

II. Millhide Management, LLC
  A. Machinery and Equipment Loan
     1.  Principal requested Total Millhide and Vanderhorst loan of $686,000
     2.  Term 36 months
     3.  Interest rate 9.5%
     4.  Security Vulcanizing equipment located at LA location 3 year lease to SWI. Lease to be assigned to lenders.

*Guarantors*: Jackson McNeil and Kalvin Tidwell

III.    Vanderhorst Management, LLC
        Machinery and Equipment Loan
     1.  Principal requested Total Millhide and Vanderhorst loan of $686,000
     2.  Term 36 months
     3.  Interest rate 9.5%
     4.  Security Vulcanizing equipment located at OK location 3 year lease to SWI. Lease to be assigned to lenders.

*Guarantors*: Jackson McNeil and Kalvin Tidwell

IV.     Beringer, LTD — Loan to Build New Vulcanizing Facility:
     1.  Principal requested $1,000,000
     2.  Term 36 months
     3.  Interest rate 9.5%
     4.  Security Land, building, equipment of Beringer. Three (3) year lease to SWI. Lease to be assigned to lenders.

*Guarantors*: Jackson McNeil and Kalvin Tidwell

**Note:** The Millhide and Vanderhorst loans are only secured by the equipment located in LA and OK Tidwell & McNeil Vulcanizing will not guarantee any loans, nor will any asset remaining at Tidwell & McNeil Vulcanizing be used as security for any loan of any other company. TMV will need to borrow funds to enlarge and add to its conveyor idler facility. The purpose of this reorganization is to create separate entities, independent of each other, created to achieve distinct business goals.

## LOANS BEFORE AND AFTER SALE OF TMV ASSETS

| | TMV | SWI | Millhide & Vanderhorst |
|---|---|---|---|
| **Loans before sale:** | | | |
| 1. Coldwell Bankers | 755,202 | | |
| 2. Fidelity Bankers | 436,596 | | |
| 3. Centura | 671,686 | | |
| **Loans after sale:** | | | |
| 1. New working capital loan | 1,177,484 | | |
| 2. New equipment loan | | | 686,000 |
| TOTALS: | 1,863,484 | | 1,863,484 |

**Note:** Centura note will not be paid off until maturity. Loan proceeds will be kept in an interest bearing account. Monthly payments will be made until the due date, 12/31/04, when the balance will be paid.

## WORKING CAPITAL AVAILABLE AFTER ASSET SALE

*South West Industries:*

| | | |
|---|---|---|
| A/R | | 1,648,190 |
| Inventory | | 1,075,035 |
| TOTAL: | | 1,975,725 |
| A/R | 80% | 1,318,552 |
| Inventory | 40% | 430,014 |
| M/L | | 1,748,566 |

# BUSINESS PLAN #14: Loan Request, Manufacturing Co.

## COMPANY HISTORY

**1975:** Louisiana Vulcanizing Company (LVC) founded by Jackson McNeil's father on October 25, 1979 as job shop vulcanizer.
**20 Employees $50,000 Annual Sales**

**1978:** LVC started carrying inventory of vulcanized bar material allowing for vulcanized steel sales in addition to service vulcanizing sales.
**40 Employees $1,000,000 Annual Sales**

**1980:** LVC started line of vulcanized synthetic and silicone rubber, with one salesman for all product lines.
**70 Employees $2,700,000 Annual Sales**

**1981:** LVC built the Hydraulic Division and installed the first high tension steel cord for conveyor belting.
**90 Employees $3,800,000 Annual Sales**

**1985:** LVC started manufacturing rubber, plastic, steel banded drainage seals and stone guards.
**187 Employees $10,000,000 Annual Sales**

**1988:** LVC purchased by Centura for its Hydraulic Division which sells high tension steel cords and vulcanized polyurethane and rubber.
**112 Employees $13,000,000 Annual Sales**

**1989:** Centura acquired hydraulic molding and frame presses.
**153 Employees $20,000,000 Annual Sales**

**1991:** Added Louisiana Vulcanizing Plant.
**175 Employees $24,000,000 Annual Sales**

**1993:** Added Oklahoma Vulcanizing Plant.
**195 Employees $27,000,000 Annual Sales**

**1997:** Centura made the corporate decision to consolidate its U.S. and European hydraulic manufacturing operations after a fire destroyed the European facility in November 1996. To finance this move and the cost of a new facility in California, Centura agreed to sell the 98-employee Hydraulic Division to Jackson McNeil and Kalvin Tidwell.
**210 Employees $32,000,000 Annual Sales**

**1997:** Asset purchase of LVC's Hydraulic Division.
**Tidwell & McNeil Vulcanizing Company begins business with 90 employees and $10,500,000 in sales**

**2002:** Tidwell & McNeil sells Vulcanizing Assets with the purpose of exiting the Vulcanizing business to enter and specialize in conveyor belting services.
- Relates to Hydraulic Division not purchased from LVC and Centura.

## HISTORY

### South West Industries

2002    SWI formed to expand in service vulcanizing and investigate other vulcanized products.

2003    SWI leases all vulcanizing assets of Millhide and Vanderhorst located in LA and OK SWI leases the new vulcanizing facility owned by Beringer.

### Millhide Management, LLC

2002    Millhide was formed in 2002 to purchase the land and buildings of TMV located in Louisiana.

2003    Millhide purchases all equipment of TMV located in Louisiana. Millhide leases all land, building and equipment for SWI.

### Vanderhorst Management, LLC

2002    Vanderhorst was formed in 2002 to purchase the land and buildings of TMV located in Oklahoma.

2003    Vanderhorst purchases all equipment of TMV located in Louisiana. Vanderhorst leases all land, building and equipment to SWI.

### Beringer, LTD

2002    Beringer, L.T.D. is a LA Limited Liability Company formed for the purpose of constructing a new, state-of-the-art vulcanizing facility near Shreveport, LA.

- Beringer, L.T.D. is 50% owned by Richard Fields and 50% owned by Kalvin Peterson, Jr.
- Beringer, L.T.D. has a three-year lease with South West Industries for the new facility. The lease will be triple net and the monthly fee will be $45,000.
- Beringer intends to assign the SWI lease to a lender for use as collateral for a three-year term loan in the amount of $1,000,000.00.

## PRODUCT INFORMATION

### SERVICE VULCANIZING

Because customers send in plastic to be vulcanized and are charged by the pound, this is a freight-sensitive, territorial business. The rubber with sulfur used in the vulcanizing process is supplied by Aulden, a European corporation and Lancaster, an importer of Sulfur. Due to the large amount of rubber purchased by SWI, the Company is able to negotiate favorable pricing significantly lower than the prevailing market price. The crude Indian rubber price is fixed under contract and negotiated annually each year. SWI will have three mature and established satellite plants located 250 miles apart. Each plant will dominate its respective market region in Texas, Louisiana and Oklahoma.

### VULCANIZED PLASTICS SALES

SWI purchases plastics and synthetic and silicone rubber from mini-mills, vulcanizes them, places the finished product in inventory, and resells to manufacturers of automobile products such as rubber tires, bearing seals, and conveyor rollers. SWI is able to purchase plastics from several regional mini-mills at competitive prices.

### NEW PRODUCTS

The market for new and used conveyor belting services is starting to develop after many years of work. The current competitive product has experienced many failures and shortcomings. SWI is uniquely positioned to take advantage of this potentially large market. SWI is currently analyzing the market for vulcanized materials such as rubber lined pipes, drums and hoppers made from raw or cured rubber. These products are manufactured for the construction market which require minimal fabrication.

## PRODUCT SERVICE INFORMATION

Vulcanized conveyor belting systems are manufactured for new facility installations as well as belt change outs. Our new facility will provide various products such as transmission belts (joined and supplied), poly belts (round or flat), lag pulleys and head drums. We will offer splicing and vulcanizing services for onsite or factory work. The standard splicing equipment will accommodate 2.2 mtrs wide in rubber and 1.5 mtrs wide. The products will be sold through agents who charge an average of 8% for their services.

**LOAN REQUEST**

We are cultivating a new vulcanized product not yet revealed. This product will be revolutionary in the automobile industry. A press release for our new product will be available after September 30, 2005 once construction of our new plant in Texas has begun. Management is completely familiar with this product.

Centura is the largest consumer of vulcanized conveyor belts in the U.S. They are located less than one mile from the Lawton production facility. Centura currently purchases all vulcanized conveyor belts from outside sources. TMV is preparing a quote to supply all vulcanized conveyor belts to Centura.

### SUMMARY OF THE PRODUCTION PROCESS

**RECEIVING**
- - - - - - - - -
1. MATERIAL UNLOADED FROM TRUCK, INSPECTED, WEIGHED, AND COUNTED.
2. MATERIAL PLACED ON RACKS.
3. RECEIVING REPORTS COMPLETED.

**SPLICING**
- - - - - - - -
1. MATERIAL IS DEGREASED
2. MATERIAL IS CLEANED TO BARE RUBBER
3. MATERIAL IS RINSED IN IN WATER

**VULCANIZING**
- - - - - - - - - -
1. MATERIAL IS SUBJECTED TO INTENSE HEAT TO CREATE DURABLE ELASTICITY, STRENGTH AND STABILITY.

**SHIPPING**
- - - - - - - -
1. MATERIAL IS CLEANED, PACKAGED, WEIGHED, AND SHIPPED.

### SCHEDULE OF MANPOWER
**2003**

| | |
|---|---|
| Direct labor: | |
| Conveyor belts | 6 |
| Indirect labor: | |
| Conveyor belts | 3 |
| Sales: | |
| Conveyor belts | 2 |
| Administrative: | |
| Accounting | 2 |
| | 2 |
| **TOTAL:** | 13 |

## SCHEDULE OF MANPOWER BY PLANT LOCATION — 2003

| | Shreveport, LA | Lawton, OK | Irving, TX |
|---|---|---|---|
| **DIRECT LABOR:** | | | |
| Group Leaders | 4 | 5 | 6 |
| Material Handlers | 17 | 18 | 17 |
| **TOTAL DIRECT LABOR** | 21 | 23 | 21 |
| **INDIRECT LABOR:** | | | |
| Plant Managers | 1 | 1 | 1 |
| Shift Managers | 2 | 2 | 2 |
| Shipping | 2 | 2 | 3 |
| Maintenance | 2 | 3 | 3 |
| Administrative Assistances | 1 | 1 | 0 |
| **TOTAL INDIRECT LABOR** | 8 | 9 | 9 |
| **SELLING:** | | | |
| Sales Manager | 0 | 0 | 0 |
| Inside Salesperson | 1 | 2 | 1 |
| Clerical Salesperson | 0 | 0 | 1 |
| Rubber Salesperson | 1 | 0 | 0 |
| **TOTAL SELLING** | 2 | 2 | 2 |
| **TOTAL:** | 31 | 34 | 32 |

**ADMINISTRATIVE:**

| | | | | |
|---|---|---|---|---|
| President | 1 | Treasurer | 1 |
| Controller | 1 | Accounting Clerks | 3 |
| Administration | 1 | | |
| | | **TOTAL:** | 7 |

### ANALYSIS OF THE COMPETITION

| Competitor | Volume | Started | Employees | Facilities |
|---|---|---|---|---|
| Fargo Vulcanizing | $3,000,000 | 1972 | 40 | 40,000 sq. ft. |
| Portland Vulcanizing | $3,000,000 | 1970 | 50 | 25,000 sq. ft. |
| Vulcan Industries | $3,000,000 | 1978 | 85 | 90,000 sq. ft. |

**Fargo Vulcanizing, Inc.** - The Company's largest competitor. Fargo is a strong competitor in the deep Northwest. The owners have been in the industry for over 20 years. Fargo is price competitive on large jobs. Fargo performs heated vulcanizing at all three plants located in Rapid City, SD, Fargo, ND, and Omaha, NE.

**Portland Vulcanizing Corporation** - A non-aggressive competitor and will not lower prices in a bidding situation. Management tends to go after low-volume, high-margin work. The owner has been in the vulcanizing business for over 25 years. The company also manufactures related vulcanizing equipment and is well capitalized. *Added a 42' kettle in 1998. We expect more aggressiveness and price competition.*

**Vulcan Industries** - An aggressive competitor. Merle Higgins, President, purchased the company in 1992 from his family. Mr. Higgins is 49 and has worked in the business since college. Vulcan Industries is squeezed between the Louisiana SWI plant in Shreveport, Louisiana, and the plant in Lawton, Oklahoma in which sales are generated by vulcanizing synthetic and silicone rubber as well as manufacturing vulcanized forklift mats and power blocks. ***Added a 42' kettle in 1999. Have become very aggressive.***

# BUSINESS PLAN #14: Loan Request, Manufacturing Co.

## GENERAL COMMENTS

The competitors listed represent companies with vulcanizing operations which have territories that, to some degree, overlap with the territories of SWI. As a general rule, all the competitors mentioned are not as aggressive as SWI. Most of the competitors focus on service vulcanizing sales and have little or no experience successfully manufacturing vulcanized products. None of the competitors have an outside sales force. They all depend on longtime customers. SWI started the Oklahoma and Louisiana plants with no customer base. It was necessary to use aggressive selling. This team of experienced salesmen has been chipping away at the foundation of the competitors in their territory. The sales force is trained to look for low-volume, high-margin products which SWI will produce and vulcanize. The SWI sales force and its aggressive approach in the market sets SWI apart from its competitors.

As noted above, our closest competitors have added larger kettles and/or replaced their existing kettles with a larger one. It is essential that SWI have a larger, better located facility. It is the management's opinion that if SWI does not put a large facility on the 85/40 corridor in TX, someone else will. There are three major manufacturers and distributors of vulcanized conveyor belts.

1. **Centura**
   Irving, TX
   Buys and sells 100,000 - 200,000 belts per month

2. **Vulcan**
   Texarkana, TX
   Produces and sells 100,000 belts per month

3. **Eppson**
   Hammond, IN
   Produces and sells 75,000 belts per month

## MANAGEMENT EXPERIENCE: OFFICERS
### KALVIN TIDWELL, *President* Age: 50

**1997 - Present**  **Tidwell & McNeil Vulcanizing Company** - Lawton, Oklahoma; President, Responsible for all operations of the company.

**1988 - 1997**  **Louisiana Vulcanizing Corporation** - Shreveport, Louisiana; V.P. and General Manager
*1992 - 1997:* Directed all Vulcanizing operations for Texas, Louisiana, and Oklahoma operations.
*1988 - 1992:* Responsible for all manufacturing and related production activities at finishing plants in Shreveport, Louisiana.

**1978 - 1988**  **Gaston Battery Company** – Kansas City, KS; Assistant Plant Manager
*1986 - 1988:* Responsible for manufacturing, maintenance, industrial engineering, and production/inventory control departments at the Kansas City complex. This plant employed 1,200 persons and produced "Energizer" brand batteries.
*1982 - 1986:* Responsible for management of the company's foreign and domestic battery chemical plant at Kansas City, Kansas.
*1978 - 1982:* Responsible for quality control, process development, and operations supervision.
**Education:** University of Kansas at Lawrence - B.S.

**JACKSON MCNEIL,** *Vice President,* Age: 44

| | |
|---|---|
| 1997 to Present | **Tidwell & McNeil Vulcanizing Company** - Lawton, Oklahoma; Vice President<br>• Responsible for finance and purchasing. |
| 1996 to Present | **Hobbs & McNeil, Attorneys** - Lawton, Oklahoma; Partner in law firm |
| 1991 to 1996 | **Centura, Inc.** – Bolivar, MO; Vice President<br>*1993 - 1996:* Designed and implemented a turnaround strategy for Centura Fastening Systems in Irving, TX. Involved in all phases of manufacturing of stud welding equipment; established new control over inventory, accounts receivable, and quality; reorganized sales management and marketing strategies; renegotiated union contracts; consolidated Missouri operation into the Texas operation resulting in a 270-employee profitable operation.<br>*1991 - 1993:* Directed manufacturing facilities in Texas, Missouri and Hawaii with total sales of $60 million. |
| 1989 - 1991 | **Louisiana Vulcanizing Corporation** - Shreveport, Louisiana; General Manager<br>• Implemented a management system for LVC which at the time had 200 employees and $23 million in sales. Actively involved in managing every department of the Company. |
| 1983 - 1989 | **Louisiana Vulcanizing Corporation** - Shreveport, Louisiana;<br>*1985 - 1989:* President: Developed operating policies and procedures that helped sustain company growth from $7 million to $15 million in annual revenues. The Company was sold to Centura, Inc. in 1988.<br>*1983-1985:* Controller: Performed various production-related responsibilities. Controlled financial functions and developed manufacturing cost system. Implemented a new management team and developed the Hydraulic Division which resulted in a 200% increase in sales in 1985.<br>**Education:** Louisiana Tech University - M.B.A., McNeese University - J.D. Louisiana Tech University - B.S., Certified Public Accountant |

### SENIOR MANAGERS

**JOHN PALLON** - Age 57. The Plant Manager at the Lawton, Oklahoma plant for over ten years. He has been employed by Louisiana Vulcanizing and Tidwell & McNeil Vulcanizing for 20 years.

**NORMAN HARPER** - Age 41. The Plant Manager in Texas. Mr. Harper has been employed by Louisiana Vulcanizing and Tidwell & McNeil Vulcanizing for the past five years. He had five years of management experience at Powell National and eight years of experience with Jasper Industries ranging from production control to assembly supervisor.

**WALTER JENKINS** - Age 38. The Plant Manager at the Lawton, Oklahoma plant for over six years. Mr. Jenkins was formerly the production shift supervisor in Texas for over five years.

**FELIX KEYES** - Age 60. Overall responsibility for Tidwell & McNeil sales and marketing program. Mr. Keyes has over eight years of experience with the Company and has had both sales and plant management responsibilities in the Lawton, Oklahoma plant.

**ROBERT POWELL** - Controller. Overall financial responsibility. CPA with 16 years of managerial accounting experience with Centura. Has managed all financial departments in several Centura companies with sales from $1,000,000 annually to $28,000,000.

# BUSINESS PLAN #14: Loan Request, Manufacturing Co.

**FINANCIAL INFORMATION**
**HISTORICALLY STRONG PROFITABILITY**

The Tidwell & McNeil Vulcanizing Company has a steady track record of profitability. Earnings before interest, depreciation, and taxes for the past six years have been as follows:

**LOAN REQUEST**

|  | 2002 | 2001 | 2000 | 1999 | 1998 | 1997 |
|---|---|---|---|---|---|---|
| NET SALES | 10,196 | 12,556 | 12,429 | 10,885 | 10,335 | 9,521 |
| COST OF SALES | 7,939 | 9,918 | 9,890 | 8,578 | 8,173 | 7,914 |
| *GROSS PROFIT* | 2,257 | 2,638 | 2,539 | 2,307 | 2,162 | 1,607 |
| *GROSS PROFIT %* | 22.1% | 21.0% | 20.4% | 21.1% | 20.9% | 16.9% |
| SELLING, GENERAL AND ADMINISTRATIVE EXPENSE | 1,417 | 1,698 | 1,441 | 1,411 | 1,485 | 1,258 |
| *INCOME FROM OPERATIONS* | 840 | 940 | 1,098 | 896 | 677 | 349 |
| Add backs: DEPRECIATION | 425 | 550 | 483 | 545 | 516 | 623 |
| EBITD | 1,265 | 1,490 | 1,581 | 1,441 | 1,193 | 972 |

**Note:** EBITD stands for "Earnings before income taxes and depreciation." All figures shown are expressed in thousands (000's) of dollars.

# PROFIT AND LOSS

| | | | | |
|---|---|---|---|---|
| P/L | 131,547 | 364,624 | 396,084 | 156,037 |
| Taxes | 43,500 | 120,500 | 130,500 | 51,493 |
| | | | | |
| *NET PROFIT* | 88,047 | 244,124 | 265,584 | 105,544 |
| Add depreciation cash available | 53,487 | 107,963 | 107,963 | 107,963 |
| | 141,894 | 352,987 | 373,547 | 212,507 |
| | | | | |
| **Principal** | 147,591 | 316,983 | 348,443 | 186,983 |
| | | | | |
| **Cash** | (5697) | 35,104 | 25,104 | 25,524 |

(for plant improvement)

**Note:** All figures above expressed in thousands (000's) of dollars.

## PROJECTED INCOME STATEMENT/CASH FLOWS

| | 2003 | 2004 | 2005 | 2006 | 2007 |
|---|---|---|---|---|---|
| **INCOME** | | | | | |
| Rent | 287,640 | 287,640 | 287,640 | 71,640 | 71,640 |
| **EXPENSES** | | | | | |
| Interest | 22,700 | 21,600 | 20,490 | 5,450 | 4,900 |
| Depreciation | | | | | |
| Building | 7,900 | 7,900 | 7,900 | 7,900 | 7,900 |
| Equipment | 98,000 | 98,000 | 98,000 | 98,000 | 98,000 |
| | | | | | |
| **Other Expenses** | 10,000 | 10,000 | 10,000 | 10,000 | 10,000 |
| | | | | | |
| **Total Expenses** | 149,040 | 137,500 | 136,390 | 121,354 | 120,800 |
| | | | | | |
| P/L | 138,600 | 150,140 | 151,250 | (49,894) | (49,160) |
| | | | | | |
| **Taxes** | 45,738 | 49,500 | 49,500 | | |
| **Net Profit** | 92,862 | 100,640 | 101,750 | (49,894) | (49,160) |
| **Add Depreciation** | 106,900 | 106,900 | 106,900 | 106,900 | 106,900 |
| **Add Principal due** | 58,864 | 64,705 | 71,128 | | |
| | | | | | |
| **TOTAL CASH AVAILABLE** | 258,626 | 272,245 | 279,778 | 57,006 | 57,440 |
| | | | | | |
| **PRINCIPAL DUE** | | | | | |
| Term loan | 207,401 | 227,987 | 250,611 | | |
| Other | 20,000 | 20,000 | 20,000 | 20,000 | 20,000 |
| | | | | | |
| *TOTAL PRINCIPAL DUE* | 227,401 | 247,987 | 270,611 | 20,000 | 20,000 |
| | | | | | |
| **NET CASH** | 31,225 | 24,258 | 9,167 | 37,006 | 37,440 |

# BUSINESS PLANS #15, 16, 17:
# Trucking Company
# Used Car Warranty Business
# Wholesale Company, Home-Based

In this final section related to business plans, you will see business plans related to the start-up of a new trucking company providing long-haul commercial services, the establishment of a company providing used car warranties, and a home-based wholesale company. Here are some of the component parts of these business plans:

Executive summary
Start-up expenses
Ownership and business concept
Management and strategic overview
Business description
Marketing plan
Business strengths and weaknesses

# BUSINESS PLAN #15: Trucking Company Start-up

I am interested in starting a trucking company that provides long haul transportation for commercial companies. I request that I be provided finances to purchase one tractor truck. I have enclosed a profit estimation after expenses. This trucking business will be a joint venture by myself and Gary Faircloth. The following contains information on his financial history:

**TRUCKING COMPANY**

| | | |
|---|---|---|
| Gary Faircloth | | SSN# 000-00-0000 |
| Salary: | Retirement pay | $550 monthly |
| | Social Security | $350 monthly |
| | Employment | $600 monthly |
| Accounts: | Bank of America #8888777766 | |
| | First Federal #9998887777 | |

## EXECUTIVE SUMMARY

I am interested in starting a trucking company that will provide quality long haul and local transportation to America's premier shipping population throughout the United States. Currently there are two leasing companies that are being considered: The Fordham Truck Line Inc., and Clayton Transportation, which both provide owner-operators/fleets owners programs that are very competitive. However, Fordham appears to be the best of the two; they are a financially strong company which first began operations in 1967. Since that time they have grown into one of the nation's premier carriers with revenues exceeding $125 million dollars in 2003. Their mileage scale is designed as a competitive package for owner-operators that are concerned with deadhead costs and productivity.

Fordham is a market-driver truckload company, with nearly forty years experience in the industry. They employ drivers to operate the equipment they own, which includes 1,300 tractors and 2,300 trailers. They are also a part of Roadster Transportation, Inc., the largest group of truckload companies in the United States. Consisting of five truckload carriers, Roadster controls more than 7,000 tractors, 10,000 trailers, and 750 field locations.

Fordham is our choice as a leasing company because they provide a more complete package that eliminates the worry over what percentage the load pays and focuses on running miles for the trucks. Their program consists of .83 cents per mile loaded and .76 cents empty. We estimate that our truck will travel 2,500-3,800 miles per week.

Fordham offers 401K and Driver Protection Plan (DPP) that covers occupational accidents, disability income, accident medical expense, non-occupational accidents and passenger accident coverage. Fordham also uses a modern computerized central dispatch system capable of effectively managing fleet through pre-planning the next load before the current load is delivered. Fordham will also advertise for a truck driver, and provide the test at no cost to the owner.

# START-UP EXPENSES

We estimate that we will require between $28,500 and $34,000 to purchase one tractor (truck). **This tractor will be a conventional vehicle that is powered by engines with 9 and 10 speed transmissions.**

The following is a breakdown of items and costs:

| ITEMS | LOW | HIGH |
|---|---|---|
| Tractor Truck 2000-01 | $28,500 | $34,000 |
| Initial Business Cost | $ 500 | $ 700 |
| Miscellaneous | $ 200 | $ 500 |

**VARIABLE COST**

| | | |
|---|---|---|
| Price of Tractor | $28,500 | $34,000 |

**FIXED COST**

| | | |
|---|---|---|
| Repairs/Maintenance per 15,000 miles | $ 200 | $ 300 |
| Payroll/Benefit and Taxes | $ 500 | $ 600 weekly |
| Insurance | $ 45 | $ 55 weekly |
| Monthly Notes Payments | $ 800 | $ 950 monthly |

**INCOME**

| | | |
|---|---|---|
| Gross | $ 2,200 | $ 2,500 weekly |

Formula:
Estimate 2500-2800
Mile per week at
83 cents per mile

**EQUITY/CAPITAL**

| | | |
|---|---|---|
| Owner's Tractor | $28,500 | $34,000 |

**OPERATIONS EXPENSES**

| | | |
|---|---|---|
| Driver Salary | $ 500 | $ 600 weekly |
| Repairs/Maintenance | $ 200 | $ 300 monthly |
| Insurances | $ 45 | $ 55 weekly |
| Miscellaneous | $ 100 | $ 150 bi-weekly |
| Net Profit after expenses estimate: | $ 750 | $ 950 weekly |

# BUSINESS PLAN #16: Used Car Warranty Business

## LAS VEGAS ELITE MOTOR CLUB

**America has always had a love affair with cars.** For the average consumer, that love is most often expressed in the purchase of a used car. Used vehicles are less expensive and the purchaser's investment doesn't depreciate as quickly. However, new cars have always enjoyed one major advantage over used cars—perceived reliability, seen as the result of the manufacturer's warranty.

**USED CAR WARRANTY BUSINESS**

Here is a preliminary proposal involving a motor club and an auction company in Las Vegas.

**Increased market for warranties on pre-owned vehicles.** The "warranty advantage of new cars" has gradually been eroded over the years, with the proliferation of "program" vehicles which still have much of their factory warranty remaining, and with the growing business in after market used car warranties. A number of companies have entered the used car warranty business in the last decade and a half, but very few of them are making full use of the latest marketing tools to expand into nontraditional areas, such as direct-to-consumer warranty sales.

**An Exciting Concept: A Pre-Owned Car Warranty Endorsed by Las Vegas Elite Motor Club!** We propose to start a different kind of used-car warranty company, one that capitalizes on the latest cutting-edge marketing technologies while benefiting from "brand-name" recognition through our proposed affiliation with the Las Vegas Elite Motor Club.

- **Elite Motor Club Affiliation:** With the skyrocketing interest in the Classic Auto Auction Company located in the heart of Las Vegas, we feel that an affiliation with the company would lend name recognition to our warranty products. In exchange for this name recognition, we propose to pay the company a set amount for every used car warranty contract sold. For their part, The Classic Auto Auction Company would give our club their official endorsement and participate as fully as possible in the marketing of our warranty products. This would be achieved through promotional materials in the print, radio, and television media, as well as through personal appearances and other joint promotions.

**Organizational Structure:** Our company would be divided into two divisions:

- **Dealer Division:** the Dealer Division would market our warranty products to all of the traditional markets, selling used car warranties to the more than 80,000 used car dealers in the United States.
- **Consumer Division:** the Consumer Division would market our used car warranty services directly to the customer; via the Internet and other cutting-edge marketing technologies, information on our products would be widely available to used car owners nationwide. The company web site would explain the benefits and advantages of our warranty products, and then offer the customer additional information on how to purchase those products. Banner ads would link our site to the Classic Auto Auction web site and other motor sports web sites, increasing the benefits realized by both the company and club.

**An easy method of obtaining the warranty:** Potential customers who wish to purchase a warranty could then make use of our products simply by taking their used vehicle to one of many inspection stations nationwide. Once the vehicle passed an initial inspection covering those areas required by our insurer, the consumer would be able to purchase a used car warranty directly from our company, without having the hassle and additional expense of going through the dealer.

**Marketing Strategies:** In addition to the Internet marketing strategies mentioned above, our warranty products would be offered through aggressive direct mail campaigns to new car customers whose factory warranties have expired. We would also offer our services through national telemarketing campaigns, point-of-purchase brochures at dealer locations and our inspection stations, etc. Contracts with established automotive service centers such as Midas, Meineke, Pep Boys, and Precision Tune would provide additional outlets for potential customers to have their vehicles certified for warranty purposes.

**Insurance Coverage:** Warranty coverage would be fully insured by an insurance carrier licensed in all fifty states. Companies we are negotiating with have vast experience in underwriting mechanical breakdown insurance and in claims handling.

**History of the Successful Entrepreneur Proposing this Concept:** The proposal is being organized and directed by Carlos Montego, the original founder, President, and CEO of Auto-Marketing Corporation. This Nevada Corporation provided marketing and servicing of used car warranties in more than 40 states between 1995 and 2001. Auto-Marketing grew from a start-up company to employ more than 120 representatives nationwide as well as a 40-person claims department. Over the course of his involvement with AMC, Mr. Montego supervised all aspects of the business including managing human and fiscal resources, marketing, claims, underwriting, and dealer liaison. In only six years, Auto-Marketing took in warranty premiums in excess of $30 million, and Mr. Montego built this start-up company into a prime acquisition target, which he then sold in 2001.

**In Summary: The Las Vegas Elite Motor Club is invited to endorse a potentially profitable and popular concept which could be of great value to the consumer and which would be implemented by knowledgeable industry professionals:** With the new technology available for marketing and purchasing, combined with the growing popularity of the Elite Motor Club and other motorsports, this venture could prove to be a tremendous profit center for them. Based on preliminary projections, we expect to generate in excess of 2,000 contracts per month between the dealer and consumer divisions.

Mr. Montego is advising a group of investors who are building a newer, stronger concept for marketing used car warranties. Clearly he and the rest of his development team have the industry experience and hands-on knowledge necessary to make this new venture an even greater success than Auto-Marketing Corporation was in the nineties. We hope that the Las Vegas Elite Motor Club will see the obvious advantages, and lend their endorsement to this exciting venture which offers much profit potential to everyone concerned.

# BUSINESS PLAN #17: Wholesale Company, Home-Based

## JCI WHOLESALE COMPANY
## TABLE OF CONTENTS

**WHOLESALE COMPANY**

This is a business plan for an organization that supplies jewelry, electronics, and various gift items.

## OWNERSHIP AND BUSINESS CONCEPT

Joseph C. Ivarsson is the President of JCI Wholesale Company. He owns 100% of this business. JCI Wholesale Company is a wholesale retail business supplying jewelry, electronics, knick knacks, and gift items. These sales (wholesale/retail) can also be done through mail orders.

## MANAGEMENT AND STRATEGIC OVERVIEW

The President of JCI Wholesale Company is directly involved in all internal and external aspects of the business. Mr. Ivarsson is responsible for inventory, advertising, budgeting and forecasting, training, and purchasing.

Mr. Ivarsson's role within JCI Wholesale is also to handle all financial matters, to train employees in quality customer service, and to make its service known to New Jersey and throughout the world. JCI Wholesale will get its exposure from the service of New York and New Jersey Ad Mail, which can reach 90,000 households. The Trenton Times' classified section, which can reach over 200,000 readers, will also be utilized.

Mr. Ivarsson's received his leadership skills from the NCO Academy, and he gained his hands-on management experience as a squad leader in the 5th Avionics Division of Fort Drum, NY. Mr. Ivarsson received the rank of Sergeant in less than three years of his service in the U.S. Army, a rank which is normally achieved in six years.

Wholesale Company is a home-based business. This will give this young business a competitive edge. By being home-based, Mr. Ivarsson does not have to pay money to rent office space at a high overhead cost. The growth potential of the market is unlimited, due to mail order aspects of this business. So, Mr. Ivarsson will spend more time and money reinvesting into the business and paying off the loan. We can conclude that a home-based business allows this business to operate "on a shoestring" and maximize the efficiency of initial working capital.

# BUSINESS DESCRIPTION

To better understand JCI Wholesale Company and its abilities, I will attempt to break this business down into three categories. These categories are Wholesaling, Direct Sales, and Mail Orders.

I. **WHOLESALING**

   A. *General Wholesaling:* Cash & Carry Wholesaling: Stocks merchandise and requires the retailer to transport and pay for merchandise which he orders. Merchandise is stocked in showroom where customers (cash & carry customers) can browse and buy on impulse.

   B. *Drop-ship Wholesaling*: Orders obtained for Sub-wholesalers and Open House (party plan) representatives. Orders are drop shipped to them or to their customers.

   C. *Catalog Jobber*: Catalog distribution at discount prices. Catalogs are distributed to consumers and retail stores. Catalogs for retailers are at wholesale prices.

   D. *Direct Mail Distribution*: Wholesaling and retail sales by mail.

   E. *Premiums and Promotional Wholesaling*: Supplies needs of business, nonprofit organizations, and professional people who purchase quantities of specialty merchandise for purposes other than retail sales (P.T.A.'s, churches, fraternal groups, such as Rotary Clubs, etc.). Premiums used by sales organizations, retail stores, and manufacturers are used to accomplish the following:
      1. Induce a prospect to buy a product.
      2. Require that a demonstration be viewed.
      3. Be present at the opening of a store.
      4. Purchase of larger than normal quantity of products.
      5. Offset competitor activity.
      6. Inspire greater effort by salesman.

   F. *Rack Merchandising*: Pre-sold products on self-service racks placed in drug stores, grocery stores, variety stores, and retail businesses.

   G. *Wagon Jobbing*: Load truck with merchandise, take orders from retail merchants, and deliver them at the same time.

   H. *Catalog Shopping Center*: Shopping centers with catalogs, orders forms, etc. These shopping centers will be placed in drug stores, grocery stores, variety stores, retail businesses, etc.

   I. *Sub-Wholesales*: Recruited wholesalers with a complete business kit. They are independent wholesalers supplied by JCI Wholesale Company.

II. **DIRECT SALES**

   A. *Fund Raiser*: Supplies the needs of PTA's, churches, schools, and other organizations that purchase quantities of specialty merchandise for the purpose of raising funds.

   B. *Party Plan (open house)*: Open House Representatives with complete kits. Open House Representatives are supplied by JCI Wholesale Company.

III. **MAIL ORDER**

   A. *Retailing and Wholesale:* Done by mail. This gives the business the opportunity to extend its service throughout New Jersey and beyond.

# BUSINESS PLAN #17: Wholesale Company, Home-Based

## MARKETING PLAN

The goal of JCI Wholesale Company is to reach 90,000 to 1.9 million customers/clients. This can and will be done by the services of New York and New Jersey Ad Mail and The Trenton Times' classified ads. These vehicles will help JCI Wholesale Company expand its boundaries by way of Direct Mail (mail orders).

This business can and will expand itself "without leaving its own back yard." Direct mail will be fastest in getting consumer and retail accounts. These orders will be drop-shipped by UPS to the consumer's and retailer's address. Cost of drop ship is included with every order, so it will not come out of our pockets.

JCI Wholesale Company believes in sharing the wealth by giving entrepreneurs the opportunity of going into business themselves. This is done by the Sub-Wholesale and Party Plan (open house) program. They have access to all of our products at wholesale prices.

## STRENGTHS

- Services not limited to Mercer County
- Business is home-based (see article attached regarding growth of home-based employment)
- Don't need to warehouse merchandise
- Order drop-ship by UPS

## WEAKNESSES

- Need phone receptionists to fill orders
- Size of work area and showroom are small
- Small selection on electronic items
- Takes one week for consumer and retailer to receive orders

## MAIL ORDER PROGRAM

GOAL: $2,000 worth of orders will produce $24,000 in gross profits.

## STEPS TO ACHIEVE GOAL

1. Price-break circulars (10)=$249.50
2. 10-Day Sale Program (100)=$300.00
3. Christmas collection (1,000)=$89.95
4. Fragrances (1,000)=89.95
5. Gift World Discount Package (100)=$250.00
6. Gift World (1000)=$250.00
7. 14K Catalog (1000)=$250.00
8. New Jersey and (90,000)=$5,305
9. New York Ad Mail (90,000)=$5,305

TOTAL = $12,189.40

## MAIL ORDERS

| # of orders | Sales Yield | Gross Profit |
|---|---|---|
| 50 | 1,200 | 600 |
| 75 | 1,800 | 900 |
| 100 | 2,400 | 1,200 |
| 300 | 7,200 | 3,600 |
| 500 | 12,000 | 6,000 |
| 700 | 16,800 | 8,400 |
| 1,000 | 24,000 | 12,000 |
| 2,000 | 48,000 | 24,000 |
| 4,000 | 96,000 | 48,000 |

- 90,000 8x10 circulars plus 90,000 2 oz. magazines will reach 90,000 households. Look at map for targeted areas.

## PARTY PLAN (OPEN HOUSE)

**GOALS:** 100 Open House Representatives will yield $1500 in profits, if each have one party per month.

## 2 STEPS TO ACHIEVE GOAL

1. Open House Master Plan Kit (100)= $595
2. Home Video Shoppe Master Package (10)= $299.50

TOTAL: $894.50

## PARTY PLAN (OPEN HOUSE)

| Parties per month | Total Sales | Monthly Profits |
|---|---|---|
| 5 | 1250 | 750 |
| 10 | 2500 | 1500 |
| 15 | 3750 | 2250 |
| 20 | 5000 | 3000 |
| 25 | 6250 | 3750 |
| 50 | 12000 | 7500 |
| 100 | 25000 | 15000 |

# BUSINESS PLAN #17: Wholesale Company, Home-Based

## SUB-WHOLESALER

**GOALS:** 400 Sub-Wholesalers will yield $20,000 in profits.

### 2 STEPS TO ACHIEVE GOAL

1. Sub-Wholesaler Recruitment Pamphlets=$129.95
2. Sub-Wholesaler Kit=$595

TOTAL: $724.95

### SUB-WHOLESALING

**WHOLESALE COMPANY**

| Active Sub-Wholesaler | Monthly Sales | Monthly Profits |
|---|---|---|
| 5 | 1000 | 250 |
| 10 | 2000 | 500 |
| 15 | 3000 | 750 |
| 20 | 4000 | 1000 |
| 30 | 6000 | 1500 |
| 40 | 8000 | 2000 |
| 50 | 10000 | 2500 |
| 100 | 20000 | 5000 |
| 200 | 40000 | 10000 |
| 400 | 80000 | 20000 |

**BORROWER:** JCI Wholesale Company

**PURPOSE:** The Loan proceeds of $16,959.45 will be used to finance the start-up of JCI Wholesale Company; $12,189.40 will be used for mail orders; $724.95 will be used for Sub-Wholesale Recruitment and Kit; $894.50 will be used for Open House Kit and Video Shoppe; and $3,150.60 will be used for supplies and printing.

**AMOUNT:** $16,959.45

**TERM:** 5 years

**COLLATERAL:** 2001 Ford Mustang, 2002 Chrysler Sebring, Various Furniture

**GUARANTOR:** Mr. and Mrs. Joseph C. Ivarsson with net worth $34,453.72.

1. Price Break Circulars (10)=$249.50
2. 10-Day Sale Program (100)=$300.00
3. Christmas collection (1,000)=$89.95
4. Fragrances (1,000)=$89.95
5. Fund-Raising Manual (100)=$30.00
6. Sub-Wholesaling Recruitment (1000)=$129.95
7. Sub-Wholesaling Kit (100)=$545.00
8. Open House Master Plan Kit (100)=$595
9. Home Video Shoppe Master Pack (10)=$299.50
10. Gift World Discount Package (100)=$250.00
11. Gift World (1000)=$250.00
12. Catalog Shopping Center (10)=$675.00
13. White Fast Action Forms (100)=$350.00
14. Blue Order Envelopes (100)=$350.00
15. 1994 Catalog Packet (1)+$7.95
16. 14K Catalog (1000)=$250.00
17. Artistic Greeting Inc.= $73.65
18. New Jersey and (90,000)=$5,305
19. New York Ad Mail (90,000)=$5,305

TOTAL = $16,959.45

Whether you have a small business or are part of a huge corporation, you always need marketing letters to communicate what you do to the outside world and to your customers in particular. In this section you will find examples of marketing letters used to promote an artist, to sell the services of a small business, and to try to interest the consumer in the service or product you are providing.

Marketing is a multifaceted function and is more a "mind set" within an organization than a specific action taken "every now and then." Many of the letters in this section were written for companies that "think marketing" all the time. There is no end to the types of letters that can be created to make the public aware of what you do as a business.

We hasten to say that this tiny section in the book can only "hit the highlights" of what we need to show you about business marketing, but you will find inside this section the following:

- A press release for an art gallery
- A press release for a new book
- A personal marketing letter
- A letter of introduction to be used in a mass mailing
- A letter of introduction used by a specialty steel company
- A letter expressing "thank you" to existing customers
- A letter saying "welcome" to new customers
- A business estimate used by a cleaning company in marketing its services
- A letter and resume used to market a mobile home repair business
- A letter marketing outplacement services

You will notice that all of these letters aim to "get to the point" rather quickly. The average person is bombarded by direct mail, and a marketing piece must usually be concise and attention-getting in order to have maximum "marketing power."

Use the ideas in this section to create your own letters, brochures, and other tools to market your business and develop awareness of your products and services.

# Art Gallery Press Release

**For release:** immediately
**Date:**
**For further information:** contact Kaley James, 910-483-6611

## CARDIAN ZIGBUAWE OPENS NEW GALLERY

The Princess Hotel in Atlanta, GA, is pleased to announce the opening of a new gallery by Cardian Zigbuawe on December 15, 1999. Mr. Zigbuawe is a world-class authority on Asian sculpture and is recognized as a authority throughout the art world on period pieces from 1975-present.

Cardian Zigbuawe found his calling in 1968 when he opened his first gallery at the prestigious Beverly Hills Hotel in Beverly Hills, CA, with a focus on Asian sculpture. In 1969 he began his extensive collection of Chinese and Japanese art, acquiring a special expertise in jade works of art. It was at this time that Cardian started to display a special talent for discovery of important overlooked art.

Because of Cardian's knowledge and love for art, his gallery outgrew its original location enabling him to relocate to a larger space in the Beverly Hills. By this time his name was becoming so well known that insurance companies started to seek Cardian's opinion regarding evaluation of various jade works of art. Numerous complex insurance claims were subsequently settled as a result of his uncommon knowledge not only of jade and oriental art, but also of paintings and sculptures as well.

In 1975, Cardian and his two partners opened a gallery at a new location in the San Francisco Fairmont Hotel. As a result of a major purchase shortly thereafter from the Arcadia Museum in San Diego, CA, the business grew tremendously in the ensuing years. Throughout this period Cardian continued to broaden his art knowledge through extensive study of world history and its major religions. It is his love for research and his drive to find the hidden truth that makes him unique among peers. A classic example is a missing masterpiece by Turner, formerly owned by the king of Poland, which was overlooked by the famous auction house, Christies. Cardian bought out his partners in 1993.

Over the last 20 years his expertise has been sought by The Smithsonian Institute and Museum of Natural History, Washington; The Los Angeles County Museum; The Asian Art Museum, San Francisco; Oakland (CA) Museum; Internal Revenue Service; United States Postal Service; and the Federal Bureau of Investigation (re: stolen art).

# Home and Commercial Cleaning Service

**AMY'S HOME AND COMMERCIAL CLEANING SERVICE**

**(910) 483-6611**

**"No job too large or too small"**

1110 Hay Street, Atlanta, GA 28305 • 910-483-6611 • preppub@aol.com

Date

To Whom It May Concern:

This letter is a formal estimate of work to be performed for Mr. and Mrs. Joe Beasley at their private residence in Atlanta, GA. The home has recently suffered smoke damage due to a fire in the back bedroom, and this estimate is being made available to both the insurance company and the Beasleys.

For the price of $50 an hour, Amy's Home and Commercial Cleaning Service will furnish all cleaning products needed to clean damage caused by grease and smoke and to complete all tasks including these:

- Clean all walls, woodwork, cabinets, doors, mantels, light fixtures, chandeliers, lamps, ceilings, fans, etc.

- Clean draperies, blinds, and windows in all rooms as well as all upholstered furniture, couches, antique chairs, needlepoint chairs, odd/miscellaneous chairs, the seats of 12 dining room chairs, bedspreads, mattresses, pillows, and accessories.

- Other items to be cleaned include a china closet filled with crystal and china as well as an Oriental curio cabinet filled with precious keepsakes, three completely furnished bedrooms, a TV, a stereo set, and VCR equipment.

- The home to be cleaned is elegantly decorated with pictures, mirrors, wall hangings, pedestals, Oriental statues, and vases as well as numerous crystal, porcelain, and wooden Oriental boxes and cabinets. The home will be dusted/cleaned.

- Other items covered in this agreement include trees and plants, silk floral arrangements, and Oriental coffee and end tables.

- The house is carpeted throughout and additionally contains Oriental rugs in the living room as well as other assorted rugs.

- Due to the large quantity of valuable and irreplaceable items contained in the house, it is impossible to list each piece separately. Considerable care will be taken to clean these valuable collectibles and keepsakes.

- We estimate it will take three people between 50-100 hours to complete this job.

Total for services rendered: 75 hours at $50 an hour — $3,750

# Personnel Placement Service

## PEOPLEFIND, INC.

1110 Hay Street, Houston, TX 28305
Telephone: (910) 483-6611
Fax: (910) 483-2439
http://www.prep-pub.com
e-mail: PREPPub@aol.com

To: Barry Wizardon
From: Dale Durgens

**BUSINESS PROPOSAL**

By a resume writing and outplacement service. This letter could be used as a template or model each time the company needs to prepare a business proposal tailored to specific customer needs.

Confidential

Schedule of Fees for Outplacement Assistance
provided to Mainline Manufacturing

PEOPLEFIND, INC., is prepared to provide the finest quality resume-writing services and job-hunting planning assistance to Mainline Manufacturing employees. Services which could be provided include the following:

**Group planning session**: During this session which PEOPLEFIND would conduct at the Mainline Manufacturing site, PEOPLEFIND will provide expert guidance on job-hunting, introduce the Personal Review Form which is an essential tool used by PEOPLEFIND in the resume-writing process, and provide for an extensive question-and-answer session by the approximately 20 participants to be laid off by Mainline.

Cost: $1,500.00 (includes preparation time by PEOPLEFIND and materials for all participants).

**Resume and Cover Letter Preparation**:

Cost: $235.00 for each person for a professional resume with 15 copies and a model cover letter

or $243.00 for a professional resume with 15 copies, model cover letter, and both on a disk
or $250.00 for a resume (15 copies), cover letter, 15 sheets of stationery & 15 envelopes
or $258.00 for resume (15), cover letter, 15 sheets, 15 envelopes, and R/CL on a disk

**Optional Group Follow-up Session with all participants on job-hunting tips and techniques and important strategies to use in getting in the door:** Such a session could be provided which would allow for all participants to get together in a strategy formulation session with PEOPLEFIND to discuss the techniques in using their professional resume and cover letter to maximum effect.

Cost: $1,500.00 ( includes preparation time by PEOPLEFIND and all materials to be distributed).

PEOPLEFIND'S services are prepaid. Satisfaction is always guaranteed.

# Racing Sponsorship Business

DEVLIN DONALDSON

### Business: CarPlus, Inc., President and Owner
FORD Service Center
Work: (910) 483-6111

- We at CarPlus Inc. are currently purchasing $60,000 worth of FORD parts from the store #910 in Greenville, SC.
- We anticipate a large sales increase in 1998.
- We travel approximately 35,000 miles along the east coast and Midwest.
- We would be very proud to display the FORD logo on the side of race car and 26' enclosed trailer.

### Accomplishments
- Started racing in 1975 as Stock Elimination 360 Plymouth Duster I/SA.
- Held N.H.R.A. national record for two years.
- Division I Champ and two I.H.R.A. national events wins.
- 16 N.H.R.A. class wins between stock and super stock; then proceeded to SS elimination in a 74 Plymouth Duster 360 SS/KSA.
- Won one I.H.R.A. national event.
- Won N.H.R.A. Gold Cup national in Lester, NY; also held national record.
- Then proceeded to the rear engine Super Comp Dragster and rear engine B-econo Dragster with Bill Jenkins of Detroit; we won several bracket races in Division 2.

### Most Recent Accomplishments
- We have recently built a new 1996 FORD Daytona IROC car which is in the class as SS/GTCA.
- We came 7th in the I.H.R.A. World Championship Points.
- In 1997 - our very first year with this car - we got into the finals of two division events and also one national event at M.I.R. as well as three semifinal finishes. We also won class 3 out of three races.
- We are planning to run the entire I.H.R.A. schedule for the 1998 season and also six N.H.R.A. races.
- We also receive a lot of publicity for having the only FORD GT/CA car on the I.H.R.A. circuit.
- We are now planning on building a new modified engine using W-7 heads and the new FORD block for the upcoming seasons.

### What we are requesting from FORD
- We would appreciate any financial help which can be provided to a vehicle and a racing expert who will bring much publicity to the FORD Corporation.
- We would be proud to repaint our car with the FORD logo if this is desired by FORD.
- Our racing schedule begins in February 2000. We are excited about putting our Daytona in the low 9 seconds to high 8.90 elapsed time in this up-and-coming season!

**BUSINESS SPONSORSHIP RESUME**

This resume is used for soliciting funds. Some activities, like racing, require sponsors. This resume is an attempt to solicit sponsorship money.

# Consulting Business

Exact Name of Person
Exact Title
Exact Name of Company
Address
City, State, Zip

**CONSULTING BUSINESS**

This is an entrepreneur with marketing and telecommunications experience.

Dear Exact Name of Person (or Dear Sir or Madam if answering a blind ad):

With the enclosed resume, I would like to make you aware of my interest in exploring consulting opportunities with your organization.

As you will see from my resume, I offer a proven ability to sell services and products while establishing strong channels of distribution throughout U.S., Canada, and South America. Although I would gladly work in a challenging sales role in the U.S., I believe my next employer would benefit most from my extensive contacts. For the past 13 years, I have worked with companies in the telecommunications, construction, manufacturing, and other industries in order to set up distribution for their products. I am accustomed to operating in an essentially entrepreneurial role, and I would cheerfully travel extensively. I am knowledgeable of the culture, customs, sports, and politics in dozens of international countries. In my current consulting assignment, I help to establish location-based service (LBS) products similar to the Global Positioning System (GPS). In previous consulting assignments, I have introduced voice processing systems, set up distribution for radio products, and sold a wireless e-mail platform and related software.

As a result of my extensive sales and marketing experience, I have come to believe that the main keys to success in sales are fourfold: (1) knowing your product, (2) knowing your market, (3) knowing your marketing program, and (4) offering good pricing. I also believe that a key to sales success is developing well-structured channels of distribution, and I believe that I am "an expert without an equal" in that area.

If you can use a dynamic and self-confident marketing executive to enhance your business, I would welcome an opportunity to discuss your needs with you. I am a loyal and trustworthy individual who subscribes to the highest principles of business ethics, and I can assure you in advance that I would hold in confidence any business opportunity which you wanted to discuss with me.

Yours sincerely,

Jeffrey D. Lockridge

## JEFFERY D. LOCKRIDGE
1110½ Hay Street, Fayetteville, NC 28305　•　preppub@aol.com　•　(910) 483-6611

---

**OBJECTIVE**

To benefit an organization that can use an experienced sales executive who offers a proven ability to establish and strengthen various channels of distribution while successfully introducing new products/services, developing new accounts, and increasing market share.

**EDUCATION**

**Bachelor of Science in Mechanical Engineering (B.S.M.E.) degree,** Florida Institute of Technology, Melbourne, FL.

Completed courses in International Business studies, Florida International University, Miami, FL.

Numerous executive development courses related to sales, export operations, and management.

**EXPERIENCE**

**PRESIDENT & SALES MANAGER.** Jeffrey D. Lockridge & Associates, Inc., Chicago, IL (1999-present). Have developed an up-to-date database of thousands of national and international contacts while acting in an essentially entrepreneurial role selling products, services, systems, and concepts.

**Highlights of customers served in telecommunications, construction, manufacturing and other industries:**

- *Kramer Industrial Kreations,* New York, NY: Provided expert advice on pricing related to selling industrial tools.
- *DataComm,* Alaska: Set up distribution in Anchorage, Alaska for OEM radio products.
- *Wire.net,* New York, NY: Sold wireless e-mail platform and related software.
- *Advanced Satellite Systems,* Los Angeles, CA: Work with companies including, Motorola, Nortel and Ericson while selling a location-based service (LBS) product which provides services similar to the Global Position System (GPS) without a satellite.
- *Inter-Market,* Detroit, MI: Performed a market study of a startup of fixed wireless companies both national and international.
- *BWI Consulting,* West Indies, NA: Established a British West Indies construction consulting company.
- *Napa Connection,* Napa, CA: Played a key role in a $2 million cable tv installation project.
- *Hargray Wireless,* Atlanta, GA: Sold fiber optic cables to Canadian telephone companies.
- *TECH Instruments,* Chicago, IL: Sold a computerized system for monitoring fiber optic cable networks.
- *NetLink Communications,* Atlanta, GA: Sold voice processing systems used by telephone companies, and successfully introduced valuable products.
- *International Electronic Supply,* Chicago, IL: Introduced more than 700 "outside plant" products to telephone and construction companies in Central America, Grand Caymans, and the Bahama Islands.

**DIRECTOR.** Dorsey Electronics, Chicago, IL (1994-99). Was recruited to introduce the company's product line on an international level; grew sales from zero to $5 million.

**REGIONAL SALES MANAGER.** United Technologies, Los Angeles, CA (1988-94). Established a distributor network with ten major markets while introducing the product lines of forty suppliers of outside plant and testing equipment.

**PERSONAL**

Outstanding references. Believe that the keys to success in sales are these: knowing your product, knowing your market, knowing your marketing program, and offering good pricing. Believe that a key to sales is developing well-structured channels. Fluent in Spanish.

# Contract for a recording studio/promotions company

## CONTRACT AGREEMENT

**CONTRACT AGREEMENT**

For a recording studio and
a promotions company
in New York City.

Agreement made and entered into as of this 12th day of June, 2003 by and between HI-FI MARKETING of 1369 32nd Avenue, Brooklyn, New York 11281 and whose Post Office Box is 11321, Brooklyn, New York 11351 ("COMPANY") and VARIETY RECORDS ("LABEL") whose address is 1165 82nd Street, Brooklyn, New York 11341.

WHEREAS Brady Thrusher and Kelly Waterson individually and jointly are known as the executive officers of Variety Records have entered into an agreement with COMPANY.

WHEREAS COMPANY is in the business of promotions, marketing, and public relations for the recording and entertainment industry, LABEL desires to hire COMPANY for such service.

NOW, THEREFORE, in consideration of premises it is hereby agreed as follows:
1.  (a)   LABEL hereby engages COMPANY to handle radio promotions for LABEL in the Northern/Northeastern District to include New York, New Jersey, Maryland, and Pennsylvania.
    (b)   COMPANY agrees to use reasonable effort to exploit the likeness of the LABEL and its artist through such mediums as radio, television, newspapers, and magazines.
    (c)   COMPANY agrees to devise and implement marketing strategies in the defined district.
2.  (a)   LABEL agrees to retain COMPANY at monthly fee of $1,200 per month. 50% to be absorbed by Kelly Waterson and 50% to be absorbed by Brad Thrusher.
    (b)   Kelly Waterson's 50% shall be paid in cash and Brad Thrusher's 50% shall be paid by in-kind contribution from Downtown Studios of which Thrusher is owner and/or monetarily whenever negotiated by COMPANY and Thrusher.
    (c)   The initial starting fees, to be paid at the signing of the contract are the administrative fee (HI-FI's fee) of one month $1,200 and the expenses as billed on invoice.
3.  (a)   Expenses shall include but not be limited to telephone, mail, shipping, travel, and entertainment as it relates to LABEL Business.
    (b)   COMPANY agrees to discuss all expenses with LABEL prior to proceeding with said expense and upon approval LABEL agrees to provide the monetary compensation.
    (c)   Travel expenses shall include but not be limited to gas, hotel, food, car rental, air travel, and ground transportation.
4.  The term of this contract shall commence the 30th day of June, 2003 and end the 30th day of June, 2006.
5.  This contractual agreement cannot be changed orally and shall be construed, governed, and interpreted pursuant to the laws of New York.

IN WITNESS THEREOF, the parties here to have executed this Contractual Agreement the 13th day of June, 2003.

_____ sig          _____ sig
_____ title          _____ title

# Health Care Plan Marketing Overview

**Hillgram Home Health Care**
**Marketing Plan**

The mission of Hillgram Home Health Care is to promote the products and services provided by the healthcare providers in the Hillgram Home Health Care Network. These provider types include the following:

| | |
|---|---|
| Respiratory Care | Medical Supplies |
| Home Medical Equipment | Physical Therapy |
| Home Health Care | Hospice |
| Residential Care | Personal Care |
| Home Infusion | Wound Care |

Hillgram Home Health Care's business plan is to encourage patient care referral sources to use the Hillgram Home Health Care network of providers for the home care needs of their patients. Hillgram Home Health Care will receive referrals using several means of communication.

- Develop & maintain the relationships with referrers
- Maximize potential by meeting with referrers to educate them about products & services
- Distribute prescription pads
- Periodic phone calls to all referrers to increase satisfaction
- Prioritize leads for additional sites
  - Physicians
  - Hospitals
  - Discharge Planners/Social Workers
  - Emergency Rooms
  - Physical Therapy Departments
  - Facilities
  - Schools
  - Teams
  - Clinics Gyms/Private Clubs
  - Ambulance Companies
- Institute Ongoing Communication Pieces
  - Blast Fax
  - Information Pieces
  - Press Releases
  - Newsletter: describe manufacturer relations, product updates, back orders
- Marketing Collateral
- Advertising
- Manufacturer Relations
- Web Site development: Promote ease of use of program:
- Links to manufacturers
- Provide all necessary forms to distribution network
  - Certificate of Medical Necessity
  - Prescription On Line
  - Pre-authorizations
  - Billing Forms

# Group Home Plan

Exact Name of Person
Exact Title
Exact Name of Company
Address
City, State, Zip

Dear Exact Name of Person (or Dear Sir or Madam if answering a blind ad):

**EXECUTIVE DIRECTOR OF OPERATIONS**

This resume and cover letter are both designed to be sent to important decision makers in an attempt to obtain contracts.

    With the enclosed fact sheet describing Columbia Care Center, I would like to make you aware of my interest in obtaining a contract with your county for a target population of males 10-18 who are seriously emotionally or neurologically disturbed, mentally handicapped, or substance abused. Columbia Care Center is a residential treatment facility licensed by the State of South Carolina (License MHL—060-805).

    When I graduated from University of South Carolina, it was my intention to pursue a career in the corporate world. After working in corporate sales and mortgage banking, I became employed as a supervisor of mildly disabled clients and then subsequently worked as a High Risk Intervention Technician working one-on-one with male youth ages 10-15/16. My experience in working with High Risk client inspired my desire to establish a facility which provides residential treatment programs for High Risk youth. As the founder of Columbia Care Center, I have assembled a quality, well-trained staff which is ready to provide round-the-clock care to four High Risk clients in a facility which offers a 2-4 ratio of client to staff. As the enclosed fact sheet describes, the Columbia Care Center utilizes the widely accepted Behavior Modification Process tied to a point system and will provide a mentoring program as well as an exciting program of planned summer activities. The newly constructed facility is located in a quiet neighborhood which has quality elementary, middle, and high schools nearby. A nurse and therapist will be on call 24 hours a day.

    Already licensed by the State of South Carolina, we are now seeking contracts with counties such as yours so that we can become a provider.

    I hope you will review the enclosed fact sheet and then call me to suggest the next step I should take in seeking a contract to become a provider with your county. If you wish, I would be happy to make a PowerPoint slide presentation to your staff about the Columbia Care Center. I hope you will welcome my call next week when I attempt to get your guidance about the next step I should take in becoming a provider. Thank you in advance for your time and professional courtesies.

Yours sincerely,

Damian R. Baldwin

**COLUMBIA CARE CENTER**
**Damian R. Baldwin, Owner**
2021 Atlas Drive, Columbia, SC 22781-1075
Phone/Fax: 999-999-9999

---

**OBJECTIVE**

The Columbia Care Center seeks to become a provider of residential treatment programs for High-Risk male children and adolescents aged 10-18 who have been diagnosed by a licensed physician or psychologist as seriously emotionally or neurologically disturbed, mentally handicapped, or substance abused.

**WHAT'S DIFFERENT ABOUT COLUMBIA CARE CENTER?**

- Equipped with an on-call nurse 24 hours a day and equipped with a therapist on-call 24 hours a day.
- Utilizes the widely accepted Behavior Modification Process tied to a point system.
- Continuous updating of client files by therapists.
- A 2-4 ratio of client to staff.
- A Mentoring Program which matches kids with caring mentors.
- An exciting program of planned summer activities to help kids develop new skills, interests, and competencies. Summer activities: horseback riding and museum visits.
- A structured environment in which tutors and counselors are provided as needed.

**THINGS YOU CAN COUNT ON:**

- A newly constructed facility with three bedrooms and two bathrooms within 1100 square feet. Built in 2003, Columbia Care Center at Atlas Street has a big back yard! The home has passed sanitation and fire inspections, state structural inspections, and meets all state requirements.
- A quiet neighborhood in a nice community.
- Quality schools nearby: David Manning Elementary School and Hillcrest Elementary School; S. M. Fairley Middle School; and R. M. Stall High School.
- A facility licensed by the State of South Carolina, Department of Health and Human Services, Division of Facility Services: Facility ID is 020058 and License Number is MHL-060-805. (License valid until July 31, 2005).

**A STAFF YOU CAN COUNT ON:**

- **Executive Director of Operations Damian R. Baldwin** is the founder of Columbia Care Center. Earned a B.S. degree, University South Carolina, 1999. Worked in corporate sales and mortgage banking prior to becoming involved in social services. Worked as a Supervisor for Tri-County Industries where he supervised up to 25 mildly disabled clients, the major of which were mentally impaired individuals aged 18-43. Subsequently worked as a High Risk Intervention Technician for Harden County Rehabilitation in Florence, SC, where he worked one-on-one with male youth ages 10-15/16 who suffered from ADD, ADHS, schizophrenia, substance abuse, and other problems.
- Columbia Care Center's **Residential Manager is Monica Lucey,** who is an experienced teacher who is certified in SC to teach in middle school.

**Training of Damian R. Baldwin, Director of Operations,** and **Monica Lucey, Residential Manager,** includes the Medication Administration Course, the Protective Intervention Course (PIC), Confidentiality and Clients Rights Training, Incident Reporting.

- Carla James, Third Shift staff member, is trained in all required areas.
- Fourth staff member Damian R. Baldwin, retired businessman, trained in all areas.

**OUR GOAL & PHILOSOPHY:**

We want to make a difference in the lives of youth and offer them the best care possible.

# Independent Subcontractor Agreement

## LETTER OF UNDERSTANDING & AGREEMENT
## WITH INDEPENDENT SUBCONTRACTOR

This Agreement made this _____ day of _____ in the year 2000 by and between Therapy Plus Speech doing business at this address: 3567 Avery Street, Suite 150, Morganton, SC (hereinafter referred to as the "contractor") and _____, an Independent Subcontractor of Therapy Plus Speech whose address is _____ (hereinafter referred to as Subcontractor).

**INDEPENDENT SUBCONTRACTOR AGREEMENT**

This is a business providing services utilizing subcontractors, and an agreement may need to be drawn up to clarify responsibilities and obligations of the respective parties.

## AGREEMENT

### 1. TERM

The term of this Agreement shall be nine (9) months from the date of its execution. Either party hereto may at any time during the term hereof terminate this Agreement upon thirty (30) days written notice to the other party of such termination. At the end of said thirty (30) day notice period, this Agreement shall forthwith terminate for all purposes, as if said date were the date set forth herein as the termination date of this Agreement, provided that any obligations arising prior to the termination of this Agreement shall be governed by the terms hereinafter set forth until satisfied.

### 2. SERVICES

The parties agree that the Subcontractor is to provide speech pathology services under the terms and conditions of this Agreement and in accordance with The South Carolina Guidelines for Speech and Language Programs and with any applicable requirements of federal, state or local laws, rules and/or regulations.

### 3. COMPENSATION

The Subcontractor will be compensated by Therapy Plus Speech for speech and language services rendered from the first to last day of each month (hereinafter referred to as the "billing period") according to invoices submitted to Therapy Plus Speech no later than three (3) working days following the end of the billing period in which said services were rendered. Therapy Plus Speech agrees to pay for the foregoing services at the consultation rate of $35.00 per hour for five (5) days per week ____ not to exceed 6 hours ____ per day. Therapy Plus Speech Services shall pay the Subcontractor upon the conditions hereinafter set forth, for all services rendered by the Subcontractor within fifteen (15) days following the date in which the Subcontractor's invoices have been received by Therapy Plus Speech Services for the applicable billing period.

Any amendments or changes to the schedule of fees herein above stated shall be effective thirty (30) days following the date upon which the parties agree to such amendment or change in writing. Upon the parties' mutual acceptance in writing, the amended schedule of fees shall become part of this agreement.

### 4. INDEPENDENT SUBCONTRACTOR

It is the parties' intention that so far as shall be in conformity with the law the Subcontractor shall be an independent Subcontractor. In conformity therewith Subcontractor shall retain sole and absolute discretion and judgment in the manner and means of providing speech services to the Meridian County Schools. This agreement shall not be construed as a partnership and Therapy Plus Speech Services shall not be liable for any obligation incurred by the Subcontractor. However, Subcontractor shall comply with all policies, rules and regulations of Therapy Plus Speech Services in

# Independent Subcontractor Agreement

connection with provision of Speech Pathology services. All services rendered by the Subcontractor shall be rendered in a competent, efficient and satisfactory manner and in strict accordance with currently approved methods and practices of Subcontractor's profession.

## 5. SUBCONTRACTOR QUALIFICATIONS

All services to students in Meridian County Schools shall be performed by the speech pathologists who are holders of current licenses of the state in which they are practicing and of the Certificate of Clinical Competence (CCC) in their area of specialization, as issued by the American Speech-Language-Hearing Association. The only exception to the above shall be employees of the Provider who are in the process of completing their Clinical Fellowship Year as specified by the American Speech-Language-Hearing Association and who are supervised by a certified and licensed speech pathologist.

## 6. INSURANCE

Therapy Plus represents that it has in effect appropriate liability coverage, including coverage for any acts of professional malpractice.

## 7. RESTRICTIVE COVENANTS

The employee agrees for a period of one (1) year following the termination of this Agreement, whether such Agreement is terminated by the Employee or Employer, that the Employee will not, directly or indirectly, engage in either as an Employee or Employer, or in any manner whatsoever, the private practice of speech and language pathology which in any manner whatsoever would be competitive with the Employer within a 25-mile radius of the Morganton office of Therapy Plus Speech.

## 8. MISCELLANEOUS

Each party to this Agreement acknowledges that no representations, inducements, promises or agreements, orally or otherwise, have been made by any party, or anyone acting on behalf of any party, which are not embodied herein, and that no other Agreement, statement or promise not contained in this Agreement shall be valid or binding.

Any modification of this Agreement will be effective only if it is in writing and signed by all parties to this Agreement.

In WITNESS WHEREOF, we the undersigned, duly authorized representatives of the parties to this Agreement herein above expressed, have entered into this Agreement without reservation and have read the terms herein.

By_____

Director, Therapy Plus                    Date_____

By_____

Independent Subcontractor                 Date_____

# Customer "Thank you" Letter

**BOOK DESIGNERS, INC.**
1110 Hay Street
Post Office Box 66
San Diego, CA 28302
910-483-6611
Pager: 910-483-6611
Fax: 910-483-2439

Date

**LETTER EXPRESSING "THANK YOU" TO EXISTING CUSTOMERS**

A letter is also a nice way to tell customers that you appreciate their business and value them. This letter is sent to each customer from a book design and binding firm. In a competitive marketplace, customer retention is often a high priority, and this type of letter helps to keep customers coming back.

Dear Exact Name:

In all the hustle-bustle of life, isn't it easy to forget to appreciate the people we value the most? That is why I'm writing you this letter. I want you to know how deeply appreciative I am to you for the business relationship we have enjoyed, and I want you to know that we are committed to helping you achieve your future business goals in whatever way we can. It is our company goal to be known as the most reputable and most quality-conscious bookbinding producer in the business today.

**We've come a long way since 1989...**

I think you already know that Book Designers, Inc. was founded in 1989 by Cayton Williams and has grown into a business that operates at the highest level of technical sophistication. Our highly professional staff now consists of the following key individuals, all of whom have Your Total Satisfaction as our foremost goal:

- Grace Williams, President
- Winston Turner, Sales Representative
- Caison Matthews, Office Manager

**Our goal—Your Total Satisfaction at all times...**

Providing the best service possible at all times while guaranteeing a quality product is our number one goal. We are committed to a Total Quality Management approach to product performance and customer service.

**We're here when you need us...**

If you have a potential project coming up and want some expert consulting and advice at an early stage, please call us and we'll make ourselves immediately available to provide advice or a bid. I personally guarantee your total satisfaction with our price, product, quality control, customer service, and follow-through. But, in the meantime, let me again just say "thank you" for the privilege of serving your business needs.

Yours sincerely,

Grace Williams
President

## ALL-PURPOSE CLEANING AND REPAIR

Owners: Jan and Robert Abernethy

P.O. Box 87, St. Pauls, MN 90234

(910) 483-6611

Date

Mr. Michael Foster
Vice President
Nexus Construction Company
P.O. Drawer 9034
St. Pauls, MN 90234

Dear Mr. Foster:

I enjoyed talking with you in your office on March 18, and I am responding to your request for a formal expression of our desire to provide extensive cleaning services to Nexus Construction. Here is what I propose:

**Services to be performed:**

For a price of .09 (nine cents) a square foot, the following cleaning services could be provided:

Cleaning of interior and exterior windows

Cleaning of store fronts

Cleaning of interior glass and frames

Vacuuming of carpet

Dustmop wood floors

Mop vinyl floors

Clean and mop bathrooms

Dust and clean casework

Clean food prep areas

For complex architectural building designs, we would reserve the right to provide a separate quote on a project basis.

As you know, we pride ourselves on our reliability and dependability, and you are aware of the quality services we have performed for you for various jobs on a project basis. It is our desire to handle as much of your cleaning business as possible, and I believe we can of valuable assistance to you in this area. We do take pride in our work, and you can certainly depend on our reliability at all times.

From our discussions I understand that you will be discussing this concept with your colleagues, and I will look forward to hearing from you.

Yours sincerely,

Robert Abernethy

**LETTER FOLLOWING UP ON AN INITIAL VERBAL PROPOSAL**
A business marketing letter often finalizes deals which have been discussed verbally or in concept. By putting in writing the details of a prior discussion, the company is committing to specific prices and terms and can "close the sale."

# Customer Letter: Welcome to New Customers

**COMMERCIAL INDUSTRIES, INC.**

1110 Hay Street, Columbia, SC 28302

Telephone: (910) 483-6611                    Fax: (910 483-2439

Date

Exact Name of Customer
Exact Title of Customer
Exact Name of Company
Address
City, state zip

Dear Exact Name of Customer:

It is my great pleasure to welcome you "on board" as a valued customer of Commercial Industries! You will see that we will be committed to your needs for rapid distribution of your products and to your business success, and we will attempt to serve your needs with an emphasis on Total Quality Management in every aspect. A permanent and long-lasting relationship with you is our goal, and we intend to achieve that goal by providing the finest service available for your needs.

**Good communication is the key...**

Commercial Industries was founded by Dillon Extasis in 1984, and there's one thing we have learned during those years when we've grown from a three (3)-warehouse operation into a twelve (12)-warehouse company. We have learned that **good communication is the key to satisfying you and making sure that you are completely happy with the quality product we intend to deliver.**

Please help us to serve you best by communicating freely with me about anything you may not be sure of as your business develops. I not only want our distribution services to be of outstanding quality, but I also want your experience to be an enjoyable one. We are committed to the highest quality standards in our customer service.

Let me close this brief letter by telling you again, **"Welcome!"** We appreciate your business, we will do our best to serve you, and we look forward to putting all of our resources and knowhow at your disposal. Thank you for your confidence in Commercial Industries.

Yours sincerely,


Davida Smith
Manager,
Customer Relations

# Letter Introducing a Service

**Lightning Courier Service**

325 Bladen Drive, Chicago, IL  28305

Office: (910) 483-6611                    e-mail: preppub@aol.com

"For a quick trip, call Lightning"

Date

Dear Sir or Madam:

**LETTER INTRODUCING A COURIER SERVICE**
How does a new business get started? Often the marketing help can come in the form of a letter such as this one, which the new business can mail or distribute by hand to businesses which it has targeted as potential customers.

Do you have important documents and time-sensitive materials which require immediate delivery by a fast, reliable courier service with extensive experience and an outstanding reputation?

Locally owned and operated, Lightning Courier Service is positioning itself to serve the needs of Chicago's business, financial, and legal communities by providing fast, reliable, same-day delivery of your materials to any location within 200 miles.

**Convenient hours, emergency availability**

As a service business, our primary concern is to make ourselves available to meet the needs of our customers. We are available for "emergency" deliveries on Saturday, in addition to our regular hours of 8:00 A.M. to 5:00 P.M., Monday-Friday.

**Experience in servicing commercial accounts**

From 1979-1993, I ran Zip Courier Service in Vallejos, CA, servicing major accounts which included North American Title, Home Federal Savings & Loan, Bank of America, and Fidelity Savings & Loan, as well as AmeriMac Advent Mortgage and NMS Mortgage Service, Inc. These and other satisfied customers came to rely on our prompt, courteous, and dependable service. **In over fourteen years of business, we never missed a deadline or misplaced a package**. I can provide letters of recommendation from these customers, and I'm certain that any of our previous accounts would be more than happy to provide outstanding references upon request.

**Integrity and dependability**

When you choose a courier service to handle your most important, most sensitive documents, you want to ensure that you are dealing with someone you can trust. In more than twenty years of service to the Criminal Investigation Division of the U.S. Army, and in 30 years as a minister, pastor, and Christian education leader, I have proven time and time again that my integrity is beyond reproach.

It would be my pleasure to meet with you at your convenience to discuss your priority delivery needs and how Lightning Courier Service could meet them. To schedule an appointment, please call me at the numbers provided above, and I will be happy to provide a price quote on the services you require. Thank you for allowing us the opportunity to serve your needs in this area.

Yours sincerely,

William Jenkins, Owner

# Letter of Intent and Investment Agreement

Date

**LETTER OF INTENT & INVESTMENT AGREEMENT**
XYZ Check Cashing Facility, Inc.
82 Monton Street
Decatur, GA 34509

The following agreement is made on the date which appears on this letter of understanding between McKenzie Phillips (SSN: 000-00-0000) of 42 Enterprise Circle, Decatur, GA, and XYZ Check Cashing Facility, Inc. of 82 Monton Street, Decatur, GA.

It is acknowledged that on December 30, 1999, XYZ Check Cashing Facility, Inc., will accept from McKenzie Phillips a cash investment in the amount of $4,500.00. This will serve as an investment to be placed in the account towards operation of XYZ Check Cashing Facility, Inc., 82 Monton Street, Decatur, GA, beginning on February 28, 2000.

It is acknowledged and understood that this investment equates to 5% of profit and for losses in above business beginning February 28, 2000. Under no circumstances may this be inferred or interpreted as a "guarantee" on a definitive return for the above investor (McKenzie Phillips) or company (XYZ Check Cashing Facility, Inc.).

This agreement is made in good faith demonstrated by all parties. It is understood that all efforts possible will be made to turn the business and above investment into a profitable venture. All Alcohol Law Enforcement rules are to be adhered to by all parties. Any deliberate violation of these policies will be considered a breach of contract.

A monthly financial statement will be made available upon request.

The above is agreed upon by the following parties and officers:

_____          _____
McKenzie Phillips                         Clyde Taunton, President
Investor                                  XYZ Check Cashing Facility, Inc.


_____
Marybelle Taunton
Vice President, XYZ Check Cashing Facility, Inc.

# Services Agreement

## JANITORIAL SERVICES OF BUENA VISTA
## LETTER OF UNDERSTANDING & SERVICES AGREEMENT

This Agreement is effective as of _____ (date to be filled in by Janitorial Services of Buena Vista (herein referred to as "Contractor") and _____ (herein referred to as "Client").

Contractor agrees to furnish the following services (check services which are applicable):

Install Flooring _____    Refurbish Bathrooms _____

Replace Roofing _____    Refurbish Kitchen _____

Replace Shingles _____    Refurbish Plumbing_____

Room Additions _____    Build/Remove Walls _____

Other (Specify) _____

_____

**SERVICES AGREEMENT and LETTER OF UNDERSTANDING**
Agreeing on the details when an agreement is entered into can do much to deter problems later on about what was promised and what was expected.

Contractor agrees to remove all work-related material from the site at the completion of the job.

Contractor guarantees the aforementioned work for a period of_____ from the date of its completion. All work will be performed in accordance with drawings and specifications submitted by Client.

Client agrees to pay the full contract price of $_____ in the following manner:

(a) 50% down payment
(b) Remaining balance at the completion of the job

**IN WITNESS WHEREOF,** the parties have executed this Agreement to be effective on the day and year first above written:

Janitorial Services of Buena Vista:

Name _____ Signature _____ Date _____

Client:

Name _____ Signature _____ Date _____

# Letter of Introduction to Customers

**PREMIUM SPECIALTY STEEL CO.**

1110 Hay Street

Post Office Box 66

Worcester, MA 28302

910-483-6611

Pager: 910-483-6611

Fax: 910-483-2439

Date

Dear Exact Name:

With this letter, I would like to introduce you to the most reputable and most quality-conscious specialty steel fabricator in the business today. We have recently learned of your possible business interest in our region, and we want to put our considerable resources and knowhow at your disposal.

### Who we are

Premium Specialty Steel Company was founded in 1974, and it has grown from a fleet of three trucks into a 12-truck operation supported by a completely computerized batching system, state approved and fully compatible with all current regulations. Our highly professional staff consists of the following key individuals, all of whom have Your Total Satisfaction as our foremost goal:

- James Franklin, President
- Judith Franklin, Sales and On-Site Representative
- Amy Beasley, Dispatcher
- Donna Gaskins, Accounts Receivables Manager

### Our goal: Your Total Satisfaction at all Times

Very simply, providing the best service possible at all times while guaranteeing a quality product is our number one goal. There is no other company in the specialty steel fabrication business that can come close to matching our Total Quality Management approach to product performance and customer service.

### The next step

In the expectation that we will be able to "make you an offer you can't refuse," I would like to call you next week to introduce myself by telephone and verify a few details of your upcoming project in this area. I hope you will give me an opportunity to bid on the job you have coming up, because I can guarantee in advance **your total satisfaction** with our price, product, quality control, customer service, and follow-through. I hope you will welcome my call in a few days.

Yours sincerely,

Judith Franklin

Sales Representative

# Letter of Introduction to Customers

**ROPER MASONRY**

**Company Background:**
Roper Masonry (formerly Andrea Roper Construction) has been in the masonry business since 1988. This launched a fifteen-year career as a husband and wife team in the masonry construction business. The company's primary business concern is concrete & brick retaining walls, drainage structures, and incidental concrete (sidewalks, curbs, gutters, etc.). The permanent location of the business is Warren, MI.

**Principals:**
Andrea Roper, a native of Michigan, is the owner and General Manager of the company. She is certified as a DBE, MB, and WB under the Michigan Department of Transportation. She attended Detroit College of Business and received an Associate's degree in General Business. She is also a trained Brick Mason.

Phillip Roper is the Field Project Manager of the company, with over 35 years experience in the masonry business. He studied Brick Masonry at Brentwood High School in Dearborn, Michigan and Construction Technology at Henry Ford Community College. He is now on the Brick Masonry Board of Directors at Henry Ford Community College.

**Financial & Suppliers:**
The financial stability of the company is strong, and the company has a good reputation within the community. Financial or business references include:

      Banking ————— Union Planters Bank
      Accounting——— Wallace Green, CPA
      Suppliers————Peterson Rentals
                Hendrick's Block Industries
                Calhoun Concrete, Inc.
                Saginaw Construction Co.

**Clients:**
Roper Masonry is proud to mention a few of our satisfied clients as references:
1. Brandywine Concrete & Metal, Warren, MI
2. Saginaw Construction Co., Warren, MI
3. Washington Construction, Dearborn, MI
4. K&K Ramsey, Inc., Dearborn, MI
5. Northwestern Paving, Warren, MI
6. William Elmhurst, Dearborn, MI

The diversity of the masonry work varied from job to job, but primary construction was in concrete & brick retaining walls, drainage structures, curbs & gutters, and incidental concrete.

**Conclusion:**
Roper Masonry would like to state that we are experienced and qualified to perform any projects, large or small, within the masonry business. We thank you for your consideration.

**MASONRY BUSINESS**
This is a press release for a family owned business with 15 years of brick masonry experience.

# Customer mailing for an electrical business

**SIMMONS ELECTRICAL SERVICES**
**Parker Simmons, Licensed Electrician**
2352 Sanderosa Avenue, San Antonio, TX 76595
Phone: 333-333-3333

**LICENSED ELECTRICIAN**

This is a mailing for a company that provides residential, commercial, and industrial services.

**Please give me one minute of your time!!**

Chances are, you have some problems in the following areas which I could help you with:

Security systems installation, repair, and maintenance
Tree trimming
Phone and computer cabling including CATV
Bucket truck services
Sign repair
Pressure washing
Fire alarm repair and maintenance
Street light repair and maintenance
Electrical work of all types including residential, commercial, and industrial
Cleaning services of all types by experienced house cleaners and building cleaners

I became a Licensed Electrician while serving my country in the U.S. Air Force, and I have lived and worked in San Antonio as a Licensed Electrician for the past 13 years.

If you would like to call my telephone number, I would be happy to visit your location and give you a **free inspection** of your electrical or other needs. Please be assured that no job is too small or too large for me.

Yours sincerely,

Parker Simmons,
Licensed Electrician

P.S. Sometimes people have problems they are not aware of. For example, I recently helped a commercial landlord by strapping up abandoned conduits which were hanging outside the building and which posed a safety hazard. My **free inspection** could benefit you. Call now to schedule a **free inspection.**

# Customer mailing for an electrical business

## SIMMONS ELECTRICAL SERVICES
### Parker Simmons, Licensed Electrician
2352 Sanderosa Avenue, San Antonio, TX 76595

Phone: 333-333-3333

---

**QUALITY SERVICES**
Security systems installation, repair, and maintenance
Tree trimming
Phone and computer cabling including CATV
Bucket truck services
Sign repair
Pressure washing and window washing
Fire alarm repair and maintenance
Street light repair and maintenance
Electrical work of all types including residential, commercial, and industrial
Cleaning services of all types by experienced house cleaners and building cleaners

**MEET PARKER SIMMONS, Licensed electrician and manager of Simmons Electrical Services:**

- TX State Electrical Contractor's License # 12345-6, valid until 2005
- Skilled in operating forklifts with attachments; 5 and 10-ton dump trucks; bucket truck; backhoes; ditchwitch; utility locating equipment; cathodic protection equipment; proficient with exothermic welding.
- Full Worker's Compensation available on all employees
- Competitive rates

**Highlights of Parker's background:**

**Dyess Air Force Base, Texas:** Provided **utility location services;** located gas, jet fuel, steam, water, sewer, storm drains, fiber optics, and abandoned utilities for construction projects on Dyess Air Force Base property. Installed and maintained interior wiring systems, security alarms, and tempest ground systems. Troubleshot and repaired high voltage distribution airfield lighting as well as interior lighting systems in buildings.

**University of San Antonio:** Installed and maintained campus fire alarms, security call boxes, street and security lighting, high voltage distribution, emergency generators, interior lighting and wiring. Performed troubleshooting of fire alarms and street lights.

**Lehman Brothers Corporation & Hall County School System:** Managed a crew of four people on numerous construction projects. Supervised the running of CATV lines in the Hall County School Systems and installed dedicated circuits in computers. Was involved in a major overhaul of Hall County School System's electrical work. Decreased number of "bad" inspections in Hall County School System.

**Alcoa Control:** Installed safety interlock and control wiring, devices, and conduits on air handling equipment, manufacturing equipment, and hospital equipment. Expertly used control drawings and mechanical drawings. Passed the company's most rigorous drug screening and was specially selected for a high-profile project.

**Dow Chemical:** Advised Dow Chemical's customers on current National Electric Codes (NEC). Prepared material takeoffs for customers.

**San Antonio Paper Mill:** Renovated the electrical system of a downtown building.

**PG&E:** Wired 3-phase rectifiers for the telephone system of a military installation.

**WHAT CUSTOMERS SAY:**

- "Parker Simmons saved me thousands of dollars with his bucket truck services." – Robert Butler, business owner.
- "I appreciated the way Parker was willing to respond to my weekend emergency." Nicholas Farnum of Southwestern Electrics.

**ABOUT PARKER:** Parker Simmons served in the Air Force and has lived in San Antonio for 15 years.

# Customer mailing for a mobile home repair business

Date

Exact Name of Person
Title or Position
Name of Company
Address (number and street)
Address (city, state, and zip)

Dear Exact Name of Person:  (or Sir or Madam if answering a blind ad.)

With the enclosed resume, I would like to make you aware of my background as an experienced Mobile Home Repair Specialist and initiate the process of being considered for work as a contractor or subcontractor as your needs require.

As a self-employed Mobile Home Repair Specialist, I operate a company called Orion Mobile Home Repair in Warsaw, Wisconsin, and serve a variety of satisfied customers in neighboring towns. Satisfied customers include the following:
Social Services/Housing & Urban Development
Warsaw County Social Services Department
American Home Star Sales
Sterling Homes
Wilfred Thompson, Jr.

I offer more than 20 years of experience in performing electrical work, carpentry, and maintenance of all types. In addition to my experience as a Mobile Home Service Technician and Maintenance Technician, I have worked as a carpenter and once owned and managed a successful auto detail shop in Georgia. I am experienced in all types of cabinet work, and there is virtually no piece of equipment or fixture in mobile homes (as well as in apartments and houses) which I have not maintained, replaced, repaired, or installed. We have all the tools and equipment necessary to perform any phase of the setup, repair, and maintenance of mobile homes as well as for all types of general construction.

If you can use a reliable and honest subcontractor for your properties, please call me to discuss your needs. Our operation is highly mobile, and we can readily travel to your job site to meet your needs. I can provide excellent credit references as well as outstanding references from individuals and organizations who are acquainted with my work and professionalism.

I would enjoy the opportunity to discuss how I could be of service to you. Remember: *"Over 20 years of experience, and we do it all."*

Yours sincerely,

Orion Hamstead Pierce

# Customer mailing for a mobile home repair business

## ORION HAMSTEAD PIERCE
## Mobile Home Repair Specialist
### OVER 20 YEARS OF EXPERIENCE
### "We Do It All"
Box 95, Warsaw, WI 28305

pager: 910-483-2439          cellular: 910-483-6611

---

**OBJECTIVE**

To serve the needs of organizations and individuals that can use a skilled mobile home repair specialist who offers an excellent personal reputation for reliability and honesty as well as proven skills in all aspects of mobile home repair, maintenance, and setup.

**EXPERIENCE**

**MOBILE HOME REPAIR SPECIALIST (Self-Employed).** Orion Mobile Home Repair, Warsaw, WI (1998-present). Am the owner and manager of Orion Mobile Home Repair, currently repair and/or replace floors, windows, doors, walls (interior and exterior), carpet, and vinyl; perform minor electrical and plumbing work.

**Offer expertise in all aspects of mobile home repair:** Handle jobs involving Kool Seal, skirting underpin, and remodeling.

**Satisfaction Guaranteed/Excellent References:** Guarantee satisfaction with all work performed, and can provide excellent references from these and other organizations whose mobile homes and apartments I service and maintain:

    Social Services/Housing & Urban Development
    Warsaw County Social Services Department
    American Home Star Sales
    Sterling Homes

**SERVICE TECHNICIAN.** Oakwood Mobile Homes, Warsaw, WI (1997-98). Was rehired by this company for which I worked previously, worked on the company's repossessions (Factory Certified Homes); repaired or replaced anything that was broken.
- Resigned under excellent circumstances to go into business for myself.

**MAINTENANCE TECHNICIAN.** Fulsome Acres Mobile Home Park, Warsaw, WI (1993-97). Repaired and rebuilt mobile homes in several parks which contained hundreds of trailers and apartments. Performed repairs and maintenance in both the mobile homes and the apartments.

**SERVICE TECHNICIAN.** Oakwood Mobile Homes (Freedom Mobile Home Sales), Warsaw, WI (1992-93). Repaired and/or replaced fixtures and equipment which was broken in existing homes and deficient in new homes.
- Selected for a special assignment to help set up a mobile home lot in FL.

**MECHANIC.** Craven Toyota, Warsaw, WI (1992). Managed the detail shop.

**GENERAL MANAGER** and **OWNER.** Scrub-A-Dub, Pensacola, FL (1988-91). Owned and managed a successful detail shop; closed the business and moved from FL to WI when my father became very ill.

**CARPENTER.** Quality Plus Construction, Sanford, NE (1986-88). Performed framing and did finishing work; became skilled in installing cabinets and cabinet tops. Handled inside and outside trim work.

# Customer mailing for a pressure washing business

Date

Exact Name of Person
Exact Title
Exact Name of Company
Address
City, State, Zip

Dear Exact Name of Person (or Dear Sir or Madam if answering a blind ad):

With the enclosed fact sheet, I would like to introduce myself and the services I can offer your company. If you answer "yes" to any of the following questions, you may be in need of my services:

- Would you like to give your exteriors a "facelift" and make your business "shine?"
- Would you like a free demonstration of how we can save you money through our quality services?

For an overview of who we are and what we do, please look at the enclosed "fact sheet" about our business and services. We can work anytime during the day or night in order to cause the least disruption to your business, customer flow, and cash flow!

Please call me as soon as you look over the fact sheet enclosed and I can schedule a time to give you a free estimate and demonstration of our services. Even if you are not sure if you need our services, let me come to see you for 15 minutes to show you what I can do for your business!

Best wishes,


Justin S. Caldwell
Owner
Caldwell Pressure Washing

# Customer mailing for a pressure washing business

**CALDWELL PRESSURE WASHING**

**Justin S. Caldwell, Owner**

1145 Village Square Road, Cleveland, MS 55566

Phone: 999-999-9999 · Pager: 888-888-8888 · Fax: 777-777-7777

---

**OBJECTIVE**   To offer quality services related to pressure washing and coating.

**THINGS YOU CAN COUNT ON:**

- Perfect safety record
- Fully insured through the Delta Credit Union licensed for all jobs; more than $1 million of protection.
- Full Worker's Compensation available on all employees
- Competitive rates, Satisfaction Guaranteed

**SERVICES, MATERIALS, AND COATINGS:**

In addition to pressure washing your exterior, we are expert in applying a variety of coatings to help you revitalize your old and worn concrete and spare you the expense of replacing it. Coatings come in a variety of patterns, designs, and colors. Pictorial portfolio available for review. Revitalize your concrete and select from the latest patterns which include rock patterns and brick patterns!

- Monthly and quarterly cleaning services provided!

**SOME OF OUR CUSTOMERS:**

We serve primarily business and commercial customers; our satisfied customers include:

- Cleveland County Schools
- Cleveland County Housing Office
- Denmark, Inc.
- Caliber Corp.
- Dupont
- Cleveland County Apartment Association
- environmental cleanup projects

**WHAT OUR CUSTOMERS SAY:**

- "Caldwell Pressure Washing saved me thousands of dollars and inconvenience by coating my concrete. Coated concrete is easier to clean and maintain!" – L. Hammonds business owner
- "I appreciated the way Caldwell was willing to work in the early hours of the morning to clean my concrete parking lot. This allowed me to give my business a clean look without causing my customers any inconvenience, and without interrupting my cash flow!" – A. Patterson, restaurant chain CEO
- Numerous other references available on request.

**EQUIPMENT USED:**

We believe the best result is achieved by utilizing the best equipment in addition to well-trained personnel. We use state-of-the-art equipment. including: Two LANDA self-contained units. Hot water units: one mounted on 16' trailer; one self-contained unit in full-size mobile van. 3,000 PSI; Temperature: 300 degrees maximum; special adapters for special jobs.

**ABOUT THE OWNER:**

Justin Salazar Caldwell holds a B.S. degree in Criminal Justice from Delta State University (2000). Started in the pressure washing business in March 1999, and formally formed and incorporated Caldwell Pressure Washing in September 1999. Experienced in all aspects of the business. Outstanding reputation. Known for integrity.

# Marketing strategy for outsourcing sales and marketing

## NATIONAL PROMOTIONAL PROGRAMS
## FOR INSURANCE PROFESSIONALS

### OVERVIEW

Stewart Geiser Insurance Inc., can develop and execute strategies for insurance group professionals so they can grow revenue, increase profitability and market share, maximize their return on investment, increase brand awareness and strengthen brand loyalty.

**PROMOTION PACKAGE**

Here is a document that provides a strategic analysis for an insurance company

We are the premier outsourced marketing and sales service provider. We are positioned to provide our clients with the solutions needed to grow a healthy, thriving business.

We can enhance your revenue and reduce your selling expenses. Marketing planning is a great exercise because you know that you must increase patient volume and differentiate your services from the competition. Many times, you need to educate the patient before your service is deemed valuable and desirable. Networking and developing referral sources are critical. Public relations and community exposure build brand recognition and credibility.

We provide comprehensive sales, marketing and contracting solutions to our clients based on our intense and detailed knowledge of the insurance coverage marketplace. We execute strategies to meet our client needs with the physician, patient, hospital, outpatient service, insurance company and employer markets. We have the knowledge and innovation to provide outstanding sales, marketing and contracting results.

Our solutions include three core services:
- Strategic analysis and measurement to develop a plan for approaching the target audience and optimizing the return on investment.
- Communications programs designed to reach your audience through education and direct messaging.
- Sales and marketing for one-to-one access to the targeted audience.

Whether you need the assistance of one core service or choose to leverage our integrated services, Stewart Geiser Insurance understands that exceeding goals and meeting deadlines are critical to success. We also appreciate that the sales and marketing challenge has never been greater nor the strategic benefits of outsourcing more evident. Our capabilities extend beyond our current offerings, as we are continually evaluating new technologies and a variety of insurance coverage initiatives to help our clients compete in today's business environment and prepare for tomorrow's. Stewart Geiser Insurance is as dedicated to your success as you are. Stewart Geiser Insurance will assist in the development and enhancement of relationships with all parties that utilize the products and services of the healthcare profession.

The target audience is:
- Insurance companies
- Non-profit disease management organizations
- Community advisory groups
- Labor groups
- Business health groups
- Physicians
- Consumers
- Employers
- Hospitals
- Retail Pharmacies

# Marketing strategy for outsourcing sales/marketing

Each of these groups involves a specific relationship plan and the interactions need to be programmed so that the message delivered to each group is effective. Our services are designed to comply with the most recent insurance marketing guidelines and to:

- Provide education on disease management and products
- Create greater visibility
- Promote public relations
- Improve patient care

How we deliver:

- Direct to Consumer Marketing to Increase Brand Awareness and Brand Loyalty
  - Insurance Coverage Management Tables
  - Group education meetings with patients
- Promotion of branded over-the-counter products and diagnostic tests
- Educational meetings with medical doctors, physicians, hospital personnel
  - Peer-to-peer Continuing Education Program Implementation
  - Physician Detailing
- Promotion of Patient Care Pathway Programs
  - Medicare
  - Low-income patients
- Function as an agent in a particular market to assist in the analysis, development, research and activity of marketing products and services
- Education for Employers and Insurance companies to influence purchasing decisions
- Seminars to introduce Insurance Coverage Management Programs, information on products

As a contract sales partner with Catabaw and Stewart Geiser Insurance will provide the following functions:

- Development of a customized referral network for insurance coverage services. This network will be constructed with geographic access and specific referrers taken into consideration.
- Development of a customized referral network for insurance coverage services. This network will be constructed with geographic access and specific referrers taken into consideration.
- Develop in-network contracts with insurance companies, workers' comp panels, case managers, etc. to assure Catabaw is an authorized, preferred provider for all payors.

The value of contracting with Stewart Geiser Insurance Group can be best described as follows:

- Once a client utilizes the sales services, all sales agents of Stewart Geiser Insurance Group begin to promote the client within the specific geographic area. This expansive sales effort can generate referrals quickly and therefore accelerate the sales plan.
- We have been in the Charleston Medical Market for over 30 years. This active participation in the insurance industry facilitates the sales effort and increases the sales success rate.
- Our fee is only based on success and performance. We are not a fixed expense. We do not need trained, prompted, managed, educated or replaced. We are a turn-key solution to increasing sales.

If you picked up this book in order to learn how to prepare financial statements as part of a business plan, you will find helpful samples in this section. You know that financial statements and operating statements are shown throughout **Part One: Business Plans**, so you should also return to these pages to see helpful examples of financial statements on pages 6, 9, 37, 42-43, 58, 84, 97, 122, 113, and 117.

### Financial Projections

If you are seeking to obtain financing for a new or existing business, you may find that you have to supply financial projections. On the following pages you will find some examples of financial projections that you can use in preparing your own forecasts.

### Income Statement and Balance Sheet

Banks or investors will usually ask you to prepare an income statement and balance sheet as a condition of evaluating your financial condition and considering you for a loan. You will find examples of income statements and balance sheets in this section.

# Corporate financial statements

## PHILLIP'S AUTO REPAIR

## FINANCIAL PROJECTIONS

|  | Year 1 | Year 2 | Year 3 |
|---|---|---|---|
| **Sales** | | | |
| Retail Products | $ 20,000 | $ 35,000 | $ 44,000 |
| Labor Sales | 42,000 | 64,000 | 83,475 |
| **Total Sales** | $ 62,000 | $ 99,000 | $127,475 |
| **Expenses** | | | |
| Advertising | $ 1,500 | $ 2,800 | $ 3,500 |
| Bank Charges | 350 | 350 | 350 |
| Insurance | 1,450 | 1,750 | 2,000 |
| Miscellaneous | 1,000 | 1,150 | 1,200 |
| Office Expenses | 800 | 1,200 | 3,500 |
| Professional Fees | 300 | 300 | 300 |
| Rent | 10,800 | 10,800 | 10,800 |
| Repair/Maintenance | 200 | 300 | 400 |
| Telephone | 875 | 1,000 | 1,000 |
| Utilities | 2,580 | 2,900 | 3,100 |
| **Total Expenses** | $ 19,855 | $ 22,550 | $ 26,150 |
| **Profit from Operations** | $ 42,145 | $ 76,450 | $101,325 |
| **Other Expenses** | | | |
| Equipment Lease | $ 1,200 | $ 2,900 | $ 4,500 |
| Loan Payment | 3,600 | 3,600 | 3,600 |
| Equity Line | 3,500 | 3,500 | 3,500 |
| Employee Benefits | 0 | 3,400 | 3,575 |
| **Total Other Expenses** | $ 4,800 | $ 13,400 | $ 15,175 |
| **Net Profit** | $ 37,345 | $ 63,050 | $ 86,150 |

**FINANCIAL PROJECTIONS**

These are detailed examples of how to create financial projections. One document is a three-year plan of financial projections, and the other is a five-year plan. Want to see the business plan that accompanied the three-year projection? See Business Plan #1 on page 2. Business Plan #13 on page 91 is the business plan which accompanied the five-year plan.

# Corporate financial statements

**WHITAKER JANITORIAL SUPPLY COMPANY**
**FIVE-YEAR PROJECTION**

## APPENDIX A

| | YEAR 1 | YEAR 2 | YEAR 3 | YEAR 4 | YEAR 5 |
|---|---|---|---|---|---|
| **Cash Receipts** | | | | | |
| Sales | $305,000 | $315,000 | $324,000 | $324,000 | $330,000 |
| Less-Increase in A/R | <2,000> | <2,000> | <2,000> | <2,000> | <2,000> |
| Net Cash Receipts | 303,000 | 313,000 | 316,000 | 322,000 | 328,000 |
| | | | | | |
| **Cash Disbursements** | | | | | |
| Cost of Goods Sold | $198,250 | $204,750 | $203,520 | 207,360 | 207,900 |
| Add-Increase Inventory | 5,000 | 4,000 | 3,000 | 2,000 | 2,000 |
| Less-Increase in A/P | <3,400> | <3,000> | <2,250> | <2,250> | <2,000> |
| Total Cash Expended for Merchandise | $199,850 | $205,750 | $207,110 | $207,110 | $207,900 |
| | | | | | |
| Salary - Officer | $ 10,600 | $ 12,600 | $ 14,000 | $17,600 | $ 21,600 |
| Salaries - Other | 25,800 | 27,600 | 29,400 | 31,200 | 33,000 |
| Sales Commissions | 0 | 0 | 0 | 0 | 0 |
| Other Expenses | $ 38,388 | $ 39,540 | $ 40,726 | $ 41,948 | $ 43,206 |
| | | | | | |
| **Capital Expenditures** | | | | | |
| Trade for New Delivery Van | $ 0 | $ 6,000 | $ 0 | $ 0 | $ 0 |
| Computer System | 3,000 | 0 | 0 | 0 | 0 |
| | | | | | |
| Debt Service | $ 17,848 | $ 17,848 | $ 17,848 | $ 17,848 | $ 17,848 |
| | | | | | |
| Total Cash Disbursements | $ 99,636 | $107,588 | $106,574 | $112,596 | $119,654 |
| | | | | | |
| Net Cash Flow | $<7,514> | $<4,338> | $<9,656> | $<6,294> | $<4,446> |
| | | | | | |
| Cumulative Cash Flow | $ 7,514 | $ 7,852 | $ 13,508 | $ 15,802 | $ 16,248 |

# Corporate financial statements

On this page you see examples of a balance sheet and an income statement. This hypothetical company -- XYZ Company (A Partnership) -- is engaged in the construction and sale of cabinets and other wood products.

**XYZ COMPANY, INC.**
**(A Partnership)**
**BALANCE SHEET**
**DECEMBER 31, 2003**

### ASSETS
(000's)

| | |
|---|---|
| **CURRENT ASSETS:** | |
| Cash | $ 1,176 |
| Accounts Receivable - Trade | 5,732 |
| Inventories | 1,500 |
| Total Current Assets | 8,408 |
| **PROPERTY AND EQUIPMENT - NET** | 33,699 |
| **TOTAL ASSETS** | $42,107 |

### LIABILITIES AND PARTNERS' CAPITAL
(000's)

| | |
|---|---|
| **CURRENT LIABILITIES:** | |
| Accounts Payable - Trade | $12,594 |
| Payroll Taxes Payable | 1,768 |
| Accrued Taxes | 791 |
| Sales Tax Payable | 2,201 |
| Accrued Interest Payable | 142 |
| Notes Payable | 8,981 |
| Total Current Liabilities | $26,477 |
| **NOTES PAYABLE (See Note 1)** | 32,722 |
| **PARTNERS' CAPITAL** | (17,092) |
| **TOTAL LIABILITIES AND PARTNERS' CAPITAL** | $42,107 |

Note 1: **Notes Payable:**
The company is liable under certain installment obligations as follows:

| | |
|---|---|
| First Federal Bank | $ 33,844 |
| Mark Ellison | 7,859 |
| Total Notes Payable | 41,703 |
| Less — Amount Due Within One Year | 8,981 |
| Amount Due After One Year | $ 32,722 |

**Income Taxes:** The partnership is not a taxable entity for federal and state income tax purposes, and thus no income tax expense has been recorded in the statements. Income from the partnership is taxed to partners in their individual returns.

# Corporate financial statements

XYZ COMPANY, INC.
(A Partnership)
STATEMENT OF INCOME AND PARTNERS' CAPITAL
FOR THE YEAR ENDED DECEMBER 31, 2003
(000's)

**INCOME**

| | |
|---|---|
| Cabinet and Wood Product Sales | $192,956 |

**COST OF GOODS SOLD**

| | |
|---|---|
| Inventory, December 31, 2002 | 1,500 |
| Purchases | 79,138 |
| Subcontractors | 2,228 |
| Factory Expense | 6,982 |
| Other Construction Costs | 920 |
| | 90,768 |
| Inventory, December 31, 2003 | 1,500 |
| | |
| Cost of Goods Sold | 89,268 |

**GROSS PROFIT**              103,688

| | |
|---|---|
| **GENERAL AND ADMINISTRATIVE EXPENSES (Schedule 1)** | 79,240 |
| Operating Income | 24,448 |

**OTHER INCOME (EXPENSE)**

| | |
|---|---|
| Other Income | 100 |
| Interest Income | 45 |
| Interest Expense | (2,969) |

**NET INCOME**              21,624

| | |
|---|---|
| **PARTNERS' CAPITAL, DECEMBER 31, 2002** | 22,784 |
| | 44,408 |
| **PARTNERS' WITHDRAWALS** | |
| | (61,500) |

**Income Recognition:** The financial records are maintained and the financial statements are prepared on the accrual basis.

# Corporate financial statements

## XYZ COMPANY, INC.
### (A Partnership)
### GENERAL AND ADMINISTRATIVE EXPENSES
### FOR THE YEAR ENDED DECEMBER 31, 2003
(000's)

**FINANCIAL STATEMENTS**

Other financial statements you may be asked to provide are these: a statement of general and administrative expenses, and a cash flow statement. Also shown is a statement which shows depreciation expenses.

| | |
|---|---:|
| Accounting and Legal | $24,484 |
| Auto and Truck | |
| Advertising | 6,315 |
| Depreciation (see detailed statement below) | 4,741 |
| Insurance | |
| Office Expense | |
| Payroll Taxes | 11,560 |
| Repairs and Maintenance | |
| Equipment Rent | 16,840 |
| Salaries and Wages | 6,315 |
| Taxes — Other | |
| Telephone | |
| Utilities | |
| Contributions | 3,910 |
| Miscellaneous Expenses | |
| | |
| **TOTAL GENERAL AND ADMINISTRATIVE EXPENSES** | $79,240 |

## DETAILED STATEMENT OF DEPRECIABLE ITEMS

| | Cost | Lives |
|---|---:|---|
| Office Equipment | $ 1,335 | 5-10 Years |
| Delivery Equipment | 14,434 | 3-5 Years |
| Factory Equipment | 26,111 | 5 Years |
| Building | 65,446 | 18-20 Years |
| Leasehold Improvements | 589 | 10 Years |
| | $107,915 | |
| Less Accumulated Depreciation | 74,216 | |
| | $33,699 | |

Depreciation expense aggregated $4,741 in 2003.

**Fixed Assets and Depreciation:** Fixed assets are carried at cost less accumulated depreciation. Depreciation is computed by the straight line and accelerated cost recovery systems over various useful lives of the assets. Maintenance and ordinary repairs are expensed as incurred; major renewals and betterments are capitalized. When an asset is sold or retired, the related cost and accumulated depreciation are removed from the accounts and any gain or loss recognized is reported in income.

# Corporate financial statements

**XYZ COMPANY, INC.**
**(A Partnership)**
**STATEMENT OF CASH FLOWS**
**FOR THE YEAR ENDED DECEMBER 31, 2003**
(000's)

**CASH FLOWS FROM OPERATING ACTIVITIES**

| | |
|---|---:|
| Net Income | $21,624 |
| Noncash Expenses, Revenues, Losses, and | |
| Gains Included in Income: | |
| Depreciation | $ 4,741 |
| Net (Increase) Decrease in Receivables, | |
| Inventories, Prepaid Items, and Payables | 30,912 |
| Increase (Decrease) in Accrued | |
| Expenses | 909 |
| | (36,562) |

| | |
|---|---:|
| **NET CASH FLOW FROM OPERATING ACTIVITIES** | 58,186 |

**CASH FLOWS FROM INVESTING ACTIVITIES:**

| | |
|---|---:|
| Cash Outflows for Operational Assets | (648) |

**CASH FLOWS FROM FINANCING ACTIVITIES:**

| | |
|---|---:|
| Capital Contributions (Withdrawals) | (61,500) |
| Payments to Settle Debt Obligations | ( 6,929) |
| Proceeds from Debt Acquired | 7,500 |

| | |
|---|---:|
| **NET CASH PROVIDED (USED) BY** **FINANCING ACTIVITIES** | (60,929) |
| **NET DECREASE IN CASH** | (3,391) |
| **CASH BALANCE, DECEMBER 31, 2002** | 4,567 |
| **CASH BALANCE, DECEMBER 31, 2003** | $ 1,176 |

# Corporate financial statements

### Sample Balance Sheet
### December 1, 2002

**Assets:**

| | |
|---|---|
| Cash | $ 6,600.00 |
| Real Estate (Residential) | 80,000.00 |
| Land | 35,000.00 |
| Deposits (savings) | 20,000.00 |
| Vehicles:  two (car - truck) | 25,000.00 |
| | **$166,600.00** |

**Liabilities:**

| | |
|---|---|
| Mortgage payable | 83,000.00 |

**Owner Capital:**

| | |
|---|---|
| Net Worth | 83,600.00 |
| **Total Liabilities and Capital** | **$166,600.00** |

**FINANCIAL STATEMENTS**

Here are other samples of financial documents which often accompany loan applications. On the top of the left page, you see a simple balance sheet. On the bottom of the left page is a sample business loan request. And on the facing page you see a Statement of Operations for a business which has been losing money and which the new owners hope to rescue after a new infusion of capital.

### SAMPLE BUSINESS LOAN REQUEST

The $85,000 loan will be used as follows:

| Use of Funds | $ |
|---|---|
| Initial Franchise Fee | $50,000 |
| Down Payment on Opening Inventory | $18,000 |
| Good Will Payment | $60,000 |
| Cash Register Fund | $ 1,000 |
| Licenses, Permits, and Bonds | $ 1,000 |
| Working capital (reserved, not disbursed) for the first three months: | $10,000 |
| | 140,000 |
| Minimum cash on hand | $15,000 |
| Total Use of Funds | 155,000 |
| Personal Contribution | 70,000 |
| LOAN NEEDED | $85,000 |

# STATEMENT OF OPERATIONS

## STATEMENT OF OPERATIONS

|  | 53 Weeks Ended November 31, 2001 | 47 Weeks ended November 15, 2002 |
|---|---|---|
| Net Sales | $94,475,010 | $71,081,092 |
| Other revenues, net | 2,023,132 | 2,393,548 |
|  | $96,498,142 | $73,474,640 |
| Costs and expenses: |  |  |
| Cost of sales | 76,703,618 | 60,149,917 |
| Selling, general and administrative expenses | 19,705,773 | 14,746,012 |
| Interest Expenses | 317,345 | 375,343 |
|  | 96,726,736 | 75,271,272 |
| Loss before income tax credit | ( 228,594) | ( 1,796,632) |
| Income tax credit | 14,000 | 983,400 |
| Net Loss | ( 214,594) | ( 813,232) |

Range Restaurant Size 2,500 to 5,000 sq. feet

Seating 80-250 customers self-service format

Investment in leasehold improvement $60,000-$120,000
Investment in furniture, fixtures, equipment $60,000

## Typical Wedgy's Pizza Outlet
Achieved sales $400,000 and $500,000
New Wedgy's Pizza Net $75,000 1st year

## 2001
Large Combo $9.75 to $11.50

| Company owned outlets | 56 |
|---|---|
| Franchises | 720 |
| Multi unit | 80 |

Franchise Fee/License Agreement Fee $15,000 per unit
Continuing fee of 3-5% of gross revenues

Here you see a statement of operations which shows a business which has been losing money. Wedgy's Pizza was a successful pizza chain that grew from a small seed and was then chopped down.

The owners wanted to serve a thick and juicy pizza to their customers. Even though the company grew like wild flowers, there was a lack of direction. More and more franchises were being offered. Through poor management and aggressive competition, Wedgy's Pizza was thrown into a tailspin. This company had an opportunity to remain the second largest pizza chain and even surpass Luigi's Pizza Place, but because of internal strife they opened the doors for the competition to move in. Earnings plunged 94 percent and some franchises started rebelling against management by withholding royalty fees.

Drive-through windows and home delivery was growing in popularity. Other pizza joints like Hungry Howie's, knew what kind of business they were in. There's a saying that "too many hands in the pot spoil the food." Poor planning and marketing, and lack of research and unity within the company, destroyed what could have been a long lasting relationship with the public.

# PART FOUR:
## Valuing and Selling a Business

There often comes a time when entrepreneurs or business owners decide to sell their business. The question then becomes, How do you value your business? In order to interest a potential buyer or buyers, you often need to put down on paper some facts about your business operations.

There is not only one way to prepare a business valuation. The purpose of this section is to show you several concepts or ideas which relate to valuing a business. This small section is by no means comprehensive. If you are in the process of valuing and selling your business, you may wish to consult authorities in this area.

# Example #1: Valuing and selling a business

## PHYSICAL & OCCUPATIONAL THERAPY
### VALUATION CHECKLIST

**Highly Confidential:** We submit this information to you in total confidence, and with the understanding that all the information we provide to you will not be duplicated without our permission, and will be returned to the name and address shown below at the conclusion of the communications between the two parties.

**VALUING AND SELLING A BUSINESS**

Here is a document that provides necessary information and explains reasons for wanting to sell a business.

Company Name:            Midwest Rehabilitation Center ("MRC")

Contact Name/Mailing Address:    Tonya W. Settles, c/o Staff Seekers, Inc.
                                         PO Box 5486

Springfield, MO 68302

Contact Phone:                    (111) 111-1111 (w); (222) 222-2222 (w)

### Corporate Structure/Background:

MRC started operations in July 2001 in Springfield, MO, which remains the location of its central facility and its fabrication laboratory. The primary focus of the business is Physical & Occupational Therapy (P&O), although it has provided wound care, sleep studies, and pharmacy services. A second P&O facility opens November 5, 2003. For expansion plans, see **Strategic Business Plan** in enclosed **Company Report.**

*Tonya W. Settles is the major shareholder and serves as the point of contact for any communications between your organization and MRC.*

**Entity Type:** P&O Corporation, Subchapter

### Services Provided (see enclosed **Company Report**)

Physical & Occupational Therapy services are provided, with Physical Therapy comprising the major part of our services, perhaps 80%. This is through design and not chance, as our growth has been so rapid because of the reputation of the personnel affiliated with MRC, that we have had to make a strategic decision to focus so far on the high-ticket Physical Therapy business. We turn nothing away, but we have not to date actively courted the Occupational Therapy business. This is about to change as we bring on board a second, and highly credentialed Orthopedic Specialist. We recently spoke to the principal physician and decision maker in the practice (a principal of MRC knows him and two other physicians in the practice personally), and we were asked to make a proposal to his group at their next monthly meeting.

Both segments of the business are growing rapidly. The new orthopedic specialist coming on board was Aaron Marshall's (Director of our P&O Division) instructor in school, and will oversee Orthopedic services. Mr. Marshall is firmly entrenched with the physiatrists at the local hospital, which is a major medical center. Beginning November 16, 2001, he will be taking over their pediatric work. Raymond Spears, M.D., is MRC's Medical Director. His reputation as a orthopedic specialist is second to none in the area. He is a salaried employee with no participation in ownership or profits of MRC, but he is a vital part of our business plan and philosophy (how many P&O practices have a board-certified physician as a Medical Director?), and lends tremendous credibility as we continue to expand our leadership position throughout the entire mid-western part of the state. We anticipate that the opening of our second facility (we just helped a young orthopedist establish a practice in this community, which is sorely in need of his services) could result in us fabricating several additional physical therapy devices per month, as we develop our relationship with the main orthopedist in the community, a physician with whom our Medical Director has a good relationship. We have competition in this community, but the quality of our work far exceeds that of the competition.

We have identified the three communities we intend to expand into within the next year (this represents Phase 2 of our business plan). Also, our Medical Director has expressed a desire to open a practice in one of these communities, performing his work under the auspices of MRC (we will of course make sure that any such arrangement is set up in the correct manner).

We look more at revenue generated per physical therapy device than revenue generated per visit.

It should be noted that we are in a region of the country where physical injuries are attaining what, as Mr. Marshall observes, appears to be almost epidemic proportions, and if anything it will be getting worse. The usage of physical and occupational therapy products seems to be higher than in other parts of the country. The future looks attractive for our business.

**Professional Contacts/References/Tax I.D. #'s:** We would be delighted to provide you with this information, in total confidence, should we both decide that we want to take our discussions to the next level.

**Strengths:**

- **Reputation and Technical Competence of Key Personnel:** While acknowledging that many facilities think their practitioners are top notch, we honestly believe that the practitioner does not exist who could supplant Mr. Marshall (Director, P&O Division) with his current referral base of satisfied doctors, hospitals, physical therapists, and patients—a referral base which is centered in Springfield, but is expanding rapidly throughout the entire region. Mr. Marshall, and Mr. Wilridge, who manages our fabrication lab, are highly skilled professionals, current in state-of-the art techniques, extremely hard working, and share in management's desire to create the leading P&O operation in the state of Missouri. Furthermore, the advantages of having Dr. Spears as our Medical Director are clear and have already been mentioned. Tonya W. Settles, the founder and major shareholder, is a Georgetown MBA, who has founded and built several successful businesses over the past 20 years.
- **Excellent Location:** a strength from several points of view:
  1. The market is superior for the products and services we provide.
  2. We are an excellent starting point for expansion northwards through the rest of Missouri and southwards into Arkansas.
  3. Springfield, our headquarters, is a former state capital and conveniently located on Interstate 95.
- **Our Market and the Competition:** It would be extremely difficult for anyone to displace us in our market as (a) our reputation is impeccable, (b) it is a fragmented region in which we possess specific knowledge of the opportunities and pitfalls available, (c) our management team is strong and visionary, relatively young, and aggressively committed to providing top-quality services while aggressively pursuing

growth and profitability, (d) we are in a region consisting of many rural communities where key decision makers (referring physicians, etc.) remain extremely loyal to providers they like and who serve them well (service providers such as ourselves, for example)—we'll temporarily leave alone markets such as St. Louis, Jefferson City, and Columbia, where competition is strong, as we build and strengthen our base of operations.

- **Diversity of Services:** Our philosophy of actively and creatively seeking, and being receptive to offering, other medical services that are complimentary to P&O and provide a measure of vertical integration only strengthens our overall operation.

**VALUATION CHECKLIST**

## Weaknesses:

Administrative, but not technical, inexperience is the only weakness we can think of. Our electronic billing operation has been slow to become fully functional. Our change of address in mid-February resulted in our going without receiving a Medicare-DME payment from the middle of February until early September, because of a "Do Not Forward" message on the Medicare payment envelopes, although we had followed correct procedures in establishing a forwarding address. Hopefully, most of these administrative learning experiences are behind us, but there will surely be others to handle. Fortunately, referrals, patients, and sales have never been a problem, except perhaps in the management of our continuing explosive growth.

## Opportunities:

The enclosed Company Report discusses Phase 3 of our expansion plan, which involves the establishment of four to six additional P&O facilities in 2004, after the setting up of our initial four facilities (Phases 1 and 2) by the end of 2003.

## Threats:

With the clear advantage of quality, reputation, and connections that we possess over our competitors in our region, we do not consider competition a major threat to our operations.

So what are our major threats? In our opinion, it would be the possibility of decreasing (or non-increasing) Medicare reimbursements over time, along with the potential threat in the future of an unexpected calamitous judgement awarded against us in excess of the insurance coverage we possess, no matter how comprehensive such coverage may be.

## Reasons for Selling:

One of the two principals of the business recently had a major change in his personal life situation. On March 16, 2001, his father passed away, leaving him as the primary care provider for his mother, who, although in good physical condition, suffers from Alzheimer's disease. He will be moving his mother down from Michigan to his residence in Missouri within the next few months. Prior to founding MRC, he operated a business from a location adjacent to his residence. He seeks to sell his share of the business, thus simplifying his life.

In this regard, we have already received an attractive bona fide offer from an experienced medical business entrepreneur to purchase his share of MRC. The position of Tonya A. Settles, the other principal in MRC, is that she is willing to either maintain or relinquish her ownership in MRC, depending on what is in the best interests of her fellow owner, the business itself, and the employees. Either option would work well for her. In the first case (maintaining ownership), she participates in the rapid growth of a business whose revenues are likely to double, triple, or grow even more dramatically (through additional P&O facilities, secondary modalities, and medical practices) in the next couple of years, and then has the option to (1) sell a multimillion dollar operation to an organization such as yours or (2) have what would be basically a generous annuity income stream forever. In the second case, she sells her ownership share in the near future to a large organization (e.g., you). A critical element in her decision is clearly the valuation you decide to place on the business. It is possible that you may employ a valuation method which would better value an older, more mature, but slower growing P&O business. Applying the same earnings multiple in the case of MRC, without factoring in the major strengths and anticipated high rate of growth of revenues and earnings, would probably not produce an acceptable valuation for our business.

**Payer Sources:**
Our primary payment source is Medicare-Magnum. We also receive payments from Medicaid, Workers Comp, private insurance, self pay and other traditional payment sources.

**Accounting/Financial Reporting Methods:**
As allowed by the IRS, we use the cash basis of accounting for tax purposes. We use both cash and accrual bases for financial reporting, as the dual bases of reporting are helpful for financial analysis.

**Referrals:**
Dr. Spears, board certified orthopedist, and the physiatrists at Greene County Medical Center, the leading medical facility in the region, are leading referral sources. We would be happy to provide more detailed information on physicians who refer to us as our communications with you progress to more serious negotiations.

**Staffing:**

| Name | Title | Salary/Year |
|---|---|---|
| Raymond Spears, M.D. | Medical Director | $60,000 |
| Aaron Marshall | Director, PT Division | $90,000 |
| Max Wilridge | Tech/Manager, PH Pharmacy | $60,000 |
| Shannon Barnell | Clinic Administrator | $25,000 |
| Callie Herndon | Billing Specialist | $15,000 |

- Please do not contact any of the above personnel without the expressed written permission of Tonya W. Settles.
- Mr. Marshall is certified as a orthopedist; Mr. Wilridge is planning on obtaining his certification as a orthopedist in the near future; we are planning on soon adding another orthopedist (approximately $60,000/year) and another technician (approximately $20,000/year)—both employees have been identified and are very interested in becoming part of MRC's team.

**Facilities:**
*Location 1:*
- 8742 Crawford Road, Suite 166, Springfield, MO 68302
- approximately 3,000 square feet (exclusive of a large storage building behind the facility)
- leased at $1,100/month—MRC pays utilities ($200-$300/month); owner of building would like to sell building and land to MRC

# Example #1: Valuing and selling a business

- all treatment rooms have walls; spacious administrative/billing/reception area; large fabrication/sewing/casting areas at rear of building (MRC has made major capital improvements to building)
- open 8:00 a.m. to 5:00 p.m., Monday through Friday—our employees are very dedicated and Mr. Marshall and Mr. Wilridge do not consider their jobs to be "9 to 5."

*Location 2:*
Opens November 6, 2001—we will be happy to provide further details at a later stage.

**VALUATION CHECKLIST**

### Financial Statements:

The following are provided with information current as of November 16, 2001:

- **Summary Balance Sheet:**
  1. **Accounts Receivable:** $266,634.65, comprised of P&O receivables of $216,729 and Wound Care ("WC") receivables of $45,671.37; the remaining $4,058.16 of receivables represent some self pays/payment plans which were set up in the first couple of months of operation; there are several other payment plans, self/private pay receivables not included in the $266,634.65 figure, which was taken from our billing software (which is different to our accounting software, from which these reports were prepared); also WC receivables are from only 30 of 67 patient charts—the remaining unbilled 37 charts (some of which include physician treatment procedures performed by Dr. Spears when he was overseeing the WC Division, currently dormant) could produce $50,000-$75,000 in additional receivables; it is difficult to predict the collectability of the WC receivables—only $23,945.81 has been collected to date, but a guess is that $30,000-$45,000 of the $95,671-$120,671 (receivables plus unbilled charts) will be realized—this is cash flow, as it will be nonrecurring (already generated) revenue with no associated expenses. Of the $216,729 in P&O receivables, perhaps 80%-90% will be realized as most patients have supplements and many have secondaries. It should be noted that no allowance has been made for uncollectables/bad debts in the Accounts Receivable figures, but when you add the unbilled charts plus the receivables not included and subtract an allowance for uncollectables/bad debts, you could arrive at a figure close to $266,634.65.
  2. **Other Current Assets:** $60,000: This is Mr. Marshall and Mr. Wilridge's best estimate of inventory in stock.
  3. **Accounts Payable:** $91,593.63, includes P&O inventory/cost of goods sold of $64,818.78, General payables of $1,758.28, (where "General" refers to balance sheet, income, and expense items not specifically allocated to P&O or Wound Care—items such as rent, administrative salaries, office expenses, etc.), and Wound Care/Pharmacy payables of $25,016.57 (this $25,016.57 figure is also shown on the Profit and Loss statement as Clinical Supplies, for purposes of simplicity, although some of this amount is for equipment—also, and this is important, many of these supplies/equipment are returnable and will be returned, but they have already been charged against income—a conservative treatment). The net result here is that true Accounts Payable has been overstated, and Net Income understated, by approximately $20,000.
  4. **Other Current Liabilities:** $193,060.82, includes Loans to Shareholders of $174,218.98 and Payroll Liabilities of $18,841.84, reduced on November 12, 1999 by deposit of 941 tax.
  5. **Equity:** $141,504.94, includes Net Income of $66,662.42 from the Profit and

Loss statement and Capital Stock of $74,842.52.

- **Profit and Loss:**

    Net Income of $66,662.42 is for all operations, including Wound Care/Pharmacy operations, which generated substantial losses, and are not currently being pursued by MRC. For factors affecting this Net Income value, see notes above under <u>Summary Balance Sheet.</u>

- **Profit and Loss (P&O and General):**

    Net Income of $113,224.92 is for P&O and General categories. This figure could be lower (or higher) if you think uncollectable receivables is greater (or smaller) than the receivables not included, as described above. The Net Income figure should be increased because not all of the General expenses would have been incurred (and are not currently being incurred) if P&O alone was being operated. For example, Dr. Spears received $10,000/month for the first six months of operation—he currently receives $5,000/month. This adds $30,000+ to the P&O bottom line, and there are other such items. Net Income should be increased by another approximately $10,000 from the amount included in Building Repairs, an amount which should really be capitalized as a Fixed Asset. Another key factor is that this Net Income figure has effectively been generated only since March, when MRC received its Medicare-DME provider number.

- **Profit and Loss (P&O):**

    Net Income of $249,215.86 is for P&O only. This is a hypothetical figure for your information— Total Expense includes expenses attributable to P&O only. Again this is basically for operations since March. The Net Income figure is revealing in that it shows what could be generated from the just opened Facility #2, a facility with very low overhead.

## Other Factors:

- Owner salaries are not included here. The principal seeking to sell his share of the business was very instrumental in the construction/set-up work, which has been largely accomplished; his daily role is currently minimal. Mrs. Settles is not critical to the daily functioning (during the day) of the business. She is an entrepreneur with several business interests. Her contributions are primarily strategic and developmental. She, or someone like her, would probably be required as the number of facilities grows, but she need not be figured as an expense in the Balance Sheet and Profit and Loss statements included, which just apply to one facility.

- Additional receipts of $25,000 have been taken in between November 6 (report date) and November 16, 2001 (today).

- As of the first of November, Accounts Receivable Aging Schedule is as follows:

| >120 days | 90-120 days | 60-90 days | 30-60 days | Current | Total |
|---|---|---|---|---|---|
| $28,109.04 | $25,675.76 | $44,921.70 | $113,472.40 | $108,102.11 | $320,281.01 |

    We would be happy to show details of the aging schedule as discussions progress. We are comfortable with the schedule as is, but additionally there are some mitigating factors: old Wound Care claims, Medicare checks returned and not yet reprocessed during our location change, move, etc.

- ***Please refer to Company Report enclosed for projections for 2003 and 2004.***

Reminder: please be totally confidential with all information submitted. Sole individual authorized to deal with your organization is:

Tonya W. Settles, Treasurer/Secretary

(111) 111-1111 (work number at Staff Seekers, Inc.)

(222) 222-2222 (home number)

# Example #2: Valuing a Business

**AMERICAN HEALTHCARE, INC.**

**Company Report**

American Health Care, Incorporated (hereinafter referred to as "AHC") is a California corporation headquartered in Long Beach, CA. AHC began operations in March 2002. AHC's primary modality (or principal area of business) is Orthotics and Prosthetics ("O&P"). The company's O&P fabrication laboratory in Long Beach ("Facility #1") has already gained a reputation as the best such lab in the county, and in only its sixth month of operation generated gross sales receipts in excess of $100,000. Indeed, O&P received its Medicare Provider Number (a prerequisite for doing business with Medicare, which is the primary insurer of a major portion of O&P's patients) only in June 2002, and we are pleased that within three months of receiving this number, the O&P Division attained a six-figure gross sales receipts month in September 2002.

AHC has in place provider numbers, insurer relationships, licenses, etc. to provide other medical, pharmaceutical, and durable medical equipment services in various modalities. As of 10/20/02, Wound Care ("WC") and Sleep Study ("SS") services had generated $23,945 in revenue received, $45,671 in billings outstanding (reimbursements for which will be low), with 37 patient charts remaining to be billed (perhaps totaling $50,000-$75,000, which amount will not be included in Accounts Receivable until it is actually billed). WC and SS fall under AHC's Clinical Services ("CS") Division. Clinical Services have not been provided since October 2002, as AHC pursues its focus on its rapidly expanding O&P business.

AHC's third division is Pharmacy ("PH"). There are several viable service areas within Pharmacy which we are considering and which we have been approached to provide by home health agencies, hospitals, and other health care providers. Projections and assumptions in this report give no consideration to the potential of the Pharmacy Division, as it is not currently a primary focus of AHC.

## Orthotic and Prosthetic Services

Orthotic rehabilitation includes the fitting, design, fabrication, and use of custom-made braces and support devices for treatment of musculoskeletal conditions resulting from illness, injury, or congenital abnormalities. Prosthetic rehabilitation entails the fitting, fabrication, and use of custom-made artificial limbs usually required by people who have suffered the loss of a limb from vascular diseases, diabetes, cancer, and trauma.

The principal referral source for orthotic rehabilitation services is the orthopedic surgeon, with the podiatrist being an important secondary referral source. The principal referral source for prosthetic rehabilitation is the vascular surgeon, with the physiatrist being an important secondary referral source. Other specialized physicians, managed care payors, physical therapists, orthopedic nurses, orthopedic technicians, and other rehabilitation professionals are also important sources of referrals for O&P.

**Strategic Business Plan**

AHC's strategic business plan is to establish several O&P mini-facilities, each headed by a certified orthotist (CO) or a certified prosthetist (CP), initially in communities within a 100-mile radius of the Long Beach lab (Facility #1). We have identified the locations for Facilities #2, #3, and #4, which constitute Phase II of AHC's expansion plan, with Phase I being the establishment and development of Facility #1. Phase II is currently being implemented, with Facility #2 opening on June 6, 2003.

Phase III will be implemented beginning in 2004. It will include the setting up of at least six additional O&P mini-facilities. A second O&P lab will probably be required during Phase III.

In each O&P mini-facility, HCC will evaluate which secondary modalities are needed and have little competition in the particular community. A secondary modality has been identified for each of Facilities #2, #3 and #4. A podiatrist who is extremely highly credentialed (in terms of surgical training and expertise—surgery being the higher ticket area of podiatry) will work closely with AHC's Facility #2 (the podiatry practice is structured as a separate corporation). The additional income and cash flow, and the reduced overhead, which will result from synergies between podiatry and O&P in this community have not been fully considered in our projections. With a podiatry practice in place in Facility #2, we have established the critical link with the key vascular surgeon in the community, a surgeon with whom our own Medical Director is already on very close terms. Although Facility #2 is open for business as of June 6, 2003, we are assuming, for the purpose of simplifying the projections in the exhibits, that Facility #2 will open in 2003.

It should be noted that we have not included projections for potential income and cash flow which could be generated by secondary modalities in any of Facilities #2, #3, #4, #5, #6, #7, and #8.

## The Market

Southwestern California, the initial focal point of AHC's business, is a market with a relatively high diabetic population, possibly due to various genetic and dietary factors. Although we have a population with an above average incidence of diabetes and vascular diseases, the supply of services available to meet these needs is greatly lacking in several communities in our principal and immediate market area. We thus have a situation of high and unmet demand combined with low levels of competition, to which we add our ability to provide state-of-the-art design and fabrication services along with our commitment to total quality patient care.

## Key Personnel

Cynthia Barnes (entrepreneur, Yale M.B.A.-1988) is the major shareholder of AHC, and is the AHC representative authorized to deal with individuals and companies interested in investing in, acquiring ownership of, or establishing a joint venture with AHC. Charles I. McCormick, M.D. (board-certified vascular surgeon), serves as Medical Director of AHC. Paul Rolon, certified orthotist-prosthetist, directs the O&P Division. Anthony Gaines oversees the O&P lab. Yolanda Sykes is the Clinic Administrator. Dr.

# Example #2: Valuing a Business

McCormick provides great credibility as AHC's Medical Director, while serving as an excellent referral source and link to other medical providers in the region. Mr. Bryant is extremely knowledgeable of state-of-the-art orthotic and prosthetic design and fabrication techniques, with a fine reputation and an extensive patient base and connections throughout our target market.

## Assumptions and Projections

**ASSUMPTIONS & PROJECTIONS**

The May and June assumptions of $80,000 per month in billings were exceeded, as May O&P billings were $126,305 and June O&P billings were $107,427. Of course, projections can only be as accurate as the assumptions turn out to be. Nowhere in this report does AHC or anyone affiliated with AHC guarantee or promise that any of these assumptions or projections will come to pass. Indeed, we encourage any person who reads this report to make his or her own assumptions and projections based on the information provided, and to request any additional information he or she feels is needed.

## Business Valuation

This plan makes a net income projection of $720,955 for 2004, based on certain assumptions. At ten times net income, this equates to a value of $7,209,550 for AHC in 2002. Applying an appropriate discount rate (discounting back from December 2002 to the present) could provide a current value for the business.

*Exhibit 6* shows a net income projection of $1,497,642 for 2003, based on certain assumptions. At ten times net income, this equates to a value of $14,976,420 for HCC in 2003. Applying an appropriate discount rate (discounting back from December 2003 to the present) could provide a current value for the business.

## Other Factors

Principal shareholder compensation has been deferred for work performed to date, which will be paid at some future time. As cash flow permits, they will begin to receive compensation for work performed from this time on. Charles McCormick, M.D., has deferred compensation of $20,000 which is payable in August 2003.

As mentioned earlier, this report does not consider any potential revenue and cash flow which could be generated by secondary modalities. Secondary modality income could more than outweigh the above mentioned deferred and future compensation factors.

# Example #1: Selling a Business

**BILL OF SALE**

February 7, 2003

I, Phillip W. Samuels, owner of K&K Partnership, Express Video, on this 7th day of February 2003 am selling the Express Video business located at 17375 Millboro Boulevard, Los Angeles, CA 90781 to Lily V. Thompson.

Payments are as follows:

| | |
|---|---|
| Total Price of Business: | $46,000 |
| Down Payment: | $ 9,000 |
| **Amount to be financed** | **$37,000** |

Remaining balance will be broken into two payments — one payment of $25,000 to be financed over two years and one payment of $13,000 to be financed over four years. The payment of $25,000 is financed at monthly payments of $1,166.67 over 24 months. The $13,000 is financed in monthly payments of $292.50 for 48 months.

Payments of $1,166.67 will be paid to Carl T. Samuels at 2017 Bradford Avenue, Santa Ana, CA 93576, and the payments of $292.50 will be paid to Phillip W. Samuels at 3762 Callaway Road, Los Angeles, CA 90762.

Payments will start on 3/1/04 and will be paid on every first day of the month with a 10-day grace period.

This contract is written on 2/7/04 in the presence of the following persons.

**SELLER:**
Phillip W. Samuels
3762 Callaway Road,
Los Angeles, CA 90762

**BUYER:**
Lily V. Thompson
1037 Ravenhill Drive
Santa Monica, CA 93171

**BILL OF SALE**
Here is an example of a simple bill of sale.

# Example #2: Selling a Business

## BILL OF SALE

August 1, 2003

We, Allan C. Kerr, Vice President and Phillip W. Samuels, Secretary with Harbor Video, on this 1st day of August 2003, are selling the Motion Pictures Express business located at 4170 Hwy 52, Los Angeles, CA 90775 to Lily V. Thompson.

Payments are as follows:

**BILL OF SALE**

Here is another example of a simple bill of sale.

Total price of business: $68,000.00
Down Payment: $9,999.99
Balance: $58,000.01

The remaining balance of $58,000.01 will be paid in 48 monthly payments at 6% which brings payments to $1,491.67. This payment will be paid at the first of every month and with the 10 day grace period. First payment will be due September 20, 2003. After the ten-day grace period, a 5% late fee will be due.

All payments will be made to the Allan C. Kerr at 1711 Saratoga Road, Los Angeles, CA 90784.

If Lily V. Thompson defaults on payments for three months (90 days), then we the Harbor Video, Inc. will take over the business on the 91st day. At the time of takeover all 4,000 tapes should be accounted for.

This contract is written on 8/25/03 in the presence of the following people:

**SELLER:**
Allan C. Kerr
2340 Fairway Lane
Los Angeles, CA 91062

Phillip W. Samuels
3762 Callaway Road
Los Angeles, CA 90762

**BUYER:**
Lily V. Thompson
1817 Hwy 12
Los Angeles, CA 90512

**WITNESS:**
William Bunce

Kenneth V. Dawkins

Witnessed by me this 1st day of August 2003.

Notary Public

# Example #3: Selling a Business

## TERMS OF BUY-SELL AGREEMENT: Florida Eye Institute

Dr. Mason Langley (hereinafter referred to as "Buyer") and Karen S. Wyatt/James R. Wyatt (hereinafter referred to as "Seller") have agreed in principle to the following terms:

- Buyer will establish a corporation which will purchase the assets of the Florida Eye Institute (hereinafter called "FEI"); these assets include current assets (deposits, accounts receivable, etc.) and fixed assets (medical equipment, office equipment and furniture, etc.), as well as going concern value (goodwill, the use of the name "Florida Eye Institute," etc.); purchased assets are depreciable (e.g., fixed assets) or amortizable (e.g., goodwill) resulting in more favorable tax treatment for Buyer, thus resulting in stronger cash flow for debt service and other purposes.
- Buyer will assume liabilities of FEI, including bank line of credit, accounts payable, etc.
- Buyer will indemnify Seller from all potential future damages/liabilities resulting from operations of FEI prior to the date of sale (professional liability insurance provides coverage for such occurrences).
- Buyer will pay Seller $250,000.00 in cash.
- Seller will pay Buyer $5,000.00 towards Seller's assumed line of credit.

{At the close of the purchase transaction, Buyer will have received Net Assets (i.e., Assets minus Liabilities or Total Equity) of $50,960.00 as per Balance Sheet (as of 7/31/03).}

**TERMS OF BUY-SELL AGREEMENT**
Here is a simple document stating the terms of a buy-sell agreement.

## ABOUT THE EDITOR

Anne McKinney holds an MBA from the Harvard Business School and a BA in English from the University of North Carolina at Chapel Hill. A noted public speaker, writer, and teacher, she is the senior editor for PREP's business and career imprint, which bears her name. Early titles in the Anne McKinney Career Series (now called the Real-Resumes Series) published by PREP include: *Resumes and Cover Letters That Have Worked, Resumes and Cover Letters That Have Worked for Military Professionals, Government Job Applications and Federal Resumes, Cover Letters That Blow Doors Open,* and *Letters for Special Situations.* Her career titles and how-to resume-and-cover-letter books are based on the expertise she has acquired in 20 years of working with job hunters. Her valuable career insights have appeared in publications of the "Wall Street Journal" and other prominent newspapers and magazines.

# PREP Publishing Order Form

You may purchase any of our titles from your favorite bookseller! Or send a check or money order or your credit card number for the total amount*, plus $4.00 postage and handling, to PREP, 1110 1/2 Hay Street, Fayetteville, NC 28305. You may also order our titles on our website at www.prep-pub.com and feel free to e-mail us at preppub@aol.com or call 910-483-6611 with your questions or concerns.

Name: _____

Phone #:_____

Address: _____

E-mail address:_____

Payment Type: ☐ Check/Money Order   ☐ Visa   ☐ MasterCard

Credit Card Number: _____ Expiration Date: _____

Put a check beside the items you are ordering:

☐ Free—Packet describing PREP's professional writing and editing services

☐ $16.95—REAL-RESUMES FOR RESTAURANT, FOOD SERVICE & HOTEL JOBS. Anne McKinney, Editor

☐ $16.95—REAL-RESUMES FOR MEDIA, NEWSPAPER, BROADCASTING & PUBLIC AFFAIRS JOBS. Anne McKinney, Editor

☐ $16.95—REAL-RESUMES FOR RETAILING, MODELING, FASHION & BEAUTY JOBS. Anne McKinney, Editor

☐ $16.95—REAL-RESUMES FOR HUMAN RESOURCES & PERSONNEL JOBS. Anne McKinney, Editor

☐ $16.95—REAL-RESUMES FOR MANUFACTURING JOBS. Anne McKinney, Editor

☐ $16.95—REAL-RESUMES FOR AVIATION & TRAVEL JOBS. Anne McKinney, Editor

☐ $16.95—REAL-RESUMES FOR POLICE, LAW ENFORCEMENT & SECURITY JOBS. Anne McKinney, Editor

☐ $16.95—REAL-RESUMES FOR SOCIAL WORK & COUNSELING JOBS. Anne McKinney, Editor

☐ $16.95—REAL-RESUMES FOR CONSTRUCTION JOBS. Anne McKinney, Editor

☐ $16.95—REAL-RESUMES FOR FINANCIAL JOBS. Anne McKinney, Editor

☐ $16.95—REAL-RESUMES FOR COMPUTER JOBS. Anne McKinney, Editor

☐ $16.95—REAL-RESUMES FOR MEDICAL JOBS. Anne McKinney, Editor

☐ $16.95—REAL-RESUMES FOR TEACHERS. Anne McKinney, Editor

☐ $16.95—REAL-RESUMES FOR CAREER CHANGERS. Anne McKinney, Editor

☐ $16.95—REAL-RESUMES FOR STUDENTS. Anne McKinney, Editor

☐ $16.95—REAL-RESUMES FOR SALES. Anne McKinney, Editor

☐ $16.95—REAL ESSAYS FOR COLLEGE AND GRAD SCHOOL. Anne McKinney, Editor

☐ $25.00—RESUMES AND COVER LETTERS THAT HAVE WORKED. McKinney. Editor

☐ $25.00—RESUMES AND COVER LETTERS THAT HAVE WORKED FOR MILITARY PROFESSIONALS. McKinney, Ed.

☐ $25.00—RESUMES AND COVER LETTERS FOR MANAGERS. McKinney, Editor

☐ $25.00—GOVERNMENT JOB APPLICATIONS AND FEDERAL RESUMES: Federal Resumes, KSAs, Forms 171 and 612, and Postal Applications. McKinney, Editor

☐ $25.00—COVER LETTERS THAT BLOW DOORS OPEN. McKinney, Editor

☐ $25.00—LETTERS FOR SPECIAL SITUATIONS. McKinney, Editor

☐ $16.95—REAL-RESUMES FOR NURSING JOBS.  McKinney, Editor

☐ $16.95—REAL-RESUMES FOR AUTO INDUSTRY JOBS. Patty Sleem

☐ $24.95—REAL KSAS--KNOWLEDGE, SKILLS & ABILITIES--FOR GOVERNMENT JOBS. McKinney, Editor

☐ $24.95—REAL RESUMIX AND OTHER RESUMES FOR FEDERAL GOVERNMENT JOBS. McKinney, Editor

☐ $24.95—REAL BUSINESS PLANS AND MARKETING TOOLS ... Samples to use in starting, growing, marketing, and selling your business

_____ **TOTAL ORDERED**

_____ **(add $4.00 for shipping and handling)**

_____ **TOTAL INCLUDING SHIPPING**

*PREP offers volume discounts on large orders. Call us at (910) 483-6611 for more information.*

THE MISSION OF PREP PUBLISHING IS TO PUBLISH
BOOKS AND OTHER PRODUCTS WHICH ENRICH
PEOPLE'S LIVES AND HELP THEM OPTIMIZE THE
HUMAN EXPERIENCE. OUR STRONGEST LINES ARE
OUR JUDEO-CHRISTIAN ETHICS SERIES AND OUR
REAL-RESUMES SERIES.

Would you like to explore the possibility of having PREP's writing
team create a resume for you similar to the ones in this book?

For a brief free consultation, call 910-483-6611
or send $4.00 to receive our Job Change Packet to
PREP, 1110 1/2 Hay Street, Fayetteville, NC 28305. Visit our
website to find valuable career resources: www.prep-pub.com!

QUESTIONS OR COMMENTS? E-MAIL US AT PREPPUB@AOL.COM